Naturalized Epistemology and Philosophy of Science

Rodopi Philosophical Studies

7 .

Edited by
Francisco Miró Quesada
(University of Lima)

Ernest Sosa
(Brown University)

Rodopi

Amsterdam - New York, NY 2007

Table of contents

Preface

Naturalized Epistemology and Philosophy of Science

Much has happened in the field of contemporary epistemology since Quine's "Epistemology Naturalized" was published in 1969; furthermore, before Ronald Giere published his article "Philosophy of Science Naturalized", naturalized philosophy of science had been pushed by the so-called historical approach. Kuhm, Lakatos, Feyerabend and Laudan's historical philosophy of science can be regarded as a form of it. Without a doubt, philosophy of science is closely related to epistemology. There is an intimate connection between (normative or descriptive) knowledge in this naturalistic approach and norms, values, reasoning, and knowledge in science and technology.

The naturalistic approach to epistemology and philosophy of science has been gaining an ever more dominant role. However, with respect to the following questions, it is not totally uncontroversial. Both in naturalized epistemology and in naturalized philosophy of science debates continue. The papers in this volume address the following questions in particular. In naturalized epistemology questions include: What exactly is naturalized epistemology? What is the significance of this investigation? How can this naturalistic approach be further developed and applied? Can the normative aspect of epistemology really be replaced by the descriptive psychology or science in general? In naturalized philosophy of science the following questions arise: Should philosophers of science propose any methodological rules or norms for scientific inquiries? What roles do norms and values play in scientific decision, choice and reasoning? What are those different forms of cognition appearing in the scientific practice?

The 2006 Soochow International Philosophy Conference and Workshop: "Naturalized Epistemology and Philosophy of Science", held in Taipei, Taiwan, aimed to address these questions over four days (May 31 to June 3) of papers presentations, workshops, panel discussions, and informal conversation. The papers collected here bring together the keynote lectures and some highlights of the conference overall.

We would like to take this opportunity to express our gratitude to all those who have made both the meeting and this publication possible, not least to the Taiwan National Science Council, the Taiwanese Ministry of Education, and the Soochow Philosophy Centre (SPC) who jointly funded the conference and workshop, and the keynote speakers Ernest Sosa, Ronald Giere, Hilary Kornblith, and Joseph Rouse, for their much appreciated contributions. We are particularly grateful to Ernest Sosa for his help in publishing this work, as well as to Chao-Shiuan Liu, the President of Soochow University for his continued encouragement of the SPC. Finally, we must express our sincere thanks to the Friends of Soochow Foundation for presenting us with the Edward L. Rada Award, which substantially supported the publication of this volume.

Chienkuo Mi
Ruey-Lin Chen

Ernest Sosa

Sources and Deliverances

Rutgers University

1. Animal Knowledge and Dependent Tracking

Animal knowledge requires a belief that is "apt," in that the believer gets it right not by accident but by tracking the truth, in the following sense.

> *Tracking.* One tracks the truth, *outright*, in believing that p IFF one would believe that p iff it were so that p: i.e., would believe if it were so and only if it were so.[1]

If suitably constituted and environed you might also have an ability to track over a certain range when appropriately related to facts in that range. Good eyesight can so relate you to a facing surface's color and shape (when it is not too far, well enough lit, unoccluded, etc.) that with respect to any relevant proposition <p> about the color or shape of the surface, you would believe <p> iff it were so that p.[2] Often there is more than one way to track a truth: you might hear the bells toll, for example, without seeing them, or you might see them toll without hearing them.

If I see that a bird flies by, but only because I happen to look out the window, which I might easily not have done, am I then in a condition where the bird would now be flying by iff I believed it? Obviously I am not. Might not the bird easily have flown by without my taking any note of that fact, because I was then looking in another direction? Even when I am in fact looking in the right direction, so long as I might too easily have looked in another direction, it remains too easily possible that the bird might have flown by without my seeing it; in which case I do know about the bird as I look out the window despite the fact that it might easily have been there unnoticed. Outright tracking therefore cannot be a necessary condition for knowing.

It might be thought that we avoid our problem through strategic relativizing. Thus the knower *would* believe that p if <p> were a fact to which he was suitably

---

1 This is Cartesian tracking, not the Nozickian tracking which requires, not that one would believe that p only if it were so that p, but rather that if it were not so that p then one would not believe it. It is defended in my "Postscript to 'Proper Functionalism and Virtue Epistemology'," in J. Kvanvig (ed.), *Warrant in Contemporary Epistemology* (Lanham, Maryland: Rowman and Littlefield, 1996), pp. 271–280.

2 Here and in what follows '<p>' abbreviates 'the proposition that p'.

related. The relevant relation for the bird watcher, for example, might be that of having looked in a certain direction with an unobstructed line of sight, etc.[3] That apparently gives the right result for Russell's case of a clock that has been stopped exactly 24 hours. *Relative to its being stopped*, it is false that one *would* acquire true beliefs by reading a clock, but relative to its working, it would of course be a source of truth.

So we might introduce a concept of relativized tracking, and thereby a concept of dependent tracking, through this preliminary concept:

> *Relative to* $<r>$, *it would be so that p iff it were so that q.*

defined as follows:

> $<r\&p>$ would be so only if $<q>$ were so, and $<r\&q>$ would be so only if $<p>$ were so.

In these terms we can define our more complex conceptions of tracking:

> *Relativized tracking.* One tracks the truth, *relative to a fact* $<r>$, in believing $<p>$ IFF relative to fact $<r>$, one would believe $<p>$ iff it were so that p.

> *Dependent tracking.* One tracks the truth, *dependently on a fact* $<r>$, in believing $<p>$ IFF (a) one does not track the truth outright in so believing, but (b) one does track the truth relative to fact $<r>$ in so believing.

What if a clock is working only by accident? Suppose the evil demon at random intervals sets it to the right time and allows it to work for three seconds. The 3-second intervals when the clock works are rare, however, occurring perhaps once a week. Within them the clock would yield true belief but no knowledge, surely, and hence no sufficient warrant.

Another example. From a darkened room one looks through a window onto a scene beyond. The window occasionally becomes an opaque screen, however, on which nearly always a VCR puts a show unrelated to the scene beyond. Just once by chance the show matches the scene outside. Anyone who mistakes the screen for a transparent window can hardly know in just that instant through beliefs just then miraculously true. What now if instead of the screening's matching the scene, the VCR/screen is randomly disabled for an instant, allowing one a view through the now transparent window? Hours of illusion could hardly frame both sides of an instant of knowledge, even if they do so seamlessly, *especially* if they do so seamlessly.

The subjects who rely on the clock or on the VCR/window are denied knowledge because they do not know sensitively enough when to believe, when to

---

3   Compare Plantinga's requiring for the warrant of a belief B that it has been formed by an exercise E of cognitive powers (or intellectual virtues) in a mini-environment MBE *favorable* for that exercise, i.e., one such that if S were to form a belief by way of E *in MBE*, S would form a true belief . See his "Warrant and Accidentally True Belief," *Analysis* 57(1997): 140–45; p. 144.

disbelieve, and when to withhold judgment. They would too easily be misled, would too easily believe incorrectly in too many similar situations that they would not discern appropriately. The clock gazer would be misled too easily about the time, as would the subject in the darkened room about the scene beyond.

Contrast with these unfortunates the perceiver who happens to see the bird's flight. She too gets it right only by accident, but this does not preclude knowledge. Why not? Because she is sensitive regarding the factors whose combined presence favors her knowledge. Sensitive to their absence, the subject would withhold her assent. Here the unfortunates are different: the clock gazer would continue to trust the clock even when stopped, which too easily might have happened; while the perceiver through the accidentally transparent window would still believe even with the window turned into a VCR-controlled screen, which again too easily might have happened.

Favored subjects enjoy a sensitivity to what puts them in touch with the truth, a sensitivity denied to the unfortunates. Favored subjects not only track dependently on a relevant combination of factors; in addition, they believe as they do *driven* by the presence of these factors specifically, which is not true of the unfortunates. Believing the clock when it happens miraculously to be running is not driven by the factor, among others, of the clock's running, nor is the belief from the darkened room driven by the factor, among others, of the subject's access through the fleetingly transparent window. On the contrary, these subjects might too easily have believed the same even absent the factors that by luck aid their tracking, for what really drives their believing is not the real presence of those factors—including the transparency of the window, or the working of the clock—but only their *appearing* to be present. They believe as they do driven by the appearance of a transparent window before them, or a working clock (in combination with other factors). However, in the circumstances they do *not* track the truth dependently on such appearances. In each case too easily the appearances might have remained, and with them the belief, even absent its truth. So the subjects do not track dependently on the appearances, although it is the appearances that drive their believing. As for factor combinations dependently on which they *do* track, none drives their believing. This divergence between the factors dependently on which they track and the factors that drive their believing helps explain why they fail to know, or so I am suggesting. To track through a virtue by believing that p one must thereby track the truth either outright or else dependently on factors that also in combination drive one's believing.

2. Sources and Their Deliverances

Traditionally our knowledge is said to have "sources" such as perception, memory, and inference. Epistemic sources are said to issue "deliverances" that we may or may not accept. Our senses may issue the deliverance about two adjacent lines that one is longer, for example, a deliverance rejected by those in the know about the Müller-Lyer illusion.

A deliverance of <p> to a subject S is a saying that p witnessed by S. Different sources correlate with different ways in which it may be said that p. Someone may say it literally, of course, in person or in writing, and S may hear it or read it. If we can believe our eyes or ears, moreover, it's because they tell us things. We experience visually or aurally as if p. Normally we accept such deliverances of our senses, unless we detect something untoward. When someone or something tells us that p, we normally know who or what is doing so. We can tell at least that a certain voice or a certain stretch of writing is doing so or that we seem to *see* the bells toll, or seem rather to *hear* them toll. And so on.

Deliverances thus conceived make up a realm of the ostensible: ostensible perceptions, ostensible memories, ostensible conclusions, ostensible intuitions, and the like. We may or may not believe our eyes or ears, we may or may not trust our senses, or our memory, or our calculations or other reasonings.

In virtue largely of a subject's constitution and positioning vis-á-vis a fact <p>, and of the subject matter or field of that fact, a deliverance to that subject, D_S<p>, will or will not track the truth as to whether p. It is largely such factors, that is to say, which determine whether or not <p> would be so delivered to S if and only if it were true. A subject in possession of the concept of a headache would ostensibly introspect that he suffered a headache if and only if he did, and this deliverance of introspection would thereby track *outright* the truth that it delivers. Unlike perception, introspection needs no medium, so it tracks without benefit of any special relation between the subject and his headache, except only for the fact that it is *his* headache. In perception, by contrast, a deliverance will track only because the subject is appropriately positioned. If I ostensibly perceive that a bird flies by, for example, this deliverance will track the truth that it delivers only because I am looking in the right direction. My ostensible perception of the bird's flight by my window does not track the truth (that the bird does fly by) *outright*. Admittedly, I would not ostensibly perceive thus unless a bird *was* flying by, except in the remote possibilities of illusion, hallucination, or a skeptical scenario. However, a bird might easily have flown by without my ostensibly perceiving it. This is why my ostensible perception does not then track outright the truth of its content. But it does track that truth *dependently* on my looking out the window, etc. That is to say, if while looking out the window, etc., I ostensibly perceived that a bird was flying by, a bird would in fact be flying by; and if while I looked out the window, etc., a bird flew by, I would in fact ostensibly perceive that this was so.

A deliverance's tracking *in virtue* of certain conditions must be distinguished from its tracking *dependently* on those conditions. Thus I may now track that there is no loud noise in my presence *in virtue* of the facts that I am not deaf, that my ears are not plugged, and so on, but not *dependently* on those facts, since my present ostensible perception of there being no such noise tracks the truth of its content *outright*; and since it does so outright it does not do so dependently. I do track that truth *in virtue* of my ears being operative: were they inoperative I would be unable to detect the presence or absence of loud noises. It may be thought that if this is so, then I cannot really be tracking outright that there is no such noise in my presence, as I must then be tracking that truth only dependently on my ears being operative. But this is not so. I can track outright a certain truth in virtue of the holding of a certain contingent condition, so long as the condition's absence is a remote enough possibility (in the relevant context of thought or discussion), remote enough that it *would* not in fact obtain in the circumstances, though of course *conceivably it might*.

Examples of deliverances are test results, indicator readings, eyewitness reports, media reports, perceptual appearances, and even rational intuitions and ostensible conclusions. Contents are delivered by each such source. Acceptance of a deliverance *as such*, i.e., for the reason that it is such a deliverance, constitutes knowledge only if the source is in that instance trustworthy and its deliverance accepted with appropriate sensitivity. The deliverance must track the truth, and one must be so sensitive to the trustworthiness of its source that one would accept its deliverances as such (for the reason that they are such deliverances) only if they did track the truth.[4] Any competence to discriminate a trust-

---

4   It would not be enough to require that source X's deliverances merely drive S to believe the contents thus delivered. It must be required rather that X's deliverances drive S's accepting those deliverances *as such*: in other words, S must accept the contents thus delivered as such, and it is this accepting of those contents as delivered that is required to be driven by the deliverances. Reason: What the absence of the deliverance would properly take away is its content being accepted as such; after all, that content itself might then be a deliverance of some other source, in which case it would not be renounced merely because of the absence of the first deliverance. Moreover, if X's deliverance is present but X is now untrustworthy, then, if appropriately sensitive to the trustworthiness of X, S will now modify his attitudes accordingly. How so? Not necessarily through no longer assenting to the deliverances of X. For, again, what X delivers, <p>, may concurrently be delivered by a source known to S to be perfectly trustworthy, in which case S would hardly give up believing <p> just in virtue of being sensitive to how trustworthy X is in the circumstances. What such sensitivity will affect is rather S's attitude to X's deliverances *as such*: i.e., S will no longer assent to <p> *as a deliverance of X*. S will no longer accept <p> *for the reason that it is a deliverance of X*. So what the deliverances of X will then no longer drive is S's accepting those deliverances at face value, i.e., as deliverances of X. (Your eyesight might fade while your hearing remains good; and you may respond accordingly.) As for the notion of "driving," consider images in a mirror reflecting a TV screen on which a tennis match is projected live. In a normal situation the images in the mirror are driven both by what happens on the screen and what happens on the court. Suppose the match is repeatedly halted because of intermittent rain, and in a desperate attempt to retain viewers the producers seamlessly enough (through commercial interruptions) fill in the gaps with old tape while giving no notice. Still the

worthy source and to accept its deliverances with such sensitivity (relative to the pertinent field and conditions) is an intellectual virtue (or has a virtue as its basis in the constitution of that subject's mind).

That develops the tracking-through-virtue view in a way that applies naturally to the examples before us.[5] The bird-watcher may now be seen to be favored over the unfortunates (the accidental clock-gazer and the observer through fleeting transparency) in the following respect. In all three cases the subject accepts a deliverance as such, but only the fortunate subject accepts it with relevant sensitivity. In accepting that deliverance she accepts a truth tracker. She would accept the deliverances of that source only were they trustworthy truth-trackers. Not so for the unfortunates, i.e., the accidental clock-gazer, and by the observer graced by fleeting transparency. These unfortunates accept deliverances that fail to track the truth of their contents.

One might of course know something through accepting a deliverance that does not track outright the truth of its content. A deliverance might track the truth of its content not outright but dependently on a certain condition. If one then accepts its deliverance while appropriately sensitive to the holding of that condition, one might still thereby know the truth of the content accepted. Thus a clock that is working for brief seconds might still track relative to its ticking (given the determined demon who starts it only while resetting it to the right time). The subject who accepts its deliverances while sensitive to its ticking might learn thereby what time it is, even if one who just believes the clock without hearing it tick would not share that knowledge. The difference is that, given the total set-up, that clock tracks the time dependently on its ticking. Therefore the subject who accepts its deliverances sensitively to its ticking can know thereby. However, the subject who is *not* sensitive to its ticking, and would believe the clock regardless of whether it was ticking or not, would not know the time by reading that clock.

Again the subject who knows of the bird's flight accepts a deliverance that tracks the truth of its content outright, but the subject who reads the accidentally working clock fails to know thereby because the deliverance he accepts does

---

sequence in the mirror is driven by that on the screen, but no longer by the course of the match, even in the occasional stretches when the images are *caused* by the match. Too easily now might things happen in the match with no effect on the mirror. No longer is the mirror sensitive to the relevant span of events on the court. In particular, if the match were to be halted, as might too easily happen once the rain sets in, the mirror would reflect not the relevant goings on but only play by the same players in some earlier match. In normal circumstances, then, the images in the mirror are driven both by those on the screen and by the course of the match. In the abnormal circumstances, however, the images in the mirror are *driven* by those on the screen but *not* by the course of the match, and this remains so even on the occasions when they are *caused* by the course of the match.

5   I do not deny that the view might still be improved through further development, and I will return to it elsewhere.

not track the truth of its content outright, *nor* does it track the truth of its content dependently on any condition to which the subject is appropriately responding. And the same goes for the subject who accepts his ostensible perceptions when accidentally allowed his view through the fleetingly transparent window.

A deliverance provides knowledge to a subject who accepts it, then, only if it tracks the truth either outright or else dependently on a condition to which the subject is responding, in that he accepts that deliverance as such, i.e., for the reason that it is such a deliverance, based in part on the holding of that condition.

3. Knowledge and Virtue

Knowledge requires nonaccidentally true belief; this casts some light on what knowledge is, but light dimmed by the imprecision in our notion of an accident, which itself needs explaining in the final analysis. More adequate is our notion of dependent tracking. Compare the belief that this is a ripe tomato, believed of a ripe tomato amidst a bushelful of wax replicas. Arguably, one's belief then *does* C-track the truth, dependently on the circumstances. But it is still in some relevant sense or respect true only by accident. Each of the items in that top layer is believed by me to be a ripe tomato, but I am right only in this one case, which my perspective does not distinguish in any relevant respect.

Suppose I fancy myself a connossieur of tomato ripeness, but suffer from a rare form of color blindness that precludes my discerning nearly any shade of red except that displayed by this particular tomato. Therefore my judgments of tomato ripeness are in general apt to be right with no better than even chance. But when it's the particular (and rare) shade of red now displayed, then I am nearly infallible. Oblivious to my affliction, I issue judgments of tomato ripeness with abandon over a wide spectrum of shades of red. Assuming that, unknown to me, the variety of tomato involved always ripens with this shade of red, my belief that this tomato is ripe *is* in step with the truth. Nevertheless, in some relevant sense or respect I am right only by accident. The problem is that I am not adequately sensitive to the presence of the conditions on which my tracking of ripeness is dependent. I still issue my verdicts of ripeness even when those conditions are absent. In this respect I am like Magoo in his perceptual judgments, which he does not restrict to the very narrow bounds within which they are reliable.

Compare a basketball B held by S at the top of an incline I. It is true, let us suppose, that (C) if B were released by S at t, it would roll down I. And this is true for reasons of two sorts: because of factors pertaining to the internal or intrinsic make-up of B at t: e.g., that it is rigidly round at the time; and because of factors external or extrinsic to B: e.g., because it is not glued to the top of the incline, because it is in a gravitational field, etc. Moreover, the truth of the conditional might be dependent on factors of two sorts: the external and the internal.

While cradled in S's hands, B's internal pressure may hover at the limit above which, if released by S it would explode upon contact with the incline, rather than rolling down. So it may be true that if it were released by S at t it would roll dependently on its condition at t, since its being in just that internal condition is too precarious a matter for it to be the case outright that it would roll if released. Alternatively, incline I may be in a moment of calm at t, even though at t − e and at t + e it is swept by winds that would blow B away rather than allowing it to roll down. So conditions of two sorts may be involved in the truth of a conditional such as C, in such a way that C is true not outright but only dependently on the holding of the conditions; some such conditions are "internal," while others are "external."

Virtues are internal conditions that enable an entity to attain desirable ends (of the entity or of its users) relative to certain circumstances, conditions in virtue of which it is true that the entity *would* succeed in those circumstances. So a condition may be a virtue relative to one end-circumstance pair $<E, C>$ while it is not a virtue relative to another $<E', C'>$. Of course, the context of thought or discussion may set the relevant ends and circumstances well enough that they need not be mentioned specifically, in which case we may and do speak of virtues without qualification. But there is always a danger of ambiguity, especially when we range in thought or speech through the realm of the possible: do we then retain the relativization to our actual ends and circumstances, or do we shift to our ends and circumstances in the supposed possible situation? This distinction is a source of ambiguity.

There are virtues of two sorts: those included in one's fundamental nature, constituted by one's innate capacities and aptitudes; and those part of one's "second nature," one's character pliable at least to some degree, at some remove. Of these, some may derive from blind habituation, from one's earliest upbringing perhaps, subject to very limited rational control. Nevertheless, at least in normal human development, there is much in one's character, moral and intellectual, due to one's own rational control. The acts, practical or theoretical, that derive from such components of one's character, from one's rational second nature, are under one's motivational control, at least to some extent, at some remove. These acts reflect on one's character, moral or intellectual, and specifically on those components of one's character for which one is to some extent, at some remove, responsible. With regard to such acts and the character they reveal, one is subject to suasion, and thus a proper participant in rational deliberative dialogue, and properly subject to praise and blame.

4. Sources, Virtues, and Habits of Thought

When one believes that here is a hand, one believes one's eyes, one believes that things are as they appear, that if it looks somehow, then that is really how it is.

This goes beyond just trusting one's eyesight on a hand appearance specifically; it involves, rather, visual appearances more generally, and sensory appearances even more generally. One believes that, absent specific signs to the contrary, reality fits how it appears in one's experience, that if it seems experientially a certain way, that is how it really is. Of course one rarely formulates such a belief in words, even in the very general way just suggested. Nearly all of one's beliefs remain unformulated at any given time, and plenty of beliefs exert a powerful influence on our thoughts and actions with no benefit of formulation. Since when must beliefs be so much as formulable by those who hold them? Surely I can believe and even know that someone looks somehow, has a certain facial appearance, even if I could not come close to capturing in words the full content of my belief. Moreover, beliefs that are easily formulable might be held even without ever being formulated. Here I have in mind not just the deep beliefs that surface only under couch analysis, but much more common beliefs revealed through one's conduct, either physical or intellectual. Thus one might believe to be G whatever one believes to be F, which might be no accident: at the time in question one might be such that one *would* believe a thing to be G upon believing it to be F. This jibes with one's holding an implicit belief that if something is F then it is (likely to be) G. Such beliefs can operate beneath the surface, even if not so deeply buried that only persistent analysis would uncover them. Some biases and prejudices, for example, are more easily uncovered than are their more Freudian underworld mates. One is shown to believe that F's are or tend to be G's through one's persistent tendency to attribute G-ness to what one takes to be F. Thus one is revealed as believing that people of a certain sort are ipso facto inferior by persistently attributing inferiority to whomever one takes to be of that sort. Even if one denies the generalization when it is formulated explicitly, and one is deemed sincere to the extent that one is not *consciously* lying, one's protestations might still be dismissed in the light of the evidence.

Freudian beliefs, biases and prejudices, beliefs about how people look and react, about how dishes taste, about how a song goes, etc., etc., operate in the background, unformulated, but guide our more particular beliefs and choices as we navigate an ordinary day. Despite being unformulated and, often, unreasoned, and certainly not *consciously* reasoned, such beliefs can vary significantly in their degree of epistemic justification. Some biases are *just* biases, formed on inadequate evidence or none at all. We are all familiar with irrational mechanisms that fix beliefs without justification. Some ways of acquiring a belief are not defective or inadequate, however, despite involving no reasoning from epistemically prior premises. Nor can we require that all beliefs whatever must be acquired through appeal to prior premises. That way lies vicious regress, and a very simple and direct route to the deepest skepticism. So there must be ways to acquire epistemically justified beliefs without reaching them as conclusions from premises known with epistemic priority.

Ernest Sosa

If that is so, might not beliefs acquired perceptually attain epistemic justification precisely by being so acquired? Such beliefs might be "directly" justified, in the sense of acquiring justification but *not* through a process of reasoning that leads to their acceptance as a conclusion.

Suppose we agree that there is some sort of "implicit inference" when we believe our eyes, some sort of processing that begins with how things seem experientially and ends with a corresponding belief about our surroundings. In that case, we might think of the processing as an inference from an implicit belief to the effect that, absent any sign to the contrary, things would normally be pretty much as they seemed. Alternatively, we might think of it as just a "habit" of thought that has us believe that things are a certain way whenever things appear that way and there is no apparent sign to the contrary. Either way an issue of "justification" arises, surely. Can anything very substantive be seen to turn on how we choose to frame the issue? Either we shall face a question of the justification of such a habit, or we shall face an issue of the justification of an implicit belief. And in neither case is there much hope that we shall be able to explain the epistemic justification involved by appeal to some abductive or "inductive or analogical" argument.[6]

In a broad sense, the issue of epistemic justification that arises in either case is that of what makes it epistemically right (or good or valuable or desirable or reasonable or of positive value) for us to be a certain way, whether that way is a belief or whether it is a "habit." In either case we are contingently a certain way (either through our nature or through our second nature), and this way seems epistemically evaluable. We may explain why it seems thus evaluable if we consider that the way we are, whether by hosting a certain belief or by hosting a certain "habit," is a way that bears on the "health" of one's intellectual life, on what sorts of beliefs we have and will acquire, correct ones or erroneous ones, and systematically so, given a fixed environment. Even Magoo may thus be seen to have "justified" beliefs, so long as the epistemic value of the relevant habits is to be assessed relative to the species, and not relative to the individual. (We abstract in any case from whatever other values may be promoted in the life of Magoo and others.)

---

6   Here is CS Peirce: "That which determines us, from given premises, to draw one inference rather than another, is some habit of mind, whether it be constitutional or acquired. The habit is good or otherwise, according as it produces true conclusions from true premises or not; and an inference is regarded as valid or not, without reference to the truth or falsity of its conclusion specially, but according as the habit which determines it is such as to produce true conclusions in general or not. The particular habit of mind which governs this or that inference may be formulated in a proposition whose truth depends on the validity of the inferences which the habit determines; and such a formula is called a *guiding principle* of inference." (From his *Collected Papers* V, par. 265.)

Moreover, beliefs depend for their epistemic quality on how they are ingrained, even when they are part of our nature, or our second nature, perhaps in a way that reflects some even deeper character of oneself or of one's community. Since we are interested in keeping track of these, we evaluate beliefs and habits by reference to the sources that yield them and the virtue of these sources. Suppose I acquire the habit of inferring in accordance with a rule that if one gets wet and cold one will catch cold, and manage to make many true predictions that way. Suppose further that I acquire this habit of thought just insensibly, over the years, so that it becomes second nature to me, through the influence of grownups who are quite unreliable. Do my true predictions amount to knowledge? Suppose that those better positioned have the best of reasons to think that getting cold and wet has nothing to do with it; given that my habit was acquired through the insensible social pressure of an unreliable community, surely I do not know, nor would beliefs acquired through the exercise of such a habit amount to "epistemically justified" beliefs. And it makes little apparent difference whether the generalization that corresponds to the habit ("cases where one gets cold and wet tend to be cases where one catches cold") is actually true or not. (If it turns out that there is after all a previously undetected but real connection after all, that need not show that those who had relied on the corresponding habit had after all known what the rest of us had been precluded from knowing by our rational scruples.)

Are the only habits of inference that can be fundamentally justified those that people have tried to codify when they have viewed themselves as elaborating a logical organon, e.g., a set of rules of inference, deductive or inductive? That seems a mistake, for several reasons: first, because there is no such simple set of rules; what one is justified in believing is too holistic and context dependent a matter to be codified in any formal system. Here the Duhem/Quine considerations bear, as does Goodman's gruesome tale. It also seems a mistake, secondly, because if restricted to the following of such rules (were there such rules, which probably there are not), we would be unable to acquire much by way of justified beliefs, nor would it help much to give ourselves data restricted just to the character of our sensory experience, etc. And it seems a mistake, finally, because there is no apparent reason why the so-called inductive habits would enjoy any special status superior to the status of believing our eyes in conditions that seem normal, etc.

As we work our way back to the sources of our good habits, and to the sources of the sources, etc., we shall eventually reach a set of ingrained ways that are not acquired or sustained by sources outside the set. And the question will remain: why are we characterized by that set of ingrained ways, when, presumably, we could have been at least somewhat different. Is it good that we are that way? Is it just an accident that we are thus characterized? These are reminiscent of the issues in the free will controversy. Positions open up in epistemology that are familiar from the free will controversy; proper philosophical coherence and integration will no doubt require that our philosophy of freedom and autonomy be in harmony with our philosophy of knowledge. Right, virtuous action will require conditions of freedom and autonomy likely to be matched by conditions demanded by belief nonaccidentally enough correct to count as epistemically justified and indeed as knowledge.[7]

Bibliography

Alston, W.P., "An Internalist Externalism," in his *Epistemic Justification* (Ithaca, NY: Cornell University Press, 1989).

BonJour, L., *The Structure of Empirical Knowledge* (Cambridge, MA: Harvard University Press, 1985), esp. ch. 3.

Foley, R., *Working Without a Net: A Study of Egocentric Epistemology* (Oxford, UK: Oxford University Press, 1993).

Fumerton, R., *Metaepistemology and Skepticism* (Langham, MD: Rowman & Littlefield, 1995).

Goldman, A., *Epistemology and Cognition* (Cambridge, MA: Harvard University Press, 1986), Part I.

Greco, J., "Internalism and Epistemically Responsible Belief," *Synthese* 85(1990): 245–77.

Kornblith, H., "How Internal Can You Get?" *Synthese* 74(1988): 313–27.

Lehrer, K., "Externalism and Epistemology Naturalized," ch. 8 of his *Theory of Knowledge* (Boulder, CO: Westview, 1990).

Moser, P., *Knowledge and Evidence* (Cambridge, UK: Cambridge University Press, 1989).

Plantinga, A., *Warrant: the Current Debate* (Oxford, UK: Oxford University Press, esp. chs. 1–3.

Sosa, E., "Reflective Knowledge in the Best Circles," *Journal of Philosophy* 94(1997): 410–30.

---

7   The way in which and the extent to which beliefs are not actions should not constitute an insurmountable obstacle to our exploiting the analogy between justified (right, reasonable) action and justified (right, reasonable) belief.

Ronald N. Giere

Modest Evolutionary Naturalism

Department of Philosophy and Center for Philosophy of Science
University of Minnesota
giere@umn.edu

Abstract

I begin by arguing that a consistent general naturalism must be understood in terms of methodological maxims rather than metaphysical doctrines. Some specific maxims are proposed. I then defend a generalized naturalism from the common objection that it is incapable of accounting for the normative aspects of human life, including those of scientific practice itself. Evolutionary naturalism, however, is criticized as being incapable of providing a sufficient explanation of categorical moral norms. Turning to the epistemological norms of science itself, particularly those governing the empirical testing of specific models, I argue that these should be regarded as conditional rather than categorical and that, as such, can be given a naturalistic justification. The justification, however, is more cognitive than evolutionary. The historical development of science is found to be a better place for applying evolutionary ideas. After briefly considering the possibility of a naturalistic understanding of mathematics and logic, I turn to the problem of reconciling scientific realism with an evolutionary picture of scientific development. The solution, I suggest, is to understand scientific knowledge as being "perspectival" rather than absolutely objective. I first argue that scientific observation, whether by humans or instruments, is perspectival. This argument is extended to scientific theorizing which is regarded not as the formulation of universal laws of nature but as the construction of principles to be used in the construction of models to be applied to specific natural systems. The application of models, however, is argued to be not merely opportunistic but constrained by the methodological presumption that we live in a world with a definite causal structure even though we can understand it only from various perspectives.

Keywords: Naturalism, Evolutionary Naturalism, Scientific Models, Testing Scientific Models, Scientific Theories, Scientific Observation, Scientific Realism, Perspectivism.

1. Naturalism

If evolutionary naturalism is understood to be a general naturalism informed by the facts of evolution and by evolutionary theory, then no responsible contemporary naturalist could fail to be an evolutionary naturalist in this modest sense. On the other hand, if evolutionary naturalism implies that the *whole* content, or even *most of* the content, of naturalism is exhausted by evolutionary ideas, one might well object that there is much to naturalism that is not particularly evolutionary. My own primary commitment is to naturalism in general. How extensive the contribution of evolutionary ideas to naturalism in general might be remains to be seen.

My first problem, then, is to characterize naturalism in general. This turns out to be far from easy. In keeping with evolutionary ideas, I agree that nothing outside the realm of abstract constructions, such as a geometrical circle, has anything like an essence to be captured in an explicit definition. So there can be no strict definition of naturalism. To begin, we can hardly do better than consider a passage from the later writings of the foremost American champion of naturalism, John Dewey.

> Naturalism [he wrote in 1939] is opposed to idealistic spiritualism, but it is also opposed to super-naturalism and to that mitigated version of the latter that appeals to transcendent a *priori* principles placed in a realm above Nature and beyond experience. (Schilpp and Hahn 1939: 580)

This passage is typical of commentaries on naturalism in emphasizing what naturalism opposes over what it proposes. It is also typical in that it does not specify the form of the opposition to super-naturalism.

Here is a suggestion for at least the form a positive characterization: Naturalism is the position that all aspects of the world can be given a naturalistic explanation. Scientific explanations are the obvious exemplars for naturalistic explanations, but I would not want to rule out historical explanations in the form of narratives expressed in every-day concepts, or, indeed, every-day explanations themselves, so long as they make no overt appeals to a transcendent realm.[1]

What, one might reasonably ask, constitutes a scientific explanation? The best general answer a naturalist can give is: A scientific explanation is an explanation sanctioned by a recognized science. To say more is to risk going beyond the bounds of naturalism. At the most general level, not being willing to appeal to essences, naturalists cannot attempt to solve the demarcation problem by providing a definition that separates science from non-science.

---

1   This characterization assumes that scientific theories themselves do not embody *a priori* claims.

At a less abstract level, naturalists know that what counts as a scientific explanation changes over time. For most of the seventeenth century, for example, mechanical explanations appealing to action at a distance would have been rejected. In the eighteenth century, after the impact of Newton's *Principia*, such explanations became commonplace. Ultimately, naturalists can do no more than follow such historical developments. This does not mean that naturalists cannot criticize current scientific practices. Such criticism, however, can only be based on common sense or on a critical understanding of other scientific practices, there being no extra-scientific basis for any other sort of appeal.

The problem with the above positive characterization of naturalism is that it is very difficult to defend against the charge of simply begging the question against all those who would appeal to the super-natural or to *a priori* principles. How could anyone know that all aspects of reality have a scientific explanation? Here the great danger is that the would-be naturalist will fall into the trap of trying to provide an *a priori* argument for naturalism. That would be self-defeating. So the problem is to find a way of defending a naturalistic stance from *within* that stance.

My recommendation for naturalists is to take a *methodological* turn. Characterize naturalism not as a doctrine, but as a method. A general formulation of the method would be something like this: For any aspect of the world, seek a naturalistic rather than a super naturalistic explanation. It is a virtue of a methodological stance that its adoption does not even seem to require an *a priori* justification. Commitment to the method can be somewhat justified by appeal to past successes at finding naturalistic explanations. One might even argue that the success rate has been going up for the past three hundred years. More than that one cannot do without going outside a naturalistic stance. I think would-be naturalists should settle for the methodological stance. But again, naturalists remain free to *criticize* non-naturalistic explanations as being unjustified, incoherent, vacuous, contradicting established science, and so on. One must only not pretend to an *a priori* refutation of non-naturalistic pretensions.[2]

2. Naturalistic Priority

In order to further develop a conception of methodological naturalism, I will present and illustrate several more specific methodological maxims intended

---

2   For a survey of philosophical approaches to naturalism in the twentieth century, see Kitcher (1992). Rosenberg (1996) provides an account more focused on naturalism in the philosophy of science.

as additions to the general maxim stated above. The first of these I call "Naturalistic Priority." It is best illustrated by the historically most important exemplar for naturalistic explanations, Darwin's explanation of the origin of species.

The historical background to Darwin's theory included a strong tradition of natural theology in which the design of nature, particularly the design of animals and humans, was taken as evidence for a super-natural designer and creator. Darwin did not provide direct evidence *against* the existence of such a god. Rather, his theory of evolution by natural selection provided an *alternative,* scientific explanation of the acknowledged facts of, for example, the fit between the functional anatomy of animals and their environment. The arguments of natural theology were thereby undercut. The existing adaptation of organisms to their environments could be explained without recourse to a divine designer. Ordinary causal mechanisms producing variation, selection, and transmission of traits could do the job.[3]

The methodological principle I am calling "naturalistic priority" may be stated as follows: The availability of a *naturalistic* explanation of a recognized phenomenon renders unnecessary any non-naturalistic explanation. Obviously this principle is not neutral as between naturalistic and non-naturalistic explanations. It is not intended to be otherwise. It is part of a methodological strategy for developing a thoroughgoing naturalistic approach to an understanding of the world.

My statement of the principle of naturalistic priority makes reference to *available* scientific explanations. What makes a scientific explanation "available"? On the one hand, logical possibility is too weak an interpretation, for that makes application of the naturalistic strategy too easy. Presumably any phenomenon could logically be the result of the fortuitous coming together of natural causes. On the other hand, one cannot require a fully confirmed scientific hypothesis. Darwin's original theory of evolution was notoriously lacking a satisfactory account of inheritance, something essential to his account of evolution. Yet that did not prevent many serious minded people from regarding it as a viable alternative to special creation. So an "available" scientific explanation must be one that, relative to the science accepted at the time, is plausible enough that something not too different is likely eventually to prove correct. This remains somewhat vague, but seems about as good as one can do.

---

3   Historians of science debate just how deep Darwin's own commitment to this form of argument might have been. There is no doubt that later thinkers embraced the argument as I have here presented it. See, for example, Chapter 3 of William James' famous lectures on Pragmatism (1907).

3. Naturalistic Explanation of Normative Claims

One of the standard objections leveled at naturalism is that it is powerless to deal with the *normative* elements of human conduct. Indeed, it is claimed, naturalism is powerless to account for the norms that underlie scientific practice itself. The basis for this objection is the assumption that science is only descriptive and that one cannot derive anything normative from something merely descriptive.

Here one must distinguish two kinds of norms, *categorical* and *conditional.* Categorical norms prescribe or proscribe various actions unconditionally. They simply say, "Do this." or "Do not do that." Conditional norms have the form: If you want to achieve G, do A. It is true, I think, that within a naturalistic framework, one cannot *justify* categorical norms. One can however, *explain* them. Conditional norms, on the other hand, can be justified naturalistically. Everyday morality includes many categorical norms. Science, however, requires only conditional norms. Let us look at morality first.

For a dramatic example, consider a case featured in the international news media early in 1997 (French 1997). In the Ju-Ju religion, practiced in southeastern Ghana, young girls are given over into slavery by families seeking to atone for sins committed by family members. The slave holders are local fetish priests. The slaves are known euphemistically as slaves of the gods. The particular case in point involved a twelve year old girl given to a local priest by her father to atone for his sin of raping his young niece, who was the little girl's mother. The practice is supported by the whole community which fears retribution by the local gods if the sins of family members are not atoned for. Indeed, an international group has succeeded in buying the freedom of several such girls from their priest owners, a practice allowed by Ju-Ju morality. The families, however, refuse to take them back, fearing the wrath of their gods.

Although its precise origins are obscure, this practice has been traced back at least to the seventeenth century. It is all too easy to speculate as to how it came about. Surely, one thinks, the practice reflects the power of men over women. How else could a society develop a practice in which a man atones for his sin of raping a niece by giving the girl child resulting from that crime to another man who will then be empowered to command sexual favors from the slave? Even if the details remain forever hidden in the mists of history, there seems little doubt about the availability of a naturalistic explanation for the existence of these moral practices. Nor is there any difficulty in explaining the normative force of these practices for the community. It is based on fear of their gods. The implicit categorical norms are: Thou shalt not bring the wrath of the gods down upon your family, and, Sins must be atoned for.

We inheritors of western civilization, of course, are prone to regard this case as an atrocious example of the most innocent of victims being punished for the crimes of others. On what do we base that judgment? On our own historical tradition. The awkward question is whether there is any ultimate basis for that tradition beyond its own history. The naturalist says "No." The history of western civilization provides ample resources for several plausible, naturalistic theories of how our moral systems came to be.[4] Nor is there any problem explaining their normative force. Even without appeal to our gods, there is sufficient basis in the power of the family, the community, local governments, and, in recent centuries, the nation state.

The methodological principle for naturalism is this: When confronted with a categorical normative practice, seek to explain the existence of that practice, and its normative backing, using scientific and historical categories. Do not attempt to *justify* any particular norms in scientific terms. No such justification is possible. One cannot infer "ought" from "is". One can at most explain how particular "oughts" originated, what natural powers sustain them, and what the consequences of following such practices are likely to be.[5]

The modesty in naturalism's positive program does not carryover to its negative program. It is not the case that naturalists renounce attempts to justify categorical norms while admitting that others can. On the contrary, a naturalist is suspicious of the claims of others to justify categorical norms in any way that, as Dewey put it, "appeals to transcendent *a priori* principles placed in a realm above Nature and beyond experience." It is, therefore, part of the naturalist's method to challenge any arguments of this sort. This does not mean, however, that a naturalist must reject attempts systematically to reconstruct the morality of a culture in terms or more or less general principles. Such reconstructions may be a useful preliminary to criticism of a particular moral system and to the suggestion of alternative principles which may be put forward as ideals to be pursued by social or political means. And they may be supported by arguments that the alternative principles are more likely to produce shared goals than principles currently in force. But they cannot be justified *a priori*.

4. Evolutionary Naturalism and Categorical Norms

I have just argued that naturalism in general has ample resources to explain the existence of categorical norms. What about *evolutionary* naturalism? Here one

---

4   Apart from the background history itself, there are several types of theories that have been used to provide a naturalistic explanation for the moral practices of western civilization. One is psychological, going back to Hume and those primarily English psychologists who appealed to naturally existing moral sentiments. Another, favored by German speaking philosophers such as Marx and Nietzsche, appeals to sociology, economics, or culture more generally.

5   The views expressed in the second half of this paragraph echo those of John Dewey.

must distinguish two different approaches to evolutionary naturalism. One approach tries to *reduce* cultural activities to biological. Wilson's (Lumsden and Wilson 1981) program of epigenetic rules, further developed by Michael Ruse (1986, 1995), is an example of this sort of strategy. A second approach applies evolutionary models at the cultural level. Hull's (1988) account of conceptual evolution is an example of this type of approach.

Any reductionist approach seems to me highly unlikely to work very well for any but a very few cultural norms. Incest taboos are an obvious possibility, since one can easily imagine group selection favoring human groups that discouraged incest. But as for the particular content of a specific incest taboo, that seems massively underdetermined by any biology. How, for example, could one possibly give a reductionist explanation of the particular practices of Ju-Ju culture?

The problem with higher level structural approaches is different. It is that they necessarily operate at too abstract a level to explain what interests us. Our interest in culture focuses more on the *content* of cultural norms than on abstract patterns of variation, selection, and transmission. In the organic realm, evolutionary models have no serious naturalistic rivals for explaining the variation in organic forms of life. So we do not demand they explain the details of how particular forms came to be. In the cultural realm, by contrast, there is a powerful naturalistic rival, namely, historical narrative. It deals with the content of particular cultural forms. I do not see how evolutionary models could ever explain the content we want explained at the cultural level. But, as a modest evolutionary naturalist, I remain open to the possibility that scientifically successful models of this type might be developed.[6]

5. Naturalistic Justification of Epistemological Norms

Whether one can give a naturalistic justification of the epistemological norms of science itself depends on the assumed character of those norms. If one presumes that such norms are *categorical* methodological rules, then no satisfactory naturalistic justification is possible. Here I take it that the deep relativism a naturalist finds among categorical cultural norms is not acceptable for science. On the other hand, if one understands the norms of scientific epistemology to be *conditional* norms, a naturalistic justification is possible.

Before saying anything more about the epistemological norms of science, I must say something about my conception of the objects to which those norms apply. Much philosophy of science presupposes a framework in which the focus is on linguistic entities, statements, and in which the connection between

---

6   For a recent discussion of the differences between biological and cultural evolution, including a critique of dynamic systems approaches, see Griesemer (2000).

statements and the world is understood in terms of the notions of reference and truth. For many reasons, which I will not develop here, I think these notions too crude a basis for a satisfactory understanding of science. A richer, more satisfactory, picture results from introducing intermediate representational entities, for which I use the designation "models." Models may be characterized using statements, but these function in this context merely as definitions. Models may also be characterized, often only partially, using non-linguistic means, such as diagrams or actual scale models.

On this view, the empirical representational relationship is not directly between statements and the world, but between models and the world. Here the operative notion is not truth, but similarity, or "fit," between a model and world. Of course one can formulate the hypothesis that the model fits the world and ask whether this hypothesis is true. But such uses of the concept of truth can be understood in a purely semantic, redundant fashion. To say it is true that the model fits is merely a meta-linguistic way of saying that the model fits. The former phrase adds no content not already contained in the latter.[7]

Returning to the problem of providing a naturalistic justification for epistemic norms, I will focus on the special case of a crucial experiment with two rival models. The experiment is assumed to have an observable output which, for purposes of illustration, we can represent schematically as a one dimensional range, R, of numerical values. The models and the experimental set-up should be related as follows:

i)   If the model M_1 provides a good fit to the real world, then it is very probable that the experiment will yield an outcome in the range R_1, and very improbable that it will yield an out come in the range R_2.

ii) If the model M_2 provides a good fit to the real world, then it is very probable that the experiment will yield an outcome in the range R_2 and very improbable that it will yield an outcome in the range R_1.

The decision rule is: If the set-up yields a reading in the range R_1, choose model M_1 as the best fitting model. If the set-up yields a reading in the range R_2, choose model M_2 as the best fitting model.

The conditional epistemological norm is: If one wishes to decide empirically which of two rival models better fits the world, design an experiment satisfying the conditions stated above. The justification for the usefulness of this norm is that an experiment satisfying these conditions provides a basis for a reliable decision between the two models. To see why this is so, one need only review the situation as presented above. Given the stated design features, if M_1 does provide a good fit to the world, it is very likely that one will observe a

---

7   For an elaboration of these ideas see Giere (1988, ch 3; 2006, ch 4).

reading in the range R_1 and, correctly, choose M_1. Similarly if M_2 in fact best fits the world. In either case one has a good chance of making the correct choice. Of course there is always the possibility that neither model fits the world very well and the experiment yields a result in some intermediate range. In that case, the whole experiment is simply inconclusive.

It is important to realize that the conditional norms for deciding which of two models best fits the world do not require any backing by categorical norms. We do not require a categorical norm such as: Thou shalt decide which of two models best fits the world, or, more generally, Thou shalt do science. There is no such categorical imperative. One always does science because of some other goal.

I would not claim that this is the only way of understanding the epistemology of science that can be justified naturalistically. That there is one way is enough to show that a naturalized epistemology of science is possible. The only major possible philosophical objection to this explanation is that it is subject to a regress. That is, applying the principles of design requires substantive knowledge of the physical probabilities of the experimental set-up. If this knowledge were based on previous experiments, they would require similar assumptions, and so on. Pursuing this line of argument leads to a quest for a foundational inductive method that can be applied with no prior general knowledge whatsoever and whose use can be justified *a priori.* I do not think that such a quest could be successful. Rather, I recommend the Pragmatist stance that one can justify any particular empirical claim if the need arises, but not all claims at once.

It will be noted that there is nothing particularly evolutionary about my understanding of scientific epistemology. Indeed, I must confess that I have always been skeptical of the pretensions of evolutionary epistemology because it often seems to imply that questions of epistemology can be totally replaced by evolutionary notions. I do not think this is at all the case.

6. Evolutionary Change in Science

What may be evolutionary is not so much the epistemology of science as the nature of historical change in science. Here, as in Darwin's time, the primary alternative is a teleological view of science—science as progressing by accumulating ever more comprehensive and ever more detailed truths about the world. The goal is the whole truth about the universe.

Kuhn's *Structure of Scientific Revolutions* (1962) provided the major challenge of the twentieth century to the teleological picture of science. Numerous historical and sociological studies have since confirmed the importance of historical contingencies for producing all sorts of changes in science—some small, some large. It is useful, in a modest way, to organize these historical contingencies into an evolutionary pattern of variation, selection, and transmission.

Most evolutionary accounts of science emphasize the evolution of *conceptual* objects such as theories. I would put the focus elsewhere, namely, on the evolution of research groups within research specialities. The models with which individual scientists are committed can then be seen as *traits* of the individuals. The relative distribution of these traits within the research group evolves over time. The central issue is: What are the *mechanisms* underlying the variation, selection, and transmission of these intellectual traits within research groups. Most of these mechanisms, I think, are *cognitive* or *social*. It is thus cognitive and social mechanisms which determine whether any particular research group grows or declines in importance within a research speciality.

If one wishes to maintain any sort of realist view of science, *one* of these mechanisms must be the outcomes of experimental tests of various models. Individuals must be differentially motivated to switch their allegiance from one sort of model to another as a result of experimental outcomes. Similarly, the experimental success of some types of models must provide a positive motivation for new recruits into the general area to join the corresponding research group. Experimental success, however, remains but one mechanism relevant to the differential growth of one research group over others. Access to material resources to support graduate and post-graduate students is also an important mechanism. So is the participation of inspiring teachers and enterprising academic organizers.[8]

In general, applying an evolutionary model to the changes that take place in scientific fields provides a good way of organizing our understanding of science, a far better way than that provided by the old teleological model. But the evolutionary model, by itself, provides little basis for understanding the details of any changes in science. For that one must look at the *mechanisms* operative in the processes of variation, selection, and transmission. And these mechanisms are by and large not evolutionary, but cognitive and social. So evolutionary models provide only a part of our total picture of science. To invoke a biological analogy, the cognitive and social mechanisms provide the genetics for an evolutionary model of science. Just as evolutionary theory was incomplete until the synthesis with genetics in the twentieth century, so any evolutionary model of science will remain incomplete until it incorporates appropriate cognitive and social models.

7. Logic and Mathematics

Logic and mathematics represent the last and most formidable stronghold of non-naturalism. The argument is that, since science cannot now be conceived of as not utilizing logic and mathematics, it is impossible for a philosophy of science

---

8   I have developed these ideas in greater detail in (Giere 1990).

ever to be fully naturalized because logic and mathematics cannot be fully naturalized. This is a very big subject about which I can say only a few words here.[9]

As in the case of morality, it strikes me as a mistake for a naturalist to attempt to provide an empirical justification for the truth of the sorts of claims that have traditionally dominated the study of logic and mathematics. Following my second methodological principle, it is enough, I would say, to *explain* the existence and effectiveness of these claims. I would prefer, therefore, to understand mathematics as a practice of creating formal models which might provide a structure for models used in the sciences. The truths of mathematics, then, would be truths only about the models, and have only the status of definitions. The applicability of such models to situations in the real world would be an empirical question, of course, but not a question of the truth of mathematical statements. Whether one could develop this approach into a full-fledged naturalistic account of mathematics I do not know. I am encouraged that such a program might be carried out by a simple analogy much discussed in debates over the foundations of mathematics a century ago. The game of chess is clearly a human invention. No one thinks the truths about chess, for example, that a King can move only one space at a time, require an *a priori* justification. Yet one can prove quite complicated, and even surprising, results about particular positions in chess, for example, that a forced mate in fewer than ten moves is impossible.

Here one might argue that, although such an account might work for mathematics, it will not work for logic, which even any chess proof requires. My reply would be that a similar account should work for logic as well. Our systems of logic can be understood as merely models of languages which, within limits, can be applied to themselves. There need be no ultimate *urlogik* upon which everything else depends.

8. The Problem of Realism

I want now to focus on the problem of scientific realism as it arises even for the modest evolutionary picture of science outlined above. The problem is this. The course of science is highly contingent on accidents of history. So the models of the world we hold at any given time might have been quite different if historical contingencies had been different. On the other hand, we regard the truths about the world as being fixed. So what reason could there ever be for thinking that what we have now are truths since we could have just as well now held different models of the world. Similarly, with all the contingencies built into the evolutionary process, what reason could we have for thinking that we

---

9   Maddy (2000) provides one sort of defense of naturalism in mathematics.

are, over time, getting closer to the truth. So even a modestly evolutionary picture of science seems incompatible with scientific realism.

My solution to this problem is to keep the evolutionary picture of science and revise the conception of scientific realism. In fact, the standard conception of scientific realism is largely a carry-over from the old teleological picture of science. It is time it be revised in any case.[10]

The clearest expression of the old picture is to be found in those areas of philosophy least familiar to people outside of philosophy—the philosophy of mathematics and logic, and formal semantics. The idea is that reality has the same structure as set theory. Reality is conceived of as consisting of discrete objects, sets of discrete objects, sets of sets of objects, sets of ordered pairs of objects, and so on. True statements are those that describe objects as belonging to the sets to which they in fact belong. A complete science would be the set of all and only the true statements about a reality so structured.

This scheme works quite well for understanding purely mathematical entities where only abstract structure matters and empirical meaningfulness not at all. The assumption among philosophers of science for most of the 20th century was that the same sort of scheme works for empirical science as well. The tacit argument seems to have been that physics is the fundamental science, and physics is highly mathematical, so our understanding of notions of reference and truth developed for mathematics must work also for physics, and, by implication, for all of science. One need only openly state this argument to realize that this picture of science is not necessarily correct.

Here is an alternative picture. Imagine the universe as having a definite structure, but exceedingly complex, so complex that no models humans can devise could capture more than limited aspects of the total complexity. Nevertheless, some ways of constructing models of the world do provide resources for capturing some aspects of the world more or less well. Other ways may provide resources for capturing other aspects more or less well. Both ways, however, may capture some aspects of reality and thus be candidates for a realistic understanding of the world. So here, in principle, is a solution to the problem of finding a picture of science that is both evolutionary and realistic. It does not matter that different evolutionary paths might lead to different sciences. Each might genuinely capture some aspects of reality.

This way of presenting the alternative picture makes it seem like a piece of *a priori* metaphysics, something no naturalist can allow. The same picture can, however, be presented as a methodological precept: Proceed as if the world were this way. As such it needs no *a priori* justification. Its vindication would

---

10   Hooker (1987) and Godfrey-Smith (2002) provide further discussions of the connections
      between evolutionary naturalism and realism.

be in its success. Actually I believe that many scientists tacitly operate successfully with just such a methodological stance. This is difficult to prove, however, because their explicit rhetoric tends to reflect the traditional teleological picture codified by philosophers.

I use the term "perspective" to designate a way of constructing scientific models. Within a perspective, some models may be discovered experimentally to fit the world better than others, at least for some purposes. Comparisons across perspectives are more difficult, but I doubt one ever finds the kind of radical incommensurability that philosophers such as Kuhn and Feyerabend are supposed to have advocated. In any case, the resulting view of realism can be called "perspectival realism." I will give some examples shortly. My main task now is to make plausible a realistic understanding of science that is perspectival rather than absolute.

9. Perspectivalism in Observation

Perspectivalism is most easily appreciated at the level of observation. It is here that the metaphor of perspectives is closest to its roots. A paradigm example would be the experience of viewing a building from different angles and different distances. Each distance and angle of view provides a different perspective on the building. Two features of this simple case already exemplify the main features of a more general perspectivalism. First, there is no total or universal perspective, or, alternatively, there is no perspective from nowhere or from everywhere at once. All perspectives are partial relative to their objects. Second, each perspective is a perspective of the building. There is something real that each perspective is a perspective of. So perspectivalism is prima facie a form of realism. Additional objectivity can be built into this example by imagining a series of photographs taken from different viewpoints rather than simply a series of visual experiences.

The example of secondary qualities stretches the metaphor of perspectivalism a bit further. We perceive the world as containing objects exhibiting different colors. Yet we know it is our capacity for experiencing color that partly explains the character of our perceptions. Without perceivers like us, there would be no experiences of color. Nevertheless, our perception of color provides us access to aspects of the world apart from us, namely differential reflection of light waves of varying frequency. I would say that our capacity for color vision provides us with a perspective from which we can experience aspects of the world. It is again not an excessive extension of the metaphor to say that different species of animals experience the world from the different perspectives provided by their various sense organs.

The existence of scientific instrumentation provides a further extension of the metaphor. Radio telescopes, for example, may be said to provide us with a perspective from which to view the heavens. It is a different perspective from that provided by ordinary optical telescopes. Without this technology, the kinds of outputs provided by such instruments would not exist. Yet radio telescopes do provide us with information about aspects of the universe that may not be accessible in other ways. Similar comments apply to the gamma ray telescopes that provided the evidence for reports of a plume of anti-matter (positrons) streaming out from the center of our galaxy.

These paradigm examples suggest that all forms of observation and/or detection should be understood as perspectival in nature. They all provide access to aspects of reality, access that is nevertheless always partial.

10. Perspectivalism in Theories

The extension of perspectivalism to the level of scientific theory is more problematic, but, I think, eventually equally convincing. As an intermediate step, consider the human practice of making *maps*. Maps, I would say, represent spatial regions from particular perspectives determined by various human interests. Imagine, for example, four different maps of Manhattan Island (New York City): 1) A street map; 2) A subway map; 3) A neighborhood map; and 4) A geological map. Each, I would say, represents the island of Manhattan from a different perspective represented, for example, by a driver, a subway rider, a social worker, a geologist.

Maps exhibit the two primary characteristics I earlier ascribed to perspectives. First, they are always *partial*. There is no such thing as a complete map. Second, maps may be maps *of something*. So maps can be understood realistically. Unlike perceptual experience or the operation of physical detectors, however, the production of a map is an act of deliberate construction. If a nervous system or other physical detector is functioning properly, it automatically registers the information available to it from its particular perspective. Insuring that a map correctly represents the intended space requires much deliberate care. Mistakes can easily be made. Moreover, one can deliberately construct mistaken maps, or even maps of completely fictional places.

One is tempted to ask: How do maps represent physical spaces? Asking the question this way suggests that the answer is to be found in some binary relationship between maps and places. A better question is: How do we humans manage to use maps to represent physical spaces? This way of posing the question makes it less easy to forget that making and using maps is a cognitive and social activity of humans.

Part of the answer is that map-making and map-using takes advantage of similarities in spatial structure between features of a map and features of a terrain. But one cannot understand map-making solely in terms of abstract, geometrical relationships. Interpretative relationships are also necessary. One must be able to understand that a particular area on a map is intended to represent, for example, a neighborhood rather than a political division or corporate ownership. These two features of representation using maps, similarity of structure and interpretation, carry over to an understanding of how humans use scientific models to represent aspects of the world.

It is not too great an analogical leap, I think, to go from maps to the kinds of models one finds in many sciences. Classical mechanics provides an archetypal example. The models of classical mechanics represent only a very limited number of aspects of objects such as mass, relative position, relative velocity, and acceleration. This being so, I would say that the principles of classical mechanics provide a perspective within which one can construct a wide variety of models, some of which we have found to provide a very good fit to mechanical systems in the real world.

Consider, for example, text-book representations of a simple harmonic oscillator. These typically contain numerous equations used to characterize the model. But they also often include a number of diagrams which look a lot like maps. That is, these diagrams are made up of lines in two dimensions which represent various aspects of the motion of a simple harmonic oscillator. One need only know how to interpret them. Here, then, is a suggestion for better understanding what it means for a model to fit the world. The fit between a model and the world may be thought of like the fit between a map and the region it represents.

Evolutionary theory provides both an example of a perspectival understanding of scientific theories and a powerful analogy for understanding how models "fit" the world. The fundamental principles of evolutionary theory (briefly: variation, selection, and transmission) may be understood as defining very abstract models of an evolving population. To achieve empirical claims one must instantiate these principles in more specific models of a particular population (or kind of population). The analogy to the fit of models in general is that what counts toward the fitness of individuals in a given environment depends on the nature of the population in question, different for mice and elephants. By analogy, what counts as "fitting" the world for models of any science depends on the particular subject matter in question and the nature of the models being deployed.

11. One World as a Methodological Rule

A final problem. Suppose we have two perspectives that overlap, but disagree about the character of the world in the region where they overlap. What should we say? We might try to brush off the question with the reflection that, since we are only concerned with applying models, what does it matter if applications conflict? Use the type of model that best serves one's current purposes. I find that attitude understandable, but too instrumentalistic.

The basis for my misgiving is the supposition that there is, after all, only one world, and it has some one structure or other. Of course, from a naturalistic perspective, one cannot offer *a priori* arguments in favor of a "one world" hypothesis. One can, however, take it as a methodological rule: Proceed as if the world has a single structure. In light of this rule, the existence of conflicting applications of different types of models is an indication that one or both types of models fail to fit the world as well as they might. It is an invitation to further inquiry to find models that eliminate the conflict, although there is no guarantee that such models will be found. If arguments in favor of adopting this methodological rule are desired, the best one can do is point out the many cases in the history of science where following such a rule was fruitful in leading to the construction of better models. The eventual resolution of the early twentieth century conflict between Mendelians and biometricians seems to me a clear case in point.

12. Conclusion

I conclude that a modest evolutionary naturalism is a viable general project, capable of encompassing all of nature, including culture and the enterprise of science itself. The role of evolutionary thinking within a naturalist program is a matter for continued investigation. It cannot, I think, be all encompassing in a useful way.

One must be careful, however, how one characterizes naturalism. Presented as theses, it invites requests for justification and self-defeating attempts to construct *a priori* arguments in its favor. Vigilance is required to keep arguments for naturalism within naturalistic limitations. A better strategy, I have suggested, is to regard naturalism as a set of methodological rules for developing a consistent naturalistic picture of the world. Success in applying these rules gives comfort to those pursuing the program and encourages others to join the effort. Positively, that is the most a consistent naturalist can do.

References

French HW (1997) The Ritual Slaves of Ghana: Young and Female. The New York Times, 20 January: 1.
Giere RN (1988) Explaining Science: A Cognitive Approach. Chicago: University of Chicago Press.
Giere RN (1990) Evolutionary models of science. In: Evolution, Cognition, and Realism (Rescher N, ed), 21–32. Lanham, MD: University Press of America.
Giere RN (2006) Scientific Perspectivism. Chicago: University of Chicago Press.
Godfrey-Smith P (2002) Dewey on Naturalism, Realism and Science. Philosophy of Science 69: S25–S35.
Griesemer JR (2000) Development, Culture, and the Units of Inheritance. Philosophy of Science 67: 348–368.

Hooker CA (1987) Evolutionary Naturalist Realism: Circa 1985. In: A Realistic Theory of Science. Albany, NY: State University of New York Press.

Hull D (1988) Science as a Process: An Evolutionary Account of the Social and Conceptual Development of Science. Chicago: University of Chicago Press.

James W (1907) Pragmatism. New York and London: Longmans, Green, and Co.

Kitcher P (1992) The Naturalists Return. The Philosophical Review 101: 53–114.

Kuhn TS (1962) The Structure of Scientific Revolutions. Chicago: University of Chicago Press (2nd ed 1970).

Lumsden C, Wilson EO (1981) Genes, Mind, and Culture. Cambridge, MA: Harvard University Press.

Maddy P (2000) Naturalism in Mathematics. New York: Oxford University Press.

Rosenberg A (1996) A Field Guide to Recent Species of Naturalism. The British Journal for the Philosophy of Science 47: 1–30.

Ruse M (1986) Taking Darwin Seriously. Dordrecht: Reidel.

Ruse M (1995) Evolutionary Naturalism: Selected Essays. London: Routledge.

Schilpp PA, Hahn LE (1939) The Philosophy of John Dewey. La Salle, IL: Open Court.

Hilary Kornblith

The Naturalistic Project in Epistemology: Where Do We Go from Here?

University of Massachusetts, Amherst

W. V. Quine ushered in a new approach to epistemology in 1969 with his paper, "Epistemology Naturalized."[1] In the decades which followed, there was a great deal of work done developing that approach, both at a programmatic level, in sketching directions and lines of research which a naturalized epistemology might follow, and in filling in the details of a number of these different and promising suggestions. This was an exciting time for naturalistic epistemologists. But now, almost forty years later, much of the focus of contemporary analytic epistemology lies elsewhere. What has happened to the naturalistic program? Is there still reason to think that this kind of approach to epistemological issues is worthy of pursuit? And, if so, what are the most promising lines of research? This paper attempts to answer these questions.

1. The First Twenty-Five Years: 1969–1994[2]

Naturalism did not begin with Quine, nor did the naturalistic approach to epistemology. Nevertheless, there is no denying that the publication of "Epistemology

---

1   In his *Ontological Relativity and Other Essays*, Columbia University Press, 1969, 69–90.
2   For a selection of papers from this period, see Hilary Kornblith, ed., *Naturalizing Epistemology*, 2nd edition, MIT Press, 1994. A particularly valuable overview is found in Philip Kitcher, "The Naturalists Return," *Philosophical Review*, 101(1992), 53–114. Books published during this period include: D. M. Armstrong, *Belief, Truth and Knowledge*, Cambridge University Press, 1973; Fred Dretske, *Knowledge and the Flow of Information*, MIT Press, 1981; Alvin Goldman, *Epistemology and Cognition*, Harvard University Press, 1986; Alvin Goldman, *Liaisons: Philosophy Meets the Cognitive and Social Sciences*, MIT Press, 1992; Alvin Goldman, *Knowledge in a Social World*, Oxford University Press, 1999; Gilbert Harman, *Change in View: Principles of Reasoning*, MIT Press, 1986; Hilary Kornblith, *Inductive Inference and its Natural Ground*, MIT Press, 1993; Robert Nozick, *Philosophical Explanations*, Harvard University Press, 1981; Ernest Sosa, *Knowledge in Perspective*, Cambridge University Press, 1991; Stephen Stich, *The Fragmentation of Reason*, MIT Press, 1990.

Naturalized" brought about a radical change in analytic epistemology. The story of Quine's influence has been told many times,[3] so I will be brief.

Quine argued that, for a variety of reasons, the positivist attempt to provide a foundationalist rational reconstruction of our knowledge was doomed to failure. In its place, he offered the briefest sketch of an alternative approach:

> Philosophers have rightly despaired of translating everything into observational and logico-mathematical terms. They have despaired of this even when they have not recognized, as the reason for this irreducibility, that the statements largely do not have their private bundles of empirical consequences. And some philosophers have seen in this irreducibility the bankruptcy of epistemology ...
>
> But I think that at this point it may be more useful to say rather that epistemology still goes on, though in a new setting and a clarified status. Epistemology, or something like it, simply falls into place as a chapter of psychology and hence of natural science. It studies a natural phenomenon ...[4]

The suggestion that the study of epistemology be made continuous with science—that it be seen simply as an empirical investigation of a certain natural phenomenon—brings with it a reconceptualization not only of the subject matter and methods of epistemology, but of the epistemic status of epistemological theories as well.

> The old epistemology aspired to contain, in a sense, natural science; it would construct it somehow from sense data. Epistemology in its new setting, conversely, is contained in natural science, as a chapter of psychology. But the old containment remains valid too, in its way. We are studying how the human subject of our study posits bodies and projects his physics from his data, and we appreciate that our position in the world is just like his ...
>
> This interplay is reminiscent again of the old threat of circularity, but it is all right now that we have stopped dreaming of deducing science from sense data. We are after an understanding of science as an institution or process in the world, and we do not intend that understanding to be any better than the science which is its subject.[5]

---

3   See, e.g., Richard Foley, "Quine and Naturalized Epistemology," *Midwest Studies in Philosophy*, XIX(1994), 243–260; Roger Gibson, *Enlightened Empiricism: An Examination of W.V. Quine's Theory of Knowledge*, University of South Florida Press, 1988; Peter Hylton, "Quine's Naturalism," *Midwest Studies in Philosophy*, XIX(1994), 261–282; Bredo Johnson, "How to Read 'Epistemology Naturalized,' *Journal of Philosophy*, CII(2005), 78–93; Jaegwon Kim, "What is 'Naturalized Epistemology'?," in Kornblith, ed., *op. cit.*, 33–55; Philip Kitcher, *op. cit.*; Hilary Kornblith, "Introduction: What is Naturalistic Epistemology?," in Kornblith, ed., *op. cit.*, 1–14; Hilary Kornblith, "Naturalistic Epistemology and its Critics," *Philosophical Topics*, 23(1995), 237–255; Stephen Stich, "Naturalizing Epistemology: Quine, Simon and the Prospects for Pragmatism," in C. Hookway and D. Peterson, eds., *Philosophy and Cognitive Science*, Cambridge University Press, 1993, 1–17; Barry Stroud, *The Significance of Philosophical Scepticism*, Oxford University Press, 1984, chapter VI.

4   "Epistemology Naturalized," 82.

5   "Epistemology Naturalized," 83–4.

There is something ironic in this last remark of Quine's. The epistemological theories which he criticizes, and which sought an understanding of knowledge which would be "better than science," were, beyond doubt, unsuccessful. But it is not just these particular epistemological theories, nor just epistemology, say, rather than the rest of philosophy, which failed to achieve an understanding which would be better than science. Science is, beyond a doubt, the crowning intellectual achievement of the human species, and there is nothing to be found anywhere in the history of philosophy which comes remotely close to the achievements of science in terms of successful explanation, depth of understanding, or, to use a phrase from Descartes, "firm and lasting" results. While Descartes sought to provide an epistemological theory which would put science, once and for all, on its proper foundation so that it might achieve such secure results, the centuries since Descartes have shown that science has done quite well without the kind of foundation he sought. It is, at this point in human history, philosophy which needs a proper basis for results which might stand the test of time. Given the security which scientific results now enjoy, the prospect Quine offers of an epistemology founded on science is one for which little apology is needed. A philosophy as well-founded as science would be better founded than any which has yet been offered.

The naturalistic epistemology which Quine urged upon us, an epistemology which would be a chapter of empirical psychology, was one for which Quine laid the foundations, but to which he did not contribute in detail. The behavioristic psychology to which Quine was committed has itself not withstood the test of time, and those who would pursue Quine's project have, for the most part, looked to cognitive science instead. But in the decades immediately following the publication of "Epistemology Naturalized," epistemologists of a naturalistic turn of mind were largely engaged in other projects.

The central project which engaged such epistemologists during this period was the development of externalist theories of justification. Early work by Armstrong, Dretske and Goldman led the way here, and the issue which divides externalists from internalists remains an important focus of epistemological research to the present day.[6] Roughly, internalists believe that the factors in virtue of which a belief counts as justified are ones which are internally accessible to

---

6   See works by Armstrong, Dretske and Goldman cited in note 2. Also tremendously influential were Dretske, "Conclusive Reasons," *Australasian Journal of Philosophy*, 49(1971), 1–22; Goldman, "A Causal Theory of Knowing," *Journal of Philosophy*, 64(1967), 355–372; Goldman, "Discrimination and Perceptual Knowledge," *Journal of Philosophy*, 73(1976), 771–791; and Goldman, "What is Justified Belief?," in George Pappas, ed., *Justification and Knowledge*, Reidel, 1979, 1–23. Papers detailing the controversy between internalists and externalists are anthologized in Hilary Kornblith, ed., *Epistemology: Internalism and Externalism*, Blackwell, 2001.

the agent—that is, accessible to introspection and reflection—while externalists deny this. Classical versions of foundationalism and the coherence theory were all varieties of internalism, and the very idea that the factors which determine whether a belief is justified might be ones which are not internally accessible to an agent seemed, to many, to simply abandon genuinely epistemological concerns. Laurence BonJour's reaction was typical of many. "My conviction," BonJour wrote, "is that views of this kind are merely wrong-headed and ultimately uninteresting evasions of the central epistemological issues."[7] A great deal of interesting work was done during this period in laying out the general case for externalism, as well as the details of a number of different varieties, but for our purposes, what is particularly striking about this work is that it was, in many ways, methodologically of a piece with the kind of epistemological work which Quine sought to reject in "Epistemology Naturalized." Goldman very explicitly presented his work as a piece of traditional conceptual analysis,[8] and neither Armstrong nor Dretske appealed to empirical work in psychology in support of their accounts of knowledge. While the substance of these accounts had a distinctively naturalistic flavor, the variety of naturalism implicit in these views was quite different from that endorsed by Quine.

It is worth pursuing this point a bit further. The externalist project developed by Armstrong, Dretske and Goldman occupies an interesting position mid-way between the traditional foundationalist and coherentist views which they sought to replace and the more radical program of naturalized epistemology which was favored by Quine. On the one hand, externalist accounts sought to explain epistemic justification in terms of such naturalistically wholesome notions as causation, lawful connection and reliability. This stands in sharp contrast to more traditional views which took certain epistemic notions as simple and unanalyzed, and attempted to show how all other epistemic concepts might be explained in terms of these.[9] By explaining all epistemic terminology in non-epistemic terms, these externalist accounts offered something importantly different from traditional epistemologies. On the other hand, the methods by which these naturalistic accounts were arrived at seemed to embrace the very methods of conceptual analysis which Quine rejected, leaving philosophy as a discipline different in kind from the sciences. The synthesis between philosophy and science which Quine urged, or rather the incorporation of philosophy as a chapter of science, was no part of the externalist program.

---

7   *In Defense of Pure Reason*, Cambridge University Press, 1998, 1, n. 1.
8   See, e.g., Goldman's remarks in "What is Justified Belief?," 17–18. Goldman's views about the nature of conceptual analysis have changed considerably since that time. See section 2 below.
9   Paradigmatic of this approach is the work of Roderick Chisholm. See, for example, *Theory of Knowledge*, Prentice-Hall, 1966, 1977, 1989.

Alvin Goldman's very important book, *Epistemology and Cognition*, nicely illustrates the difficult position which this variety of naturalism attempted to occupy. The first half of the book, *Theoretical Foundations*, presented conceptual analyses of a variety of epistemic notions. Goldman argued in great detail for his preferred version of reliabilism, the view that a belief is justified just in case it is produced or sustained by a reliable psychological process. While naturalistic in substance, this section of the book is not different in methodology from more traditional approaches, and philosophers of a traditional turn of mind found themselves very much at home with this section of the book. There is a great deal of interesting philosophical literature which engages with this material, discussing a variety of would-be examples of knowledge and justification, and would-be counterexamples to the proffered analyses. The second half of the book, *Assessing our Cognitive Resources*, presents a compendious review of empirical literature in the cognitive sciences, and discusses the ways in which the various cognitive processes we tend to draw upon meet, or fail to meet, the epistemic standards elaborated in the *Theoretical Foundations* section of the book. Unlike the first half of the book, this second part received relatively little attention in the philosophical literature. It was as if many philosophers thought that Goldman had written an important philosophical book—the section on *Theoretical Foundations*—and appended a book on cognitive science—*Assessing our Cognitive Resources*—at the end of it. Those most sympathetic to the methodology employed in the first half of the book often simply ignored the second. It was, as they saw it, empirical work in psychology: interesting in its own right, perhaps, but not philosophy.

For those committed to a more Quinean project of naturalization, the second portion of Goldman's book was a treasure trove of information about cognition, highlighting epistemologically significant issues in the cognitive science literature. But the fact that the first section of the book was articulated and defended in a way which is entirely independent of the empirical work seemed odd. Surely the first section of the book might be integrated with the second in a way which would serve to realize the naturalistic approach which Quine outlined. Anything short of this seemed to leave the book, and the defense of externalism, in an unstable position. And in this respect, Goldman's work on externalism was not unusual; most other externalists seemed to be in the same position.

There is, I believe, a way to understand much of the work done by externalists which would place it more squarely in the naturalistic camp, viewing it as not only naturalistic in substance, but in method as well. Viewing it in this way requires us to depart from the explicitly stated intentions of some of these authors, and in other cases, from fairly clear features of their practice. Nevertheless, I believe there is a case to be made for seeing the work done on externalism as falling more clearly in line with the Quinean project of naturalization.

Consider the way in which examples and counterexamples are used to motivate externalist theories of justification. It is frequently argued that versions of
internalism lead to a broad skepticism, and this, therefore, counts against internalism and in favor of theories, such as externalism, which uncontroversially
allow for a great deal of justified belief. Now this may be viewed as simple conceptual analysis: we have intuitions about cases in which an individual has (or
lacks) justified belief, and we examine candidate analyses of justification to
see the extent to which they square with our intuitions. In this way, we come to
understand the contours of our ordinary concept of justification. But it is possible
to view the manner in which these examples are used quite differently. Suppose
we view knowledge, and justification, as Quine suggested, as a natural phenomenon. What we wish to do is investigate that very phenomenon, not our concept
of it. And in order to do that, we should begin by assembling a number of clear
instances of it, just as we begin an investigation of natural kinds by assembling
clear instances of them. Having assembled a collection of such clear instances, we
then attempt to see what it is that they all have in common. Externalist theories
of justification may be seen as offering an hypothesis about the underlying
characteristics shared by clear-cut cases of justified belief.

If we think of externalists as engaged in this kind of theory construction,
then we may view what they are doing as thoroughly naturalistic: that is, naturalistic in both content and method.[10] Admittedly, the use of common sense examples falls short of the full integration with science that Quine envisioned, but it
does at least make clear that what is going on is a bit of empirical theory construction, rather than *a priori* conceptual analysis; it thereby makes sense of
Quine's suggestion that theory construction in philosophy should be seen as
continuous with work in the sciences. More than this, it shows how the two kinds
of projects which Goldman developed in *Epistemology and Cognition* might
be better integrated. While the kind of theory construction which motivates
externalism may well begin with common sense examples of knowledge and
justification—after all, an investigation of various natural kinds, such as gold,
begins with such simple everyday classifications—the detailed psychological
work in the second part of Goldman's book may be called upon as well to aid
in the understanding of what is genuinely shared by cases of knowledge and
justified belief.

The most recent work in naturalistic epistemology has, I believe, shown the
kind of explicit integration between empirical work and philosophical theory

---

10   Dretske seems to be suggesting something like this in his description of the "bottom-up
     strategy" to studying knowledge. See his "Two Conceptions of Knowledge: Rational vs.
     Reliable Belief," in his *Perception, Knowledge and Belief: Selected Essays*, Cambridge
     University Press, 2000, 80–93. I defend this approach in detail in chapter one of my
     Knowledge and its Place in Nature, Oxford University Press, 2002.

which Quine urged. There are a large number of different lines of research which are currently being developed, and, in the remainder of this paper, I will present an overview of a number of these projects.

2. Conceptual Analysis and Experimental Philosophy

Goldman's view about the status of conceptual analysis has shifted since the publication of *Epistemology and Cognition*. In a series of papers,[11] Goldman has defended the use of appeals to intuitions about hypothetical cases as a source of insight into the nature of our concepts. The target of philosophical analysis, according to this view, is the character of our concepts. Epistemologists thus seek to understand our concepts of knowledge and justification. Concepts are viewed as real psychological entities which play an important causal role in our mental economy. Our intuitions may serve as a guide to the contours of our concepts because one of the roles our concepts play is precisely to produce these intuitions about hypothetical cases. By consulting our intuitions about cases, then, we are, in effect, performing a small-scale psychological experiment. Goldman thus seeks to defend the integrity of traditional armchair philosophical methods, while, at the same time, giving them a legitimate scientific grounding.

Goldman does not believe that traditional methods are fully adequate in getting at the features of our concepts. As a result, armchair methods need to be supplemented by experimental work of the sort now common among cognitive scientists.[12] Nevertheless, Goldman argues that the more careful experimental work, while it is likely to add detail to the conceptual analyses produced by armchair methods, and, on occasion, to provide correction as well, is unlikely to make major changes to the conceptual analyses produced by thinking about our intuitions. This is one way, quite clearly, in which philosophical theory construction may be embedded in empirical theorizing.[13]

---

11   "Psychology and Philosophical Analysis," reprinted in his *Liaisons: Philosophy Meets the Cognitive and Social Sciences*, MIT Press, 1992, 143–153; "Epistemic Folkways and Scientific Epistemology," in *Liaisons*, 155–175; "Kornblith's Naturalistic Epistemology." *Philosophy and Phenomenological Research*, LXXI(2005), 403–410; "Philosophical Intuitions: Their Target, Their Source, and Their Epistemic Status," *Grazer Philosophische Studien*, forthcoming. See also Alvin Goldman and Joel Pust, "Philosophical Theory and Intuitional Evidence," reprinted in Goldman's *Pathways to Knowledge: Public and Private*, Oxford University Press, 2002, 73–94.

12   For experimental work on concepts, see, for example, Edward Smith and Douglas Medin, *Categories and Concepts*, Harvard University Press, 1981; Frank Keil, *Concepts, Kinds and Cognitive Development*, MIT Press, 1989; Gregory Murphy, *The Big Book of Concepts*, MIT Press, 2002.

13   I have criticized this project in detail in "Naturalism and Intuitions," *Grazer Philosophische Studien*, forthcoming.

Interestingly, there is now a fairly large group of philosophers—including Stephen Stich, Joshua Knobe, Shaun Nichols and Jonathan Weinberg—who have sought to do the very experimental work which Goldman argues is relevant to conceptual analysis, and they have produced a series of results bearing on analyses of intentional action, freedom, and a variety of epistemic notions. Thus, for example, Weinberg, Nichols and Stich[14] presented a series of hypothetical cases asking subjects whether the various individuals described were ones who "really know" or, instead, "only believe." In one experiment, cases were described in order to see whether subjects had intuitions matching those standardly elicited by Gettier examples. In another, hypothetical cases were used to test whether subjects' intuitions tended to favor internalist or externalist accounts of knowledge. Intuitions varied considerably across different cultural groups. North Americans of European descent were found to have quite different intuitions from East Asians, as well as from those of Indian, Pakistani and Bangladeshi descent. This kind of cultural variation should not be surprising, as Weinburg, Stich and Nichols argue, in light of the recent work by Richard Nisbett on cognitive differences between Westerners and East Asians.[15]

The upshot of these differences, should they prove genuine, has an important bearing on the project of conceptual analysis in epistemology. Epistemologists often write as if there is a single concept of knowledge, or of justification, which is the object of epistemological theorizing. We seek to understand that folk concept, and consulting our intuitions is designed to aid in the project of making clear what its boundaries are. More than this, our assessment of beliefs as justified or unjustified carries normative force: when we discover that a belief is unjustified, this gives us reason to give it up. But if it should turn out that there are many different concepts of justification, and these concepts vary from one culture to the next, then the normative force of claims of justifiedness becomes more tenuous. It is tremendously implausible to think that the appropriate standards for how one ought to arrive at one's beliefs should vary from culture to culture, in the way, say, that matters of etiquette do. But if we reject this simpleminded relativism, and the concept of justification does vary from culture to culture, then the connection between our concept of justifiedness and epistemic norms must be reevaluated. Some more objective basis for epistemic normativity must be found.[16] I will return to this theme below.

---

14   "Normativity and Epistemic Intuitions," *Philosophical Topics*, 29 (2001), 429–460. See also Nichols, Stich and Weinberg, "Meta-Skepticism: Meditations on Ethno-Epistemology," in Stephen Luper, ed., *The Skeptics*, Ashgate, 2003, 227–247.

15   *The Geography of Thought*, The Free Press, 2003.

16   Stich presented this argument on the basis of a thought experiment in chapter 4 of *The Fragmentation of Reason*. The experiments done by Weinberg, Nichols and Stich are designed to show that the worry presented in *The Fragmentation of Reason* turns out not to be merely imaginable; instead, the standards implicit in folk concepts actually do vary across cultures.

One might, of course, attempt to undermine the claim of the experimental philosophers that their data genuinely do support the view that concepts of justification or knowledge vary from culture to culture.[17] Those who see the target of philosophical analysis as residing in our concepts, however, cannot simply reject this data out of hand as irrelevant. And once the relevance of this data is granted, this moves the subject of philosophical theory construction exactly where the experimental philosophers wish to see it located: well within the empirical domain.

3. Virtue Epistemology

There is an approach to epistemological questions which sees the notion of intellectual virtue as a fundamental concept of epistemic evaluation. This idea has been developed in quite different ways by Ernest Sosa and Linda Zagzebski, on the one hand, and James Montmarquet, on the other.[18]

On Sosa's view, something counts as a virtue only if it "would produce a high ratio of true beliefs," that is, only if it is reliable.[19] A belief is justified only if it is produced by the exercise of a virtue.[20] Note that the requirement that a belief have its source in an intellectual virtue is a necessary condition for justification; it is not, however, sufficient, but I will be concerned here only with the part of Sosa's account that ties justification to the possession of a virtue. Zagzebski also defines justified belief in terms of the possession of intellectual virtues,[21] but for her, the virtues have a more complicated structure than we see in Sosa. According to Zagzebski, a virtue has both a motivational component and a reliability component. Thus, to take one of her examples, "Courage is the virtue according to which a person is characteristically motivated to risk danger to himself when something of greater value is at stake and is reliably successful in

---

17　Ernest Sosa has presented objections of this sort, among others, in "A Defense of Intuitions," in Michael Bishop and Dominic Murphy, eds., *Stich and his Critics*, Blackwell, 2005.

18　See Sosa, *Knowledge in Perspective,* and also Sosa's contribution to Laurence BonJour and Ernest Sosa, *Epistemic Justification: Internalism vs. Externalism, Foundations vs. Virtues,* Blackwell, 2003; Zagzebski, *Virtues of the Mind: An Inquiry into the Nature of Virtue and the Foundations of Knowledge,* Cambridge University Press, 1996; James Montmarquet, *Epistemic Virtue and Doxastic Responsibility,* Rowman and Littlefield, 1992. There are three useful volumes of essays on this approach: Guy Axtell, ed., *Knowledge, Belief and Character: Readings in Virtue Epistemology,* Rowman and Littlefield, 2000; Abrol Fairweather and Linda Zagzebski, eds., *Virtue Epistemology: Essays on Epistemic Virtue and Responsibility,* Oxford University Press, 2001; Michael DePaul and Linda Zagzebski, eds., *Intellectual Virtue: Perspectives from Ethics and Epistemology,* Oxford University Press, 2003.

19　*Epistemic Justification: Internalism vs. Externalism, Foundations vs. Virtues,* 156.

20　*Ibid.,* 157.

21　*Virtues of the Mind,* 241.

doing so."[22] The intellectual virtues, according to Zagzebski, all have the motivation of attaining knowledge,[23] and thus the reliability component of these virtues will also necessitate that they tend to produce true belief. This aspect of Sosa's and Zagzebski's view, then, is naturally seen as having an important affinity with reliabilism.

Montmarquet, however, while also giving an account of justification in terms of intellectual virtues, insists that it is no part of an intellectual virtue that it be truth-conducive. Thus, consider what Montmarquet has to say about openmindedness, one of the intellectual traits which he regards as a virtue:

> it is the tendency, for example, to resist initial dismissals based on unfamiliarity that partially constitutes openmindedness. Whether it turns out that this resistance tracks, or nearly tracks, objective truth will certainly be of epistemological interest. But it is not part of openmindedness.[24]

Thus, while Sosa and Zagzebski offer accounts of justified belief which parallel consequentialist moral theories—they define the epistemic right (justified belief) in terms of the epistemic good (truth)—Montmarquet offers an account which parallels virtue theories of ethics, defining the epistemic right independently of the epistemic good.

Now neither Sosa nor Zagzebski nor Montmarquet present their views as based on empirical evidence, and so it might seem that they are not rightly regarded as falling within the naturalistic approach to epistemology, at least as I am construing it here. Nevertheless, these views seem to have quite substantive empirical commitments. Each of these authors argues that there are certain stable intellectual character traits which are instrumental in bringing about paradigm cases of justified belief and knowledge. Now there can be little doubt that such a claim has a great deal of initial plausibility, and thus many of the discussions of examples in these authors seem to provide a good deal of motivation for this approach. Nevertheless, empirical work in social psychology has often undermined common sense conceptions of human psychology, and since there is a good deal of work being done by psychologists on the nature of human character traits, it is thus worth examining the extent to which this literature either supports or undermines the virtue-theoretic picture.

Indeed, John Doris has argued in some detail[25] that the kinds of character traits to which virtue-theoretic accounts of ethics are committed are ones which

---

22   *Ibid.*, 165.
23   *Ibid.*, 166–197.
24   *Epistemic Virtue and Doxastic Responsibility*, 25.
25   *Lack of Character: Personality and Moral Behavior*, Cambridge University Press, 2002. See also Gilbert Harman, "Moral Philosophy Meets Social Psychology: Virtue Ethics and the Fundamental Attribution Error," *Proceedings of the Aristotelian Society*, 99(1998–9), 315–331, and "The Non-Existence of Character Traits," *Proceedings of the Aristotelian Society*, 100(1999–2000), 223–226.

the best current empirical theories tell us do not genuinely exist. The source of our behavior does not reside in traits which have the stability and scope which virtue theories of ethics presuppose. And Doris has suggested[26] that these results may perhaps be applied to the epistemological case as well. This is certainly a suggestion worth looking into. My point here is not, however, to cast doubt on virtue-theoretic approaches to epistemology; that would certainly require the kind of detailed discussion which Doris has brought to the moral case. Rather, to my mind, the importance of Doris's suggestion lies in the way it reveals that the virtue-theoretic approach to epistemology might be subjected to empirical test. To the extent that a virtue-theoretic epistemology makes substantive empirical claims about human character, we should welcome the prospect of gaining evidence that bears on its truth or falsity.

4. Judgmental Heuristics

Work by Amos Tversky and Daniel Kahneman, beginning in the 1970's, presented an extraordinary picture of the human mind.[27] Although a casual look at the way in which individuals reason might lead one to believe that there is a good deal of variation in the ways in which individuals draw conclusions from a body of data, a more careful and controlled investigation of human inference showed something quite different: there is a great deal of uniformity in the manner in which inferences are drawn; it is possible to lay bare a large number of the judgmental heuristics which drive human inference; when these judgmental heuristics are examined, they show that human beings have a very strong tendency to reason in ways which are extremely unreliable. Tversky and Kahneman drew the obvious conclusion: Our "intuitive expectations are governed by a consistent misrepresentation of the world ..."[28] Many others agreed. Nisbett and Borgida saw this work as having "bleak implications for human rationality."[29] Human beings, it seemed, have a strong tendency to reason very badly.

This extremely pessimistic view, however, was soon replaced by a far more moderate one. As Nisbett and Ross argued in their extensive review of the

---

26 In conversation. See also Alexandra Plakias and John Doris, "Virtue Epistemology, Cognitive Science and Skepticism," in preparation.

27 Some of the most important papers in this research tradition, both by Tversky and Kahneman and others as well, are collected in Daniel Kahneman, Paul Slovic and Amos Tversky, eds., *Judgment under Uncertainty: Heuristics and Biases*, Cambridge University Press, 1982.

28 "Belief in the Law of Small Numbers," reprinted in Kahneman, Slovic and Tversky, eds., 31.

29 Richard Nisbett and Eugene Borgida, "Attribution and the Psychology of Prediction," *Journal of Personality and Social Psychology*, 32(1975), 932–943.

literature,[30] these judgmental heuristics are a mixed bag. Some of them are quite reliable in many of the contexts in which they are actually used, effecting a useful trade-off of reliability for speed and computational simplicity.[31] Others are, however, just as bad as they initially seem. Any reasonable assessment of these heuristics requires a careful evaluation of their contexts of use, their interaction with one another, and issues not only of reliability, but cost of computation.

Research in this tradition continues, and it has deepened and broadened the picture initially offered by Tversky and Kahneman and Nisbett and Ross.[32] Gerd Gigerenzer's research group at the Max Planck Institute has been working on what he calls "fast and frugal" heuristics, those heuristics which sacrifice reliability for computational ease, and they have done a good bit of work to set this approach in an evolutionary perspective.[33] Not surprisingly, there are efficient heuristics which do not come naturally to us, and yet which might be put to use in ways which would be far more effective in getting at the truth than the heuristics which we are naturally inclined to employ. Michael Bishop and J. D. Trout have made a detailed case for the use of such heuristics.[34]

There are two broader issues which this body of research raises. First, this entire literature nicely illustrates the interanimation of descriptive and normative themes. Work showing the limitations of human cognition clearly has an important bearing on normative issues.[35] More than this, even in cases where the reasonableness of certain heuristics might well have been recognizable *a priori*, it is not at all surprising that many of these heuristics were discovered not by *a priori* considerations, but rather by an attempt to accurately describe the ways in which human beings reason. While imaginary cases and thought experiments are a useful stimulus to research, actual cases quite often raise possibilities which would not otherwise have been considered.

---

30   *Human Inference: Strategies and Shortcomings of Social Judgment*, Prentice-Hall, 1980; see especially chapter 11, "Assessing the Damage". See also Kornblith, *Inductive Inference and its Natural Ground*. An extremely useful overview of these issues may be found in Edward Stein, *Without Good Reason: The Rationality Debate in Philosophy and Cognitive Science*, Oxford University Press, 1996.

31   The importance of these kinds of trade-offs was a central feature of Herbert Simon's work. See, for example, *The Science of the Artificial*, MIT Press, 1981 and *Models of Bounded Rationality*, vols. 1 and 2, MIT Press, 1982.

32   For a useful collection of more recent papers in this tradition, see Thomas Gilovitch, Dale Griffin and Daniel Kahneman, eds., *Heuristics and Biases: The Psychology of Intuitive Judgment*, Cambridge University Press, 2002.

33   Gerd Gigerenzer, Peter Todd and the ABC Research Group, *Simple Heuristics that Make Us Smart*, Oxford University Press, 1999.

34   *Epistemology and the Psychology of Human Judgment*, Oxford University Press, 2005.

35   I have discussed this issue in "Epistemic Obligation and the Possibility of Internalism," in A. Fairweather and L. Zagzebski, eds., 231–248.

Second, the heuristics which accurately describe the character of human inference are not, of course, ones which we self-consciously employ; we are not at all aware of employing the inferential strategies which this body of research has revealed. More than this, the views most people have of their own inferential processes are frequently quite inaccurate.[36] This has an important bearing on the dispute between internalists and externalists. There is, after all, a common sense picture of belief-acquisition which comports quite nicely with internalism. While much of our belief acquisition is clearly unreflective, we do sometimes turn reflective and ask ourselves what it is that we ought to believe. At such times, we examine our beliefs and their logical interconnections and, it seems, either revise our beliefs on the basis of such examination, or decide to go on believing as before. On these occasions, we seem to exert our control over our belief formation; it is in these reflective moments that we are most naturally described as epistemic agents. It is here, as well, that the internalist approach to questions of epistemic evaluation seems most compelling. But this picture presupposes a certain view about the way in which our beliefs are formed, a view which the body of literature under discussion here seems to challenge. The kinds of justifications we offer in our reflective moments may have far less bearing on the fixation of belief than it seems to the reflective agent.[37] If these justifications are typically epiphenomenal with respect to the fixation of belief, then the central position such justifications are accorded in internalist epistemologies,[38] and in any epistemology which would emphasize the role of reflection, begins to look misguided. By illuminating the ways in which our beliefs are formed, and the ways in which these processes are affected, this body of empirical literature helps us to understand some of the empirical presuppositions of our normative theories.

5. The Naturalistic *A Priori*

Quine, of course, rejected the very idea of a priori knowledge, and this has often been seen as integral to a naturalistic epistemology. It is thus particularly interesting that a number of authors have recently begun to develop the case for a

---

36   Pioneering work on this was done by Richard Nisbett and Timothy Wilson, "Telling More than We Can Know: Verbal Reports on Mental Processes," *Psychological Review*, 84(1977), 231–259(a). See, more recently, Timothy Wilson, *Strangers to Ourselves: Discovering the Adaptive Unconscious*, Harvard University Press, 2002.

37   I have argued for exactly this conclusion in chapter 4 of *Knowledge and its Place in Nature*, and also in "Distrusting Reason," *Midwest Studies in Philosophy*, XXIII(1999), 181–196.

38   For a recent attempt to connect our practice of justifying beliefs with the property some beliefs have of being justified, see Adam Leite, "On Justifying and Being Justified," *Philosophical Issues*, 14(2004), 219–253.

naturalistic a priori, something which, until recently, would surely have seemed a contradiction in terms. Philip Kitcher laid the foundation for this approach,[39] and it has been developed in some detail, more recently, by Georges Rey,[40] Alvin Goldman[41] and Louise Antony.[42]

The central idea here is quite straightforward.[43] Consider a process of belief-acquisition. If we are reliabilists, for example, then whether this process confers justification on beliefs which result from it depends on whether the process is reliable. Whether the resulting beliefs are a priori justified depends on whether the process takes any sensory input. There may well be processes, however, which take no sensory input at all and which are, nonetheless, extremely reliable. Thus, suppose that there were a reasoning module, innate in all human beings, and hard-wired with a basic deductive system. Such a module could spit out theorems in the propositional calculus, for example, without any sensory input whatsoever. The resulting beliefs would be justified, since the process which produces them is reliable; and they would be a priori justified, since the process which produces them takes no sensory input. Processes such a this would thus produce *a priori* justified beliefs, and a priori knowledge, and there is nothing in this way of viewing things to which a naturalist need object.

A few things need to be mentioned about this conception of the a priori. As these authors point out, the claim that we have such *a priori* knowledge is itself an empirical claim. Whether we should believe that this kind of *a priori* knowledge genuinely exists thus needs to be determined by experimental research.[44] Indeed, there is some work, for example, Lance Rips' extensive investigation of deductive inference,[45] which lends some support to this way of viewing things.[46]

---

39   See his "A Priori Knowledge," *Philosophical Review*, 89(1980), 3–23 and *The Nature of Mathematical Knowledge*, Oxford University Press, 1983. While Kitcher defends the naturalistic integrity of the notion of a priori knowledge, he rejects the view that mathematics is known a priori.

40   "The Unavailability of What We Mean I: A Reply to Quine, Fodor and LePore," in J. Fodor and E. LePore, eds., *Holism: A Consumer Update, Grazer Philosophische Studien*, 46(1993), 61–101 and "A Naturalistic A Priori," *Philosophical Studies*, 92(1998), 25–43.

41   "A Priori Warrant and Naturalistic Epistemology," *Philosophical Issues*, 13(1999), 1–28.

42   "A Naturalized Approach to the A Priori," manuscript.

43   The account in this paragraph both simplifies a number of complex issues, such as the role of potential defeaters, and ignores certain differences among the authors mentioned above.

44   Albert Casullo has also argued for this claim. See his *A Priori Justification*, Oxford University Press, 2003.

45   *The Psychology of Proof: Deductive Reasoning in Human Thinking*, MIT Press, 1994.

46   Rips' approach, however, is not at all uncontroversial. For an alternative way of viewing things, see Leda Cosmides, "The Logic of Social Exchange: Has Natural Selection Shaped How Humans Reason? Studies with the Wason Selection Test," *Cognition*, 31(1989), 187–276.

But even if it should turn out that we do in fact have inferential modules of the sort which this view requires, the naturalistic *a priori* would not be able to play many of the roles which traditional appeals to *a priori* knowledge were intended to provide. The project of First Philosophy, which Quine attacked in "Epistemology Naturalized," cannot be sustained by the naturalistic *a priori*, since a defense of any particular claim as *a priori* knowable is a product of scientific research, and not established prior to and independent of science. In addition, attempts to defend the view that philosophy itself is *a priori* justified do not comport well with this particular conception of the *a priori*. The scope and importance of *a priori* knowledge, on this view, is thus far more limited than it is on more traditional conceptions.

Nevertheless, the very idea that there might be a naturalistically respectable notion of *a priori* knowledge is an interesting development, and it shows that the rejection of the *a priori* turns out to be less integral to the naturalistic project than anyone could have predicted in 1969.[47]

6. Social Epistemology

Much of the early work done in naturalistic epistemology focused on processes of belief acquisition which take place within individual agents. As many have pointed out, however, a good deal of cognition is straightforwardly social, and there is now a great deal of literature examining social factors in cognition and their epistemological implications.[48]

C. A. J. Coady's important book, *Testimony*,[49] forced epistemologists to come to terms with the extraordinarily pervasive influence of other people's opinions on individual belief. What Coady made absolutely clear is that the influence of testimony is not some isolated and minor factor affecting individual opinion, and precisely how it is to be accommodated within existing epistemological theories is anything but obvious. Much of the large body of literature on this topic written since Coady's work is not at all within the naturalistic tradition, but naturalists

---

47　There are, of course, naturalists who reject this, or any other, conception of the a priori. See, for example, Michael Devitt, "Naturalism and the *A Priori*," *Philosophical Studies*, 92(1998), 45–65, and "There is No *A Priori*," in Matthias Steup and Ernest Sosa, eds., *Contemporary Debates in Epistemology*, Blackwell, 2005, 105–118.

48　Here, as elsewhere in this paper, I limit my discussion to work in epistemology proper, rather than attempt to survey the large body of related work in other areas of philosophy, such as philosophy of science. In the case of work on social epistemology, this restriction may seem even more arbitrary than elsewhere. Nevertheless, if this survey is to remain of manageable size, some restriction of this sort is required.

49　*Testimony: A Philosophical Study*, Oxford University Press, 1992.

have certainly engaged with the issues raised by testimony as well.[50] It is, in many cases, misleading to think of testimony as an epistemological transaction between two individuals. Instead, it is often illuminating to see communication between individuals against a broader background of social relations. We have a tendency to trust the testimony of individuals who are socially regarded as experts on the topic on which they are testifying, but this now raises the question of how the title of expert is socially conferred and whether the manner in which such titles are conferred allows for the reliable dissemination of true belief. Here the mechanisms for the acquisition and retention of true belief are seen to extend far more broadly than in paradigm cases of perceptual knowledge, where a focus on individual cognition seems most appropriate. It is important to recognize, however, that the move to examine the social mechanisms of belief acquisition and retention is a straightforward extension of a point long made by naturalistic epistemologists: once one recognizes the externalist point that the features of a belief in virtue of which it is justified are ones which need not be accessible to introspection or reflection, it becomes clear that social structures are as deeply implicated in the regulation of belief as are individual psychological mechanisms and various structural features of the non-social environment. While internalists about justification are understandably puzzled about how anyone might regard social factors in cognition as epistemically significant, externalists have no reason at all to treat cognition as a transaction between a lone individual and an environment physicalistically construed.[51]

Alvin Goldman's seminal *Knowledge in a Social World* sets these issues in a broad naturalistic framework and shows not only the relevance of social epistemology to an understanding of science, law, democracy and education, but also to areas traditionally regarded as wholly within the purview of individualistic epistemology, such as argumentation.[52] Goldman has investigated the importance of various economic models for understanding the social transmission of ideas,[53] and the relevance of evolutionary models for understanding the relationship between individual rationality and group rationality has been explored

---

50   *Socializing Epistemology: The Social Dimensions of Knowledge*, Frederick Schmitt, ed., Rowman and Littlefield, 1994; and *The Epistemology of Testimony*, Jennifer Lackey and Ernest Sosa, eds., Oxford University Press, forthcoming, are important collections of papers which deal with this issue from both naturalistic and anti-naturalistic perspectives.

51   I have presented this argument in greater detail in "A Conservative Approach to Social Epistemology," in F. Schmitt, ed., 93–110. See also Philip Kitcher, "Knowledge and Tradition," *Philosophical Topics*, 29(2001), 251–270.

52   See also Goldman's "Argumentation and Social Epistemology," *Journal of Philosophy*, 91(1994), 27–49.

53   Alvin Goldman and Moshe Shaked, "An Economic Model of Scientific Activity and Truth Acquisition," *Philosophical Studies*, 63(1991), 31–55 and also Goldman, *Knowledge in a Social World*, chapter 6.

by Philip Kitcher.[54] Evolutionary considerations about animal signaling have also been brought to bear on the subject of testimony in interesting ways by Dan Sperber[55] and Kirk Michaelian.[56] There is a very large body of literature on the social dimensions of scientific knowledge which is also clearly relevant, but it is impossible to canvas that here.

7. Biological and Evolutionary Approaches

In "Natural Kinds," Quine famously remarked that "Creatures inveterately wrong in their inductions have a pathetic but praiseworthy tendency to die before reproducing their kind."[57] The idea that an evolutionary approach might shed some light on the nature of cognition is, of course, an utterly natural one.[58] Indeed, it is common in textbooks on animal cognition to organize and develop the material on this topic by way of evolutionary themes.[59] As biologists frequently remark, it is impossible to understand the biological world apart from evolutionary considerations, and this applies not only to physical features of living things such as their limbs, their sensory organs and their brains, but their behavior and cognition as well. Biologists regard the environment as making informational demands on animals, and one may usefully regard cognition as an adaptive response to those demands.

Ruth Millikan's *Language, Thought and Other Biological Categories*[60] was a groundbreaking work in developing the philosophical foundations for a biological approach to the mind, and she has expanded on these themes in subsequent

---

54   See especially "The Division of Cognitive Labor", *Journal of Philosophy*, 87(1990), 5–22 and *Science, Truth and Democracy*, Oxford University Press, 2001.

55   See, e.g., "The Modularity of Thought and the Epidemiology of Representations," in L. A. Hirshfeld and S. A. Gelman, eds., *Mapping the Mind: Domain Specificity in Cognition and Culture*, Cambridge University Press, 1994, 39–67 and "An Evolutionary Perspective on Testimony and Argumentation," *Philosophical Topics*, 29(2001), 401–413.

56   "Testimony as a Natural Kind," manuscript.

57   *Ontological Relativity and Other Essays*, 126.

58   For some pioneering developments of this idea, see Karl Popper, *Objective Knowledge: An Evolutionary Approach*, Oxford University Press, 1972, and Donald Campbell, "Evolutionary Epistemology." in P. A. Schillp, ed., *The Philosophy of Karl R. Popper*, Open Court, 412–463. For a useful anthology of work on this area, see Franz Wuketits, ed., *Concepts and Approaches in Evolutionary Epistemology: Towards an Evolutionary Theory of Knowledge*, Reidel, 1984.

59   For particularly influential versions of this approach, see John Alcock, *Animal Behavior: An Evolutionary Approach*, 8th edition, Sunderland, 2005, and Sara Shettleworth, *Cognition, Evolution, and Behavior*, Oxford University Press, 1998.

60   *Language, Thought and Other Biological Categories: New Foundations for Realism*, MIT Press, 1984.

work.[61] Central to Millikan's approach is the notion of a *proper function*.[62] As Millikan tells us, the notion of proper function is defined recursively:

> ... for an item *A* to have a function *F* as a "proper function", it is necessary ... that one of these two conditions should hold. (1) *A* originated as a "reproduction" ... of some prior item or items that, *due* in part to possession of the properties reproduced, have actually performed *F* in the past, and *A* exists because ... of this or these performances. (2) *A* originated as the product of some device that, given its circumstances, normally causes *F* to be performed by *means* of producing an item like *A*.[63]

An item may have a certain function as its proper function even if it rarely or never performs that function, and even if items of that type rarely or never perform that function. To take Millikan's useful example: sperm having the proper function of fertilizing ova even though the overwhelming majority of sperm never, in fact, perform such a function. The notion of a proper function wears its biological roots on its sleeve. Millikan takes this idea of proper function and proceeds to explain the central ideas of psychology—including thought, language and knowledge—in terms of it.

Peter Godfrey-Smith[64] and Kim Sterelney[65] have also done important work in this area, showing a variety of ways in which the biological approach may deepen our understanding of cognitive phenomena. My own recent work on knowledge[66] is also an example of the influence of biological ideas on epistemology.

Work by evolutionary psychologists has taken these biological ideas in a distinctive direction. Leda Cosmides[67] argued that a number of the inferential heuristics discovered by Tversky and Kahneman could be best understood if seen from an evolutionary perspective. In particular, she argued that early hominids needed to be particularly adept at detecting cheaters in would-be co-operative social interactions, and many of our inferential tendencies are best viewed as adapted for that purpose. More than this, Cosmides has championed an approach to the mind

---

61   See especially *White Queen Psychology and Other Essays for Alice*, MIT Press, 1993; *On Clear and Confused Ideas: An Essay about Substance Concepts*, Cambridge University Press, 2000; *Varieties of Meaning: The 2002 Jean Nicod Lectures*, MIT Press, 2004; *Language: A Biological Model*, Oxford University Press, 2005.

62   See *Language, Thought and Other Biological Categories*, chapters 1 and 2, and "In Defense of Proper Functions," in *White Queen Psychology and Other Essays for Alice*, chapter 1.

63   *White Queen Psychology*, 13–14.

64   *The Evolution of Agency and Other Essays*, Cambridge University Press, 2001; *Complexity and the Function of Mind in Nature*, Cambridge University Press, 1996.

65   *Thought in a Hostile World: The Evolution of Human Cognition*, Blackwell, 2003.

66   *Knowledge and its Place in Nature*.

67   See especially "The Logic of Social Exchange: Has Natural Selection Shaped how Humans Reason?," *Cognition*, 31(1989), 187–276 and work by Cosmides and others collected in Jerome Barkow, Leda Cosmides and John Tooby, eds., *The Adapted Mind: Evolutionary Psychology and the Generation of Culture*, Oxford University Press, 1992.

which viewed its organizational structure as massively modular, i.e., nothing more than an assemblage of special purpose modules. Cosmides has thereby taken the idea of mental modularity developed by Jerry Fodor,[68] which has its origins in the Chomskian explanation of language acquisition, and attempted to explain the entire workings of the human mind in these terms, an approach inimical to that suggested by Fodor. This approach to cognition has been developed and extended by Stephen Pinker[69] and David Buss,[70] and is the source of a great deal of current controversy.[71]

8. Knowledge of Other Minds and Self-Knowledge

The question of how we come to know about the mental states of others is a traditional philosophical issue, and one which raises special problems for Cartesian views about the nature of mind and knowledge. In the mid nineteen eighties, an important vein of naturalistic work on this issue began with the development of simulationist views by Robert Gordon[72] and Alvin Goldman.[73] According to simulationists, we do not come to understand the mental states of others by, in effect, constructing theories to explain their behavior; instead, the very processes by which mental states are produced in us are run, off-line, so as to simulate the processes and states of other agents. On this view, one needn't have beliefs about psychological generalizations in order to arrive at views about the mental states of others; accurate views about others' mental life may be generated without recourse to an understanding of the regularities which govern mental phenomena. There is now a very large body of literature elaborating and defending these ideas, as well an extensive literature on the theory-theory.[74]

---

68 *The Modularity of Mind: An Essay on Faculty Psychology*, MIT Press, 1983.

69 See, for example, *How the Mind Works*, Norton, 1997; *The Blank Slate: The Modern Denial of Human Nature*, Viking, 2002.

70 *Evolutionary Psychology: The New Science of the Mind*, Allyn and Bacon, 2nd edition, 2004; David Buss, ed., *The Handbook of Evolutionary Psychology*, Wiley, 2005.

71 For useful critical work, see Richard Samuels, "Evolutionary Psychology and the Massive Modularity Hypothesis," *British Journal for the Philosophy of Science*, 49(1998), 575–602; David Buller, *Adapting Minds: Evolutionary Psychology and the Persistent Quest for Human Nature*, MIT Press, 2005.

72 "Folk Psychology as Simulation," *Mind and Language*, 1(1986), 158–171.

73 "Interpretation Psychologized," *Mind and Language*, 4(1989), 161–185.

74 For particularly useful collections of papers, see Martin Davies and Tony Stone, eds., *Folk Psychology: The Theory of Mind Debate*, Blackwell, 1995, and Peter Carruthers and Peter Smith, eds., *Theories of Theories of Mind*, Cambridge University Press, 1996. For the most sophisticated defense of the theory-theory, see Alison Gopnik and Andrew Meltzoff, *Words, Thoughts and Theories*, MIT Press, 1997.

One important outgrowth of this literature is a renewed interest among naturalistic epistemologists in questions about how it is that we come to know the character of our own mental life. Self-knowledge is, of course, at the heart of the Cartesian view of knowledge of the physical world: we are able to know about the physical world, on the Cartesian view, only because our beliefs about the world may be grounded in knowledge of our own current mental states. The Cartesian view about self-knowledge, however, presents an overly optimistic picture of the powers of introspection based on a metaphysical picture of the mind which is anathema to naturalists. A naturalistic look at self-knowledge is thus long overdue.

In the late nineteen sixties, David Armstrong suggested that introspection should be viewed on the model of an internal monitoring device, working in very much the same way that computers do when they run checks on their own internal states.[75] Armstrong's suggestion was important in that it provided a straightforward way in which naturalists might account for the possibility of self-knowledge—especially insofar as it offered an alternative to much of the Wittgensteinian work on self-knowledge which was common at the time—but it was not defended by any sort of appeal to empirical evidence. More recent work, however, has sought to ground an account of self-knowledge in the available empirical evidence.

Particularly important was Richard Nisbett and Timothy Wilson's 1977 paper on our knowledge of our own mental processes.[76] Nisbett and Wilson argued that, in a wide range of situations, we are quite unreliable in the judgments we make about our mental processes and the relations among our mental states. More than this, they argued that the appearance of the "directness" of our judgments about such things is merely an illusion; at bottom, these judgments depend on inference, often mediated by mistaken or misleading premises. Wilson has developed this idea in detail in a recent book.[77] This picture is complimented by the gradual unraveling of the view that mentally healthy human beings have a largely accurate picture not only of the physical world, but of themselves. This view is now universally rejected, and it has been replaced with the view that the emotionally healthy individual typically has an overly optimistic view of himself along many different dimensions.[78] Much of what was

---

75 *A Materialist Theory of Mind*, Routledge and Kegan Paul, 1968, chapter 15.
76 "Telling More than We Can Know: Verbal Reports on Mental Processes," *Psychological Review*, 84(1977), 231–259.
77 *Strangers to Ourselves: Discovering the Adaptive Unconscious*, Harvard University Press, 2002.
78 For a useful review of the literature, see S. E. Taylor and J. Brown, "Illusion and Well-Being: A Social Psychological Perspective on Mental Health," *Psychological Bulletin*, 103(1988), 193–210. See also Shelley Taylor, *Positive Illusions: Creative Self-Deception and the Healthy Mind*, Basic Books, 1989.

once regarded as self-knowledge thus turns out to be no sort of knowledge at all, since it does not involve true belief.

This is not to deny, of course, that we do have a great deal of self-knowledge and that we need some sort of account of how we are able to achieve it. Shaun Nichols and Stephen Stich have championed a more sophisticated and empirically informed version of Armstrong's early suggestion,[79] and theory-theorists, such as Alison Gopnik, have attempted to explain self-knowledge as a product of theory construction.[80] It may seem that the very issues which animated debate on self-knowledge a number of decades ago are being recycled yet again for another go round, but such a cynical view, would, to my mind, miss what is important about the current state of affairs: issues which were once debated from the armchair are now being addressed with the benefit of the kind of empirical evidence which might allow for their principled resolution. If the debate is not settled yet, as it most certainly is not, we may yet hope that we are at least now approaching the issues in a way which will allow for a more constructive engagement.

9. Conclusion

The initial period following the publication of Quine's "Epistemology Naturalized" was largely devoted to foundational issues, making the case for the naturalized approach to epistemology, and arguing that there are important benefits to be gained by way of it. In addition, this period was characterized by the development of a deeper understanding of the character of anti-naturalistic views in epistemology, and the debate between internalists and externalists is a product of this period. These issues are not entirely behind us; there is a good deal more to say about them. At the same time, however, I believe that work in naturalistic epistemology is moving into a new phase. Much of the work of the last decade has been concerned less with foundational issues, and more with working out the details of a naturalistic worldview. It is thus that we see the importance of work on judgmental heuristics, on social epistemology, on the various biological and evolutionary approaches to cognition, and the work on self-knowledge. The naturalistic approach to epistemology is alive and well, and there is a wide range of ambitious and exciting work within this approach under way.

---

79   *Mindreading: An Integrated Account of Pretence, Self-Awareness, and Understanding Other Minds*, Oxford University Press, 2003.

80   See, e.g., "How We Know Our Own Minds: The Illusion of First-Person Knowledge of Intentionality," *Behavioral and Brain Sciences*, 16(1993), 1–15, 90–101, and also Gopnik and Meltzoff, *Words, Thoughts and Theories*.

Joseph Rouse

Naturalism and Scientific Practices: A Concluding Scientific Postscript

Wesleyan University

Naturalism is the dominant philosophical stance in North American philosophy today. Many philosophers explicitly identify themselves as naturalists, whose philosophical work is closely aligned with the natural sciences. Yet the best evidence for the dominance of naturalism comes from those philosophers who profess to be its opponents. These critics often make very significant concessions to naturalism. They hasten to accept a broadly scientific understanding of the world. They also often disavow any philosophical constraints upon scientific inquiry. Many even express these sentiments by accepting 'naturalism' as a label for their own views: they oppose "radical" versions of naturalism, but do so by defending a more tolerant, inclusive version of naturalism.

My response to this apparent triumph of philosophical naturalism echoes the Danish philosopher Søren Kierkegaard's *Concluding Unscientific Postscript* to the triumph of Christianity in 19th Century Europe.

> Nowadays we all of us indeed are Christians. But with this, what have we all become, I wonder; and what has Christianity become by the fact that we all of us as a matter of course are Christians of a sort? This work has made it difficult to become a Christian, so difficult that among people of culture in Christendom the number of Christians will not be very great. (1941, 519–20)

My "concluding scientific postscript" advances a similar claim about philosophical naturalism. It has become too easy nowadays to profess to be a naturalist; we need to recognize how difficult it is to fulfill the philosophical demands of naturalism. I say this not to criticize naturalism, but to invite you to accept a more demanding conception of what naturalism commits us to. I then argue that a conception of naturalism which gives central place to scientific practices rather than scientific knowledge best satisfies these demands.

The paper has two main parts. The first part of the paper identifies some tensions and conflicting demands that arise within naturalist philosophy today. The second argues that shifting primary philosophical attention from scientific knowledge to scientific practices provides a constructive response to these tensions.

Part I: Making It Harder to be a Naturalist

The tensions and conflicts within naturalism stand out especially clearly in the context of the historical development of naturalism, so I begin the first part of the paper with some brief historical remarks. After a more extensive discussion of the resulting internal tensions, the first part of the paper concludes with a more detailed discussion of one prominent locus for these tensions, namely whether to think of a scientific understanding of nature in terms of natural *laws*, or whether to do so in terms of *causal* interactions and theoretical models. This issue will then play a prominent role in the second part of the paper.

Ia: Some Historical Remarks About Naturalism

Western philosophical naturalism arose in the long struggle to free science or natural philosophy from its origin within a religious understanding of the world. Most early modern natural philosophers (such as Isaac Newton in the 17th Century) placed the scientific interpretation of nature within the larger project of understanding God's creation. Reading the Christian Bible and "reading" God's creation were two sides of a single activity. During the 18th and 19th Centuries, scientific research gradually freed itself from subordination to theological concerns. Nature became a distinct domain of understanding, accountable solely to its own standards and norms. Natural science was thereby freed from the authority of church or scripture. The French mathematician Laplace famously expressed the spirit of this initial stage of naturalism. In response to the Emperor Napoleon's question about the place of God in Laplace's celestial mechanics, Laplace said, "I have no need for that hypothesis." His view expressed the "enlightened" aspiration to free our understanding of nature and ourselves from appeals to divine intervention or other supernatural elements.

When natural science had been partly freed from subordination to religion, however, naturalism took on a new dimension. New scientific disciplines in psychology and the life sciences emerging in the late 19th Century offered a more expansive naturalist vision: natural science might also replace philosophical accounts of thought and rationality. In Germany, this project had a practical import, since there were then no university chairs in psychology. If experimental study of the mind was to find a place in the university, it would have to replace logic and epistemology in university chairs previously devoted to philosophy.

For much of the 20th Century, most philosophers rejected the effort to give empirical scientific answers to traditional philosophical questions. The great anti-naturalist philosophers of the early 20th Century such as Frege, Husserl, or Carnap argued that science could not do without philosophical guidance as easily as it had forsaken religion. They agreed that only empirical science can describe the contingencies of nature, society, and human psychology.

Philosophy nevertheless had a different and supposedly vital task. Only philosophy could clarify and justify the meaning and validity of scientific understanding. Science therefore needed philosophy to fulfill its own mission of understanding nature and human society. The competing philosophical programs of logical analysis, phenomenology, and neo-Kantian philosophy agreed that some form of philosophically comprehensible necessity must provide the norms for genuine scientific understanding. The primary topic of debates over naturalism had then changed, however, from a metaphysics of nature that rejects anything "supernatural," to the semantics and epistemology of science.

How did naturalism become more acceptable to philosophers later in the 20th Century? What changes in science or philosophy allowed naturalism to achieve its current philosophical prominence? Internal criticism of the anti-naturalist philosophical programs was important, but that is less relevant to my argument. I will instead highlight three developments that made naturalism a more attractive philosophical position. I will then discuss some different conceptions of philosophical naturalism that emerged from these developments, and the difficulties of integrating these conceptions.

Sophisticated new scientific research programs in cognitive science, evolutionary biology, and neuroscience were the first development that made naturalism more attractive to philosophers. Early 20th Century psychological theories and research programs were vulnerable to philosophical criticism. Frege, Husserl, or much later, Noam Chomsky, could readily show why these research programs were unable to explain the content of thought and language or the norms of epistemic justification. In contrast, the new research programs in psychology and biology did propose a defensible basis for understanding content and justification, in terms of the cognitive or evolutionary functions of mental states. These scientific fields were also much better empirically grounded than their predecessors. Above all, however, they introduced a new relationship between natural science and philosophy. Early 20th Century naturalists sought to *replace* philosophy with empirical research in psychology. Contemporary naturalists instead typically propose *philosophical* theories for which cognitive psychology, evolutionary biology or neuroscience provide important resources. Naturalists now want to use science to do important *philosophical* work that empirical science alone could not replace. Science provides philosophers with new empirical and conceptual tools to help understand thought, language and knowledge philosophically. Moreover, these scientific resources enhance the legitimacy of naturalist philosophy. Naturalists can now plausibly claim to replace mere philosophical speculation with empirically grounded philosophical research.

A second major development occurred within the philosophy of science. Earlier opponents of naturalism argued that only philosophy could account for norms of scientific justification and understanding. Historical and contemporary studies of scientific research showed, however, that the sciences often did not fit philosophical claims about how science ought to be done. The failure of logical empiricist philosophy of science was the most widely discussed example, but phenomenological accounts of science encountered similar problems. The eventual response of most philosophers to conflicts between philosophical norms and scientific practice was to accept the self-sufficiency of the sciences. If scientific work conflicts with philosophical accounts of science, we should revise our philosophy. Philosophy of science has no standing to legislate norms governing science. Some philosophers still do offer general philosophical accounts of science, but their accounts now typically defer to how science is done. For example, recent disputes among scientific realists, instrumentalists, or social constructivists do not concern which standards *ought* to govern knowledge of nature. Proponents of these views instead claim to make best sense of science as it *is*.

Changing philosophical attitudes toward causality and necessity are the third and final historical development I consider. Under the influence of David Hume, empiricist philosophy of science was long suspicious of the notion of causal connection. Hume's followers argued that observation could only recognize empirical regularities, not causal connections. Moreover, most early 20th Century philosophers thought that all empirical truths were contingent. "Necessity" could only mean logical, rational or transcendental necessity, recognizable by reason alone. Causality and natural necessity have now become more philosophically respectable concepts, however, for several reasons. First, philosophers of science now recognize that scientific understanding and inductive confirmation seem to require some concept of necessity or causal connection; strictly empiricist descriptions of nature cannot suffice for science. Second, important technical work in modal logic has allayed earlier philosophical suspicions about the coherence of modal concepts and inferences. Finally, the empiricist philosophy that supported suspicions about causality or nomological necessity now looks like an unwarranted philosophical imposition upon the sciences. As a result of these changes, naturalists today have much more powerful *philosophical* concepts and inferences for understanding thought and knowledge than were available to their predecessors. Naturalists can now use a scientific understanding of nature that goes beyond merely contingent facts to grasp causal relations or natural laws.

Ib: Some Conflicts and Tensions Within Philosophical Naturalism

These philosophical and scientific developments have now given naturalism a central place in North American philosophy. This apparent triumph of naturalism nevertheless masks some important disagreements over what naturalism is, and what difference naturalism would make in philosophy or science. In this part of the paper, I will describe some of these tensions, and argue that they are genuine conflicts that naturalists must resolve.

The first issue concerns the argumentative force of naturalism. What difference would accepting philosophical naturalism make to how we live and think? Is naturalism a *radical* position that requires its proponents to reject many otherwise attractive beliefs or practices? Or is naturalism a *tolerant* stance that accommodates most of what people already believe and do? The first stage of naturalism, which gradually freed science from religion, was understood to be radical at that time. An autonomous natural science may leave no place in the world for God, supernatural powers, or direct revelations of knowledge. The early 20th Century attempts to replace philosophy with empirical science also adopted a radical stance. These naturalists sought to *abolish* armchair philosophical speculation about reason or cognition. They would replace all traditional philosophy with resolutely empirical methods and an unsentimental conception of human thought undisciplined by scientific methods.

Such radical orientations are still an influential aspect of philosophical naturalism today. Opposition to religious conceptions of nature is admittedly no longer a radical stance among Western intellectuals. Some radical naturalists do argue, however, that a scientific worldview has no place for a "folk" psychology of beliefs and desires, for consciousness, for reliable self-awareness, or for binding moral norms. Radical naturalists believe or hope that the progress of neuroscience, cognitive science, evolutionary biology or physics will eventually replace some or all of these aspects of human self-understanding. Indeed, some believe that current scientific theories already show that these familiar philosophical conceptions and vocabularies are otiose.

Radical naturalists are now frequently challenged by advocates of a more gentle and tolerant naturalism, however. More tolerant naturalists have an inclusive vision of a scientific understanding of the natural world.[1] They argue that the self-sufficiency of natural science within its own domain does not support a scientific imperialism that reconstructs other disciplines in natural scientific terms. The sciences are not a unified domain, and do not require the reduction or elimination of all concepts apart from a single austere scientific vocabulary. If appeals to folk psychology, conscious awareness, or rational insight offer improvements in prediction or explanation, and do not openly conflict with established scientific results, they are compatible with a naturalistic stance in philosophy. Perhaps a tolerant naturalism could even accommodate an appropriately modest theology and religious life.

Finally, there are what might be called reactionary strains of naturalism. I am thinking of philosophers such as Bernard Williams, John Searle, Thomas Nagel, or Charles Taylor. These philosophers *oppose* naturalistic approaches to

---

1   De Caro and MacArthur (2004) bring together some eloquent and influential approaches to a more tolerant philosophical naturalism.

mind, knowledge, or ethics.[2] Yet they do so on the basis of a philosophical understanding of science that early 20th Century philosophers would have regarded as
naturalist. They agree that the natural sciences are self-sufficient in their own
domain, with no need for philosophical justification. Moreover, they endorse a
relatively naive conception of science: natural science secures an "absolute conception of nature" (Williams 1985), or a straightforward grasp of natural kinds,
natural causality, or natural laws. They offer no elaborate philosophical defense
of their views of science, which they assume to be the common heritage of all
sensible participants in a scientific culture. These ostensible opponents of naturalism thus indicate how thoroughly naturalism dominates contemporary North
American philosophy. Even many critics of naturalism are now "naturalists of
a sort."

The differences between radical, tolerant, and reactionary naturalist attitudes
only concern how deeply naturalism challenges familiar conceptions of thought
and agency. A more substantial difference in the very idea of philosophical naturalism accompanies these differences in attitude. What does it mean to align philosophy with the natural sciences, as naturalists propose? For many philosophers,
naturalism is a commitment to understand mind, knowledge or morality as part
of scientifically-comprehended *nature*. I call this approach "metaphysical naturalism." A different conception of naturalism is widespread in philosophy of
science, however. Here, naturalism concerns how to do philosophy rather than
how to understand mind, knowledge or morality within nature. I call this second
conception "scientific naturalism." Scientific naturalism demands that philosophy answer to *science* rather than to nature. Many scientific naturalists give
up the aspiration to a general philosophical conception of science or nature,
and simply engage with ongoing work in a specific scientific field. Others do
develop more general philosophical views about explanation, experimentation,
or scientific theory, but hold those views directly accountable to how science is
done in different fields.

Metaphysical naturalism and scientific naturalism have different histories and
invoke different standards of philosophical adequacy. Metaphysical naturalism
inherits the Enlightenment's attempt to eliminate God and the supernatural from
our understanding of the world and ourselves. Human beings are natural entities.
If semantic, epistemic, or moral norms have content, authority or force, it comes

---

2   Searle (1983) presents his view as naturalist. Yet Searle's "naturalism" turns out to involve a
      philosophical account of intentionality developed without significant appeal to empirical
      science, coupled with an expression of faith or hope that subsequent work in the biological
      sciences will show how intentionality so construed can be shown to be a higher-level feature
      of some biological systems. I regard this view as closer to those of anti-naturalists about the
      mind, because it effectively gives primacy to philosophical analysis over empirical research,
      which is presumed to follow in philosophy's wake.

from their role in our *natural* lives. There is no normative authority apart from the natural world. This stance has important consequences for how we do philosophy. Philosophy must be empirically grounded; appeals to rational insight or philosophical intuition are no more acceptable in philosophy than are appeals to divine authority.

Scientific naturalism has a different history. It arose primarily from the failure of logical empiricism and other philosophical programs that claimed authority to legislate for science. Scientific naturalism emphasizes that science need not accord with philosophically-imposed limits upon what methods, evidence, or ontology is scientifically acceptable. Scientific naturalists make philosophy continuous with scientific work, and permit no impositions upon science that serve philosophical but not scientific ends. For example, if a scientific discipline finds it useful to refer to unobservable entities, then a prior commitment to empiricism gives philosophers no grounds to object to these references.

How do these differences in the force and content of philosophical naturalism matter to my project to make it harder to be naturalist? It is obviously more challenging to uphold the more radical naturalist positions. Radical naturalists need to give arguments that are sufficient to rule out beliefs or concepts that philosophers might otherwise accept. The more tolerant strains of naturalism hold their own dangers, however. While they seem to make naturalism easier to accept, that easy acceptance may lose its content and significance. If a wide range of opposing philosophical positions is all consistent with naturalism, what difference does naturalism make to philosophy, science, or the conduct of one's life?

A more substantial problem arises, however, if we consider the relation between metaphysical and scientific naturalism. These two views are often defended by different philosophers working in different sub-fields of philosophy. Metaphysical naturalism is more widely espoused in philosophy of mind, epistemology, and ethics; scientific naturalism is more common within the philosophy of science. Yet a coherent philosophical naturalism must answer to the concerns of both views. The rightful legacy of metaphysical naturalism is that philosophical understanding cannot appeal to anything supernatural, that is, to what is not part of a scientific understanding of nature. Scientific naturalism also constrains any aspiring naturalist, however. Naturalists should accept no *philosophical* restrictions upon science. No philosophical conception of how science *ought* to be done can block well-motivated developments within a science. The problem is that these two concerns are difficult to satisfy jointly.[3]

We must first ask why naturalists must satisfy both of these philosophical commitments. Consider metaphysical naturalism. We can easily see why

---

3   For a more extensive discussion of the internal difficulties within philosophical naturalism, see Rouse 2002.

metaphysical naturalists should also accept the central commitment of scientific naturalism. Metaphysical naturalists want to understand human thought and action as part of *nature*: we are natural beings, governed by physical and chemical laws, and shaped by natural selection. But why should we believe *that*? We believe that because we think we have learned this conception of nature and ourselves from the natural sciences. If we have not correctly acquired this conception from the sciences, but instead have imposed it upon the sciences for philosophical reasons, then the primary rationale for metaphysical naturalism dissolves. Metaphysical naturalism would then need a very different, philosophical justification that did not claim the authority of science.

The first problem confronting metaphysical naturalism is the need to justify the scientific authority of its preferred metaphysics of nature. This problem arises because metaphysical naturalism no longer seeks to *replace* philosophical arguments with scientific research. Naturalists instead offer their own philosophical theories about how scientific work enables them to answer philosophical questions about mind, knowledge or morality. In their efforts to establish the scientific credentials of their preferred metaphysics of nature, many metaphysical naturalists appeal to the laws of physics, Darwinian natural selection, or recent cognitive science to defend their philosophical views about mind, knowledge, or morality. But naturalists cannot just take a plausible story about the metaphysics of nature from current scientific theories. They must defend the much stronger claim that scientific understanding *requires* their preferred metaphysics of nature. Otherwise they risk imposing upon the sciences a philosophical theory that science itself neither needs nor wants. They would also risk falsely claiming the authority of science for a philosophical view that science itself need not endorse.

A second problem for metaphysical naturalists comes from their inability to settle upon a single philosophical account of a scientific understanding of nature. For example, some metaphysical naturalists understand "nature" to mean actual objects and their causal interactions. Others understand nature as the domain of natural *laws*, which apply not only to the actual world, but to all mutually accessible possible worlds. Still other metaphysical naturalists think that the *biological* history of natural selection that shaped our cognitive capacities is what matters to philosophy, not physical causes or laws. Alongside these alternative conceptions of nature, metaphysical naturalists also have different conceptions of *how* to "naturalize" rational agency, consciousness, or normative authority. Some philosophers still think that understanding mind, knowledge or morality as naturalists requires eliminating traditional philosophical vocabulary in favor of scientific language. Others argue that familiar philosophical concepts are reducible to or supervene upon a scientific account. The more tolerant conceptions of naturalizing mind and knowledge allow any philosophical account that has predictive utility, or does not overtly contradict current scientific theories.

Perhaps we should not worry about such differences among metaphysical naturalists' conceptions of nature and the place of mind and knowledge in nature. We might have compelling reasons to understand mind and knowledge in scientific terms, even though science has not yet settled exactly which terms we should use for that purpose. That response will not do, however, for it presumes that science *should* eventually settle this philosophical question for us. Yet many philosophers of science now challenge the presumption that the sciences need to resolve philosophical disputes about the proper metaphysical interpretation of scientific achievements. Thomas Kuhn's rejection of this presumption was an important and relatively uncontroversial part of his account of "normal" science. Kuhn insisted that "scientists can agree in their *identification* of a paradigm [for subsequent research] without agreeing on, or even attempting to produce, a full *interpretation* or *rationalization* of it. Lack of a standard interpretation ... will not prevent a paradigm from successfully guiding research" (1970, p. 44). More recently, Arthur Fine has argued that philosophers should accept and respect this diversity of scientific opinion. Fine urged philosophers to "try to take science on its own terms, and try not to read things into science.... [We should] tolerate all the differences of opinion and all the varieties of doubt and skepticism that science tolerates, [and] not tolerate the prescriptions of empiricism and other doctrines that externally limit the commitments of science" (1986, 149–50). If Kuhn, Fine, and others are correct, the success of the sciences accommodates a wide range of metaphysical views among scientists, including metaphysical agnosticism. Philosophers' attempts to claim scientific authority for a specific metaphysics of nature may therefore be an unjustified philosophical imposition upon science. Metaphysical naturalists cannot just defend the philosophical advantages of their preferred conception of nature; they must also show its entitlement to the authority of empirical science.

These difficulties confronting metaphysical naturalism may encourage us to emphasize scientific naturalism instead. Scientific naturalism seems to be consistent with a tolerant attitude toward the metaphysics of nature. No naturalist could make philosophical appeals to intuition or divine revelation, but one might accept and engage with the best current scientific work without demanding a specific metaphysics of causality, law, or biological adaptation. If so, it might be easy to be a philosophical naturalist after all.

I am sympathetic to this approach, which is very close to my own. Unfortunately, it makes it look *too* easy to be a philosophical naturalist. To see why, we need to consider more carefully what happens when we combine scientific naturalism with an inclusive and tolerant metaphysical naturalism. Two claims are being defended together:

1) The natural sciences are well-ordered practices on their own; philosophy has no independent authority to prescribe how science should be done;

2) Acceptance of the natural sciences does not require that philosophy use a single favored scientific vocabulary, or explain thought, knowledge, or action within a favored metaphysics of nature.

Philosophy and science would then seem to go together easily. Science does not need philosophical justification, yet a scientific understanding of nature imposes only minimal constraints upon a philosophical understanding of mind or knowledge.

Conjoining these two claims may nevertheless be more difficult than it seems at first. A tolerant naturalism may seem to leave wide scope for philosophical accounts of mind, language, or knowledge. Yet such accounts must also apply to *scientific* thought, scientific language use, and scientific knowledge. In seeking a philosophical theory that applies to scientific work, philosophers once again risk imposing philosophical constraints upon science. Philosophical theories are usually normative: they do not simply report what people say, do, or believe, but propose norms for what they ought to say, do or believe. If we take our philosophical theories of knowledge, thought or language seriously, and accept that they apply to science, why wouldn't we cautiously reclaim philosophical authority over the sciences? We should also ask whether our philosophical conceptions of science implicitly ascribe to us supernatural cognitive capacities, either in fixing the content of scientific claims, or in assessing their justification.

Most naturalistically-inclined philosophers minimize or ignore these concerns. They are confident that their careful, philosophically- and scientifically-sophisticated theories about knowledge, language, or mind will readily account for science, and that scientific understanding can accommodate their theories. Yet the history of logical empiricist, post-empiricist, and other philosophical theories of scientific knowledge should be a cautionary tale. The logical empiricists were equally confident that scientific knowledge was governed by the formal structures and strict empirical accountability that were central to their semantics and epistemology. Careful study of scientific practice later shattered that confidence. Part of what still makes it hard to be a naturalist today is the need to pay closer attention to the relations between philosophical theories of mind, knowledge or language and the history and current practice of science.

Ic: From Nomological Necessity to Causal Interaction

I conclude the first part of the paper by considering briefly how philosophers of science now think about one important aspect of scientific work that bears on the metaphysics of nature. This issue, concerning causality and nomological necessity, nicely illustrates the danger of taking for granted a philosophical conception of science and a scientific understanding of nature. In my earlier historical remarks about the rise of naturalism, I noted the importance of changing attitudes toward causality and necessity. These changes have profoundly affected metaphysical naturalism. Many naturalistic philosophers of mind, language and knowledge have made extensive use of the concept of a natural law, and related concepts such as "natural kinds." When they talk about 'causes', they often use the term interchangeably with talk about causal laws. These are powerful, far-reaching concepts. Many prominent naturalistic theories of mind, language or knowledge employ them extensively and effectively. Indeed, philosophers outside of the philosophy of science often simply identify scientifically-understood nature with events governed by natural laws.

Such appeals to natural laws, or to theories as systems of laws, were encouraged by work in the philosophy of science in the 1970's and 1980's. In responding to the failures of logical empiricism, philosophers of science initially emphasized the unifying role of theoretical laws in explaining diverse events. They also thought that scientific concepts are developed primarily through their systematic role in broadly explanatory theories. Many philosophers of science now think differently about laws and causes, however. I will therefore briefly consider how and why concepts such as 'law' or 'natural kind' have become less central to philosophy of science, and which concepts have begun to replace them.

Post-empiricist philosophers of science were attracted to the concept of scientific laws as empirically-discovered necessary truths for two reasons. Laws seemed important for explanation, by unifying diverse events within a more general pattern. Laws also seemed important in inductive reasoning: new predictions from prior observations are reliable when the concepts they use belong to general laws. Neither explanation nor inductive reasoning seemed to work unless the connections they found were *necessary* connections; yet the failures of logical empiricism suggested that the relevant necessity could not be merely logical necessity.

What changes nevertheless led philosophers of science to give less emphasis to laws or natural necessity? I will emphasize three reasons why philosophers of science are now less attracted to understanding laws as necessary truths: closer attention to biology; a reconception of scientific theory in terms of models rather than laws; and the separation of causes and mechanisms from general laws. Consider biology first. For much of the 20th Century, the philosophy of science was primarily a philosophy of physics and chemistry. If biology was considered at all, it was treated as an immature science because it lacked well-established theories and laws. The growing success of the biological sciences throughout the 20th Century made disregard or disrespect for biology untenable, however. More important, philosophers of biology argued that biologists' success came through modes of conceptualization and explanation that did not employ laws. There are no laws of genetics or biological development, for example. Central concepts in biology, such as 'gene' or 'species' do not fit the standard philosophical conceptions of natural kinds. Some common features of biological systems explain why. Evolution makes biology historically contingent. Biological systems often depend upon complex organization of their components, and their behavior may be sensitive to their environment. These aspects of biological systems seem to require different modes of analysis and understanding that are not conceived in terms of necessary natural laws.

Natural laws and natural necessity have also encountered hard times in the physical sciences, however. Philosophers such as Ronald Giere, Nancy Cartwright, Margaret Morrison and Mary Morgan have argued that the primary work of explanation and conceptual articulation in science is done by families of models rather than laws. Giere (1988) has shown, for example, that classical mechanics is not usually understood and used by physicists directly through a general law expressed by F = ma. Physicists instead learn standard models for various abstractly characterized systems. They analyze real systems by adding corrections and approximations to the models. Often scientists use mutually inconsistent models. Mark Wilson points out that classical physics textbooks

> usually provide accounts that work approximately well in a limited range of cases, coupled with a footnote of the "for more details, see ..." type. ... [Yet] the specialist texts [referred to] do not simply "add more details," ... but commonly overturn the underpinnings of the older treatments altogether. (Wilson 2005, 180–81)

In more complicated settings, scientists will sometimes employ models drawn from logically inconsistent theories to capture different aspects of the same phenomenon. For situations on the borders between classical chaos and quantum mechanical effects, for example, physicists shift back and forth between classical, semi-classical, and quantum mechanical models. In other circumstances, they use different, inconsistent models for different aspects of a more complicated phenomenon.

The models used in these situations are not merely derived from more general theories, either. Consider how Margaret Morrison and Mary Morgan summarize their influential book of philosophical papers on *Models as Mediators*:

> Autonomy is an important feature of models. ... Viewing models strictly in terms of their relationship to theory draws our attention away from the processes of constructing models and manipulating them. Both [processes] are crucial in gaining information about the world, theories, and the model itself. (Morgan and Morrison 1999, p. 8)

Recognizing the central role of models in scientific understanding provides a less unified and more haphazard conception of the world than that suggested by the traditional hierarchy of increasingly general laws.

This disunity is strengthened by an increasing emphasis upon causation and causal mechanisms within philosophy of science. Not so long ago, many philosophers treated causation and law as virtually interchangeable concepts. Now philosophers of science often talk about causal relations, causal structures, or mechanisms without presuming that they instantiate general laws. Nancy

Cartwright points out that philosophers of science now "describe a variety of different kinds of singular causal relations ... such as hasteners, delayers, sustainers, contributors [with] different counterfactual tests for each of the different kinds of relationship" (Cartwright 2004, p. 242). One reason for the plurality of causal relationships is that causes typically have definite effects only within a larger causal structure. How a cause works depends upon where it is placed. Moreover, models of a causal mechanism mostly help us understand what happens when that mechanism operates normally. Under other conditions, the normal outcome will not occur. Understanding the mechanism will help us understand how its normal operation can be disrupted, but will not always indicate what happens instead when disruptions occur.

Not surprisingly, these three challenges to a conception of nature as law-governed often function together. Scientists can understand complex events in the world by constructing models of simpler causal mechanisms. These models link together causal capacities whose outcome depends upon the overall structure. Models of mechanisms are especially prominent in many areas of biology. Yet scientific understanding of physical systems also often works similarly at all scales, from structured arrangements of molecules, to global climate, to collisions between galaxies. These philosophical and scientific developments challenge traditional philosophical conceptions of nature as organized by laws governing its constituent natural kinds. Nancy Cartwright offered a provocative summary of this challenge:

> [Advocates of law-like natural order] yearn for a better, cleaner, more orderly world than the one that, to all appearances, we inhabit. But it will not do to base our methods on our wishes. (Cartwright, 1999, 12–13).

To base our methods on the world we live in, not the world we wish for, is of course the only acceptable strategy for naturalists.

Part II: Scientific Practices

Philosophical attention to scientific practices is a relatively new and unfamiliar approach to the philosophy of science. Discussions of scientific knowledge are much more familiar. Much work on scientific practice is now being done, however. Philosophers of science in Europe, North America, and Australasia have formed a Society for the Philosophy of Science in Practice that will hold its first meeting in 2007. Philosophers are also relative latecomers to the topic. An emphasis upon scientific practices rather than scientific knowledge has been common among historians, anthropologists, and sociologists of science for some time.

I begin this part of the paper with some brief remarks about practices, because the concept may not be familiar. The central sections of this part then consider three important aspects of scientific practices: causal interaction with the world to create phenomena; conceptual articulation; and the role of laws in scientific practice. The final section returns to the themes of Part I by asking how a philosophy of scientific practices contributes to naturalism.

IIa: The Very Idea of a Scientific Practice

What are scientific "practices"? The concept of a practice has been widely used in philosophy, social theory, and science studies, albeit with divergent interpretations of the core notion of a "practice."[4] The following initial remarks about the concept are thus intended to clarify my own use of the term, and especially to *block* some familiar uses of the term whose implications are at odds with my own account:

1. Practices are activities. They are what people do, rather than their beliefs, or the results of what they do.
2. Practices are interactions with the world around us. We can have false beliefs, or beliefs about things that do not exist. Our practices, by contrast, cannot lose contact with their worldly surroundings. That is because practices *incorporate* those aspects of the world with which we interact. That is true even when participants in the practice misunderstand what they interact with.
3. Many people participate in a practice. People who participate in the same practice need not perform the same activities, or hold the same beliefs, however. Practices can be complicated patterns of activity; different participants may contribute to a practice in different ways. People can also participate in the same practice despite holding different conceptions of that practice. They can disagree about how its constituent performances belong together, about the aims of the practice, or about the stakes in its success or failure.
4. The activities that belong together in a single practice may have no common features. Practices are held together instead by the interactions among those activities. These linked interactions extend in space and time. A practice can therefore change over time, and be done differently in different places.
5. Language use is normally integral to practices, especially to scientific practices. The ability to use words that are repeatable and recombinable in new judgments is crucial to conceptually articulated practices. We understand a concept by understanding how to use it or respond to it appropriately, in the right circumstances. Our responsiveness to conceptual differences nevertheless goes beyond our ability to express those concepts in words.

---

4   For an extensive, critical review of the practice literature in philosophy, social theory, and social science, see Rouse 2006.

6. Philosophical attention to practices is an alternative to a philosophical focus upon knowledge. A philosophy of scientific practices can nevertheless accept and use the concept of knowledge. The sciences obviously allow us to know much about the world. Yet we still might understand science better by looking at scientific practices rather at relations between knowers and what is known.

7. Scientific practices include more than just scientists' activities. Many people participate in scientific practices, most of whom are not scientists. Talking about scientific practices also does not require a sharp distinction between scientific practices and other practices. Practices overlap and interact with one another. The term 'scientific practices' only assumes loose historical connections between sciences at different times, and different sciences at any one time.

These initial remarks about the concept of practices have been brief and abstract. These abstract descriptions are intended only to provide some initial guidance and to avoid some simple misunderstandings. The concept will become clearer in the following sections, which consider several aspects of scientific practices specifically.

IIb: Scientific Practices as Causal Interactions

I begin by discussing scientific practices as patterns of *causal* interaction with the world. A salient feature of natural science is the extensive work done in laboratories, observatories, medical clinics, and carefully prepared field sites. For simplicity, I will use the word 'laboratories' to refer to any site of scientific work, even though their differences are important in other contexts. Most philosophers recognize that laboratory work is at least an indispensable means to acquiring scientific knowledge. When considering scientific practices, however, laboratories and experimentation are integral to science, and not merely a means to something else. Attention to practices can even reverse the means/end relationship. The knowledge achieved at one stage of an ongoing research program is often mostly important as a means to further experimental research.

Laboratory work is integral to science, because the world normally does not show itself intelligibly. Scientists must instead interact with things and re-arrange them. When that interaction is successful, the world shows itself intelligibly in new respects. This way of talking about scientific work reverses the more familiar empiricist idiom. What matters is not what we can observe in nature, but what the phenomena can show us.

What is a "phenomenon"? Ian Hacking once said that Old science on every continent [began] with the stars, because only the skies afford some phenomena on display, with many more [obtainable] by careful observation … Only the planets and more distant bodies have the right combination of complex regularity against a background. (1983, 227)

Science began with observable phenomena in the night sky, but obviously did not stop there. In most scientific domains, however, very few phenomena in nature already display a clear pattern against a background. Where scientists do not find phenomena in nature, they work hard to create them. When Hacking or I say that scientists create phenomena, we do not mean that such work is dubious or unreliable. Creating significant and revealing patterns in the world is careful, skillful work. It requires extensive understanding of one's instruments, materials, and circumstances. These items are integral components of the phenomenon, and experimenters' skills must use and respond to their causal capacities.

Experimental work involves causal interaction with the world. Scientists are causally effective agents who are part of those interactions. Intelligible phenomena only occur when the causal capacities of their components are properly organized. To this extent, experimental phenomena are mechanisms. Like biological or technological mechanisms, phenomena invite normative assessment. We say an experiment runs "properly" and produces the "normal" or "correct" result, or that there were "mistakes" or "malfunctions." The most common and basic failures result in noise or confusion, rather than clear errors. A clear but misleading pattern is still a phenomenon.

We often describe phenomena briefly and abstractly. We talk about the melting point of a substance, the activation of a gene, or a synthetic pathway for a chemical. Such descriptions usefully highlight the scientific significance of the phenomenon. Yet they also abstract from crucial components of the phenomena they describe. A phenomenon includes all of the causally relevant components of a very complex, regulated interaction. We should remember just how many components must come together properly to produce a revealing phenomenon. The components of a laboratory phenomena typically include properly prepared and contained *materials*; controlled *circumstances* (e.g., temperature, air pressure, or magnetic fields); *signifying* elements (e.g., radioactive labels, biological stains, induced emissions of radiation, or antibiotic resistance); *detectors* for those signifying elements; standardized *measures* (of mass, electrical resistance, time intervals, or work); *instruments* calibrated to those measures; proper *sequencing* of events; skillfully performed or properly automated *techniques*; and above all, extensive *shielding* of these components and events from possible interference.

Recognizing the special circumstances of laboratories suggests a problem for the significance of scientific practices. The sciences seek to understand what happens in the messy, complex world around us. At their best, however, they seem to produce something else instead: a clear, precise grasp of phenomena in isolated, regulated laboratory settings. This problem has no *general* solution. The proper response is to consider what inferences can be drawn from a laboratory phenomenon to other circumstances; understanding when such inferences are good is important to scientific practice.

One further point about inferences beyond the laboratory concludes this part of my discussion. The creation of laboratory phenomena involves scientists in causal interaction with the world. These causal interactions are not confined to the laboratory, however. Inferences from laboratory phenomena to other settings are now more extensive and reliable precisely because scientific practices extend far beyond the laboratory. The sciences guide a massive, continuing effort to engineer the world partly in the image of the laboratory. We are surrounded by laboratory artifacts and procedures in our everyday lives. Our mundane surroundings include purified or synthesized substances; insulated wires in electrical circuits; complex machines and other mechanisms; standard measures and calibrated instruments; carefully timed and sequenced events; and shielding from other causal influences. The world is now more intelligible and predictable, because these extended scientific practices make it so. The scientific practices that make the world intelligible, however, are themselves causal interactions within the world.

IIc: Conceptual Articulation in Scientific Practices

We usually think of scientific progress primarily as the replacement of false beliefs with true beliefs, or beliefs that are more adequately justified. Such a conception of progress reflects a familiar philosophical emphasis upon scientific knowledge. It expresses an important achievement. Most educated people in modern scientific cultures no longer believe, for example, that sick people are possessed by demons, that fire gives off phlogiston, or that the earth is flat and a few thousand years old. Yet scientific practice also enables a more basic comparison to our predecessors. In most domains of science we can now *say* things that people before us could not say. On these subjects, people previously had no beliefs at all, rather than false beliefs. Being able to say what others cannot say is not just learning new words; it requires being able to "*tell*" what you are talking about. As philosopher John Haugeland noted,

> Telling [what something is, telling things apart, or telling the differences between them] can often be expressed in words, but is not in itself essentially verbal. ... People can tell things for which they have no words, including things that are hard to tell. (Haugeland 1998, 313)

Science allows us to talk about very many things, by enabling some of us to "tell" about them. Here are some examples. People can now tell and can therefore talk about mitochondria, the pre-Cambrian Era, subatomic particles, tectonic plates, retroviruses, spiral galaxies, and amino acid sequences. Not long ago, people were in silence rather than error on these and many other scientific topics.

How was that silence broken? To hold beliefs and to talk about something, we need concepts that can express those beliefs. Having a concept is not just knowing a word, but being able to "tell" something. W.V.O. Quine used metaphors to express one familiar account of how conceptual articulation occurs in science:

> [Scientific theory] is a human-made fabric which impinges upon experience only along the edges, or a field of force whose boundary conditions are experience. A conflict with experience at the periphery occasions readjustments in the interior of the field. (Quine 1953, 42)

For Quine and many other philosophers, concepts are parts of a systematic theory, and are developed or changed by internal adjustments in that theory. I call this view traditional because it regards knowledge as a relation between a system of verbal representation, and something unconceptualized (experience, nature, or "the world"). The world impinges upon us from *outside*, compelling us to adjust the *internal* relations among our sentences or thoughts.

On this view, having a theory allows us to be "articulate," to express thoughts in words. The English word "articulate" now primarily describes a verbal capacity, but it has a more fundamental meaning. Something is "articulated" when it has joints, like the human skeleton. Verbal articulation is simply our most powerful and fine-grained way of finding or (as I prefer) *telling* "joints" or boundaries in the world. Familiar philosophical views of science regard the primary work of articulation as verbal. On one version of this claim, the world is already articulated into kinds of things and properties. Verbal articulation just tries to match words to those kinds. On another version, the world comes more-or-less adaptable to different verbal articulations. I think understanding scientific practices requires rejecting either version. More fundamentally, we must reject the distinction between how the world already is, and how we represent it in words. Science *articulates* the world, allowing us to *tell* about it, by developing new patterns of interaction and new ways of talking, together.

This claim is rather abstract, but some examples may help explicate it. As a first example, consider the rich vocabulary for the internal components of cells and their functions now available in cell biology. Modern cell biology began, many historians would argue, when Albert Claude spun pulverized chicken sarcoma cells in the ultracentrifuge at 28,000 revolutions per minute.[5]

Different materials gradually precipitated; after a week, several layers of cellular debris lay beneath a liquid. At first, Claude could only describe the layers as "small particles" or "large granules," and note when each precipitated. By itself, that is like trying to understand how an automobile works by blowing it up, and sorting the pieces by size or where they land. That does not help you say much about the automobile. Cell biology did better by interconnecting multiple interactions with cell components. Claude analyzed the different fragments biochemically. Later, he and his successors identified layers in the ultracentrifuge with

---

5   For more extensive discussion of this example, see Bechtel 2006, Rheinberger 1995.

features visible through light microscopes, and then with electron microscopes. Connecting these experimental, structural, and biochemical interactions with cell components helped locate biological functions like respiration or protein synthesis. Cell biology then had a very good start. Empiricists might think the key work came earlier, when some cell structures became visible in light microscopes. That is a mistake. Microscopes alone cannot indicate whether or how the boundaries they make visible are biologically meaningful. The visually identifiable elements need to be robustly connected to other interactions with cells. If not, they could be mere artifacts. The stains and instruments that make them visible, or the prejudices that equate visibility to us with importance, might lead science astray.

Consider another deceptively simple case that I adapt from Hasok Chang (2004). What does it mean for one thing to be hotter than another? We distinguish temperature from quantity of heat, but what is temperature? People noticed that hotter and colder correlate with expansion and contraction, and constructed thermometers. Is temperature simply whatever a thermometer measures? No. I ignore the real difficulties of defining some fixed points, such as the freezing and boiling points of water. With these points fixed, however, suppose we mark 100 equal lengths between them on a thermometer. Here are some different measures of the same temperatures with mercury, alcohol, and water thermometers:

Mercury	0°	25°	50°	75°	100°
Alcohol	0°	22°	44°	70°	100°
Water	0°	5°	26°	57°	100°

(from Chang, 2004, 58)

How should we understand these differences? Is there one concept of temperature, or many, or none? Or is temperature a purely conventional concept? Perhaps scientists could just agree to use mercury or alcohol as a standard measure. Yet we also want to understand temperature when these thermometers would melt, or their contents freeze. What is a "degree," and what is it a degree *of,* at 1000°, 1,000,000° or −250°?

I have three points to make about this example. First, scientists were able to define a unified scale of temperature *experimentally,* and use it to assess the accuracy of various thermometers. This achievement did not primarily involve internal adjustment within a theory. Second, defining the concept of temperature more precisely required connection to another experimental and practical domain, in which steam engines allowed correlations of heat with a capacity for mechanical work. Third, however, the resulting unity and coherence of the concept of temperature is highly unusual among empirical concepts. Consider by contrast the question of what it is for one solid material to be harder than another, for example. Mark Wilson (2005) reminds us of many partly conflicting empirical measures of hardness. Is hardness best displayed by resistance to denting, to scratching, to cutting, or to friction? Here there is no prospect of unifying different measures into a single scale. Materials can be harder or softer in many ways, which only partly overlap. Yet like temperature, articulating the concept of hardness involved creating phenomena more than redefining words or formulating theories.

A defender of familiar accounts of concept articulation might now object. Not all conceptual developments in the sciences are as straightforwardly empirical as temperature, hardness, or cell structure. Internal adjustments within theories might still be the main form of conceptual articulation in science. I accept the premise of this objection, but reject the conclusion. The role of theories in conceptual development does not imply that conceptual articulation is primarily verbal, because theories are not primarily verbal either. Recall my earlier discussion philosophical work on models. Theories do not just connect a general verbal representation to a situation in the world. Scientific theorizing is better understood as a *practice* of modeling various actual or possible circumstances. Although scientists sometimes formulate general theories, from classical mechanics to thermodynamics, we learn what those theories and equations say by developing and using families of models. How do we recognize the relevant forces, masses and accelerations in F = ma in classical mechanics, for example? We model specific situations, such as free fall, harmonic oscillators, or planetary orbits. We then understand more complex situations by comparison to the models, with appropriate corrections or complications. Models are even more important in sciences that describe complex interactions. When we think about the workings of a cell on a small scale, or the dynamics of global climate on a larger scale, models become stand-ins for the actual systems we seek to understand. We cannot comprehend such complex interactions except with more simplified models.

Understanding theoretical modeling helps us recognize that models and experimental phenomena play similar roles in articulating concepts. Theoretical models and experimental phenomena each establish simplified, idealized settings in which conceptual relations can be clearly displayed as telling differences. First, differences among various components or factors in a situation can be identified and highlighted within a model or phenomenon. Second, their dominant modes of interaction stand out more clearly in the simplified or idealized circumstances of the model. Understanding how the model works provides an indication of where to look and how to intervene in "real" circumstances for scientific or practical purposes.

This treatment of conceptual articulation has been long and detailed, so I conclude this section with a brief summary of its contribution to understanding the sciences as practices. Familiar images of science focus upon comparisons between knowledge claims and the world. These comparisons would stand on their own if we could independently determine what these claims say, and whether they are true. Our most familiar conceptions of knowledge do treat them independently: understanding what knowledge claims mean is mostly verbal and internal to theory; assessing truth requires looking at the world. There is no clear separation between these tasks, however. We only understand scientific concepts by interacting with the world in appropriate ways. Understanding what these concepts say, and understanding the world in those terms, go hand in hand. Moreover, by creating and using experimental systems and theoretical models, we transform the world to let it show itself intelligibly to us. My discussions of experimental practice and conceptual articulation thus make the same point from different angles. Scientific practices are disciplined patterns of causal interaction that transform the world to articulate it conceptually.

IId: Laws in Scientific Practice

As I noted in the first part of the paper, philosophers of science now discuss diverse kinds of causal interaction. We are less inclined to talk about laws of nature. Many metaphysical naturalists, however, assume that nature is understood scientifically as the domain of laws. The distinction between necessary laws and merely contingent truths seems to provide useful resources for philosophical theories of mind and knowledge. These differences mark one of the tensions that make it harder to be a philosophical naturalist. Metaphysical naturalists are not entitled to understand laws as necessary truths if this conception is not part of a scientific conception of nature. Scientific naturalists, on the other hand, should not abandon the concept of law if the sciences do find it useful. In that case, a conception of "science without laws" would be an unwarranted imposition upon science.

To resolve this tension, consider how scientists understand "laws" in scientific practice. Marc Lange (2000) argues that laws work differently in scientific practice than philosophers usually recognize. Most philosophical discussions of laws treat them as a special kind of truth, such as "nomologically necessary" truth. Lange argues instead that laws have a special use in scientific practice. A scientist who regards a hypothesis as a law undertakes a strategy of inductive reasoning. Laws would support inferences from a small number of examined cases to predictions about unexamined cases. If the examined cases are instances of a law, we have good reason to expect later instances to behave in the same way. Such inference strategies are not always reliable, and must sometimes be revised in light of later evidence. Yet without committing to some inductive strategies, and the laws that express them, scientific research could not proceed. If the events we study in the laboratory or elsewhere did not tell us about events elsewhere, scientific research would be pointless.

The familiar problem, however, is that many inference strategies are consistent with any given data. Lange argues that scientists consider which possible inference strategy is *salient* in context. A salient inference strategy suggests an appropriate scope. For example, inferring from experiments with copper wires in Taipei that "all copper objects *in Taipei* conduct electricity" would be too narrow; "all solid objects conduct electricity" would be too broad. Geography is not a salient aspect of these experiments, but copper is. A salient strategy also makes no unmotivated changes in later applications. Suppose we do some elementary experiments with the pressure, volume and temperature of gases. We will likely discover that P, V, and T vary in a fairly constant relationship, expressed by $PV = kT$ (where k is a constant). To infer that the product PV will *increase* if we raise the pressure substantially would introduce an unmotivated change. I will return to this example of Boyle's Law shortly.

> I first need to say more about "salience." Lange rightly insists that [the salience of an inference strategy] is not something psychological, concerning the way our minds work. ... [Rather] it possesses a certain kind of justificatory status: [like] observation reports, this status requires that there be widespread agreement, among qualified observers who are shown the data, on what would count as an unexamined [case] being relevantly the same as the [cases] already examined. (Lange 2000, 194)

Comparing inference strategies to observation reports is instructive. The salient patterns of experimental phenomena, and the salience of an inductive strategy expressed in laws, play related roles in scientific understanding. Experimental phenomena, and the inductive strategies that extend them beyond the laboratory, work together to articulate the world conceptually. Moreover, the salience of each pattern has a normative status within scientific practice. Such patterns are defeasible, but they offer default justification. They should be accepted unless there are good reasons not to do so.

We can now return briefly to Boyle's Law of gases as an example. Boyle's Law has a problem common to many familiar empirical laws. Strictly interpreted, this "law," $PV = kT$, is false. The problem dissolves, however, when we think about scientific practices. Practices are patterns of interaction with the world. Because we are part of those interactions, their norms refer to us. In this case, the inference strategy expressed by this law is sufficiently accurate for some scientific purposes. For these purposes, Boyle's Law is both salient and reliable.

Which laws are salient also depends upon us in other ways. Different background assumptions can change which inferences are appropriate. Boyle's Law is inductively salient from how gases behave at "ordinary" pressures; predicting that the product PV rises at higher pressures would be unwarranted. Some plausible background assumptions can change our inferences, however. Suppose that gas molecules occupy part of the volume of their container, and attract one another at very close distances. A different strategy then suggests itself. On these assumptions, the van der Waals law becomes salient, and *Boyle's* Law suggests an unwarranted change in our inductions at higher pressures. Under other assumptions, even the van der Waals law becomes unreliable. Yet Lange rightly argues that both should be recognized as laws, because stricter assumptions would permit no general gas law at all. To overlook the salience of Boyle's and van der Waals' laws for certain purposes would impose unreasonable restrictions on scientific reasoning and explanation.

The aims of scientific disciplines also affect which laws express salient strategies of induction. Consider biology. Earlier, I noted that many philosophers of science now think laws play little part in biology. Biological systems evolve contingently and variably, so there are no necessary truths of biology. Lange argues that laws *are* important in biology, however, if we understand laws as related primarily to norms of scientific inference. In biological disciplines like molecular genetics, developmental biology, physiology, or medicine, scientists do draw inferences from data about one organism to others of the same species. When scientists sequence the genome of model organisms like yeast or *Drosophila*, for example, the sequence functions as a genetic law for all members of that species. For the purposes of molecular genetics, the widespread genetic variation among individual organisms is rightly ignored. In evolutionary biology and population genetics, however, that variation is important. In those disciplines, different laws express salient strategies of inference.

These references to scientists' purposes and assumptions do not compromise the objectivity of science. Scientific practices are not activities that we impose upon nature from "outside." They are instead patterns of causal interaction with nature. How a scientific practice develops is determined neither by us alone, nor by how the world is apart from us. A practice is instead shaped by ongoing interaction between scientists and the world. The "purposes" of the practice emerge from within that interaction. To show how this happens, let's return briefly to Albert Claude's experiments with the ultracentrifuge.

I mentioned earlier that Claude's experiments were the beginnings of the modern discipline of cell biology. That is not how Claude conceived his own work at first, however. Claude worked in a medical school, trying to understand cancer. He put chicken sarcoma cells in the ultracentrifuge to discover how cancer cells differ from normal cells. When he compared the debris from the two kinds of cell, he found no differences between them. This result was not a failure, however. The differences among the layers of cellular debris were instead a striking and salient result. This result suggested new lines of inquiry and new inferential strategies that eventually came together in a new discipline, with new goals. When Claude pursued those new directions, however, he continued to use his familiar cancer cells. When he started, these cells were treated as pathologically abnormal. For the new purposes emerging from his research practice, cancer cells were cells like any other. The incipient "laws" of cellular structure and function were simply more salient than the cancer pathologies that first motivated the research. Their salience was neither an objective feature of cells, nor a subjective imposition by scientists, but an emergent feature of their interaction in scientific practice.

IIe: Scientific Practices and Philosophical Naturalism

We can now, at long last, return to the topic of naturalism. In the first part of the paper, I claimed that it is more difficult to be a naturalist than many philosophers recognize. There are many varieties of naturalism in philosophy. Both scientific naturalism and metaphysical naturalism make legitimate demands upon naturalists. Scientific naturalism demands that we not impose philosophical constraints upon science. Metaphysical naturalism demands that we understand mind, knowledge, and language as part of scientifically-understood nature. The difficulty is that these demands are often in tension with one another.

In this part of the paper, I have introduced a less familiar way to think about the sciences philosophically. Instead of focusing upon scientific knowledge, I invited you to think about the sciences as practices. I discussed three aspects of scientific practice. First, the sciences involve causal interaction with the world. Such interactions allow scientists to create phenomena. Phenomena are arrangements of instruments and materials, often novel arrangements, that allow the world to show itself in revealing ways. Second, by creating phenomena, the sciences also articulate the world conceptually. We can now talk about many previously inconceivable aspects of the world. We can do so, because new scientific concepts express telling differences that show up clearly in the phenomena. Systematic interconnections among these concepts give them content and enhance their reliability. Third, scientists extend these concepts to apply beyond the immediate experimental context through strategies of inductive inference. These strategies point toward a different conception of scientific laws. Laws are not necessary truths. In their scientific uses, laws express inference strategies that apply concepts within scientific practices. The scope and content of the laws reflect salient strategies of ongoing interaction with the world.

How does this conception of scientific practices contribute to naturalism in philosophy? A philosophy of scientific practices is first and foremost a version of *scientific* naturalism. It aims to avoid unwarranted philosophical impositions upon science, by attending more closely to what scientists say and do. My discussion of scientific practices today highlighted aspects of scientific work that many philosophical discussions of science often overlook. One under-emphasized aspect of science is the causal interactions that create phenomena. Scientific practice is part of the causally interactive world that science discloses. I also call attention to the future-orientation of scientific research that articulates the world conceptually and extends those concepts inferentially. Philosophers more commonly focus upon the retrospective justification and systematization of scientific knowledge.

A philosophy of scientific practices also adopts what initially seems to be a tolerant metaphysical naturalism. Along with many philosophers of science now, this approach takes causal interactions at face value. Human beings understand causal relations through our own causal involvement in the world as embodied agents. We do not need natural laws to explain the difference between genuinely causal interaction and merely accidental correlation. Yet causal interactions take many forms, and function together in more complex causal patterns. Causality is not a univocal concept, and there is not one privileged mode of causal relation that science discovers. Recognizing the diversity of causal relations, we will not be tempted to try to impose an austere and restrictive vocabulary upon philosophical understanding. Nor will we think that such metaphysical views can claim the authority of the natural sciences. In metaphysics and philosophy of science, a philosophy of scientific practices joins Arthur Fine in "tolerating all the differences of opinion and all the varieties of doubt and skepticism that science tolerates" (Fine 1986, 150).

Yet a naturalist philosophy of scientific practices also takes a radical stance in other respects, ruling out some familiar philosophical positions. I conclude this section of the paper by briefly suggesting just how radical this form of scientific naturalism may be. Giere (1999, ch. 5) and others have noted that the concept of natural laws as necessary truths arose within a theological understanding of nature as God's creation. God was the legislator who laid down the laws, and whatever happens must obey them. Giere criticized this conception of natural law, arguing that naturalists should not ascribe universality and necessity to scientific understanding. These features of a metaphysics of natural law belong to an earlier theological conception, which naturalists should avoid.

While I endorse such criticisms of a metaphysics of natural law, I also think a more basic trace of a theological conception remains in many philosophical accounts of science and nature. A theological conception of God as creator places God outside of nature. God's *understanding* of nature is also external to the world. Such a God could understand his language and his thoughts about the world, apart from any interaction with the world. Naturalists long ago removed God from scientific conceptions of the world. Yet many naturalists still implicitly understand science as aiming to take God's *place*. They interpret science as trying to represent nature from a standpoint outside of nature. The language in which science represents the world could then be understood apart from the causal interactions it articulates. A philosophy of scientific practices denies that such an otherworldly understanding of nature is possible. Scientific concepts and scientific understanding are situated in the midst of ongoing causal interaction with the world. That is why I talk about conceptual articulation in science rather than theoretical representation. We understand scientific concepts only by understanding the phenomena they articulate. We find ourselves in the midst of the world, and cannot understand it except from within. That is the radical vision of a naturalistic philosophy of science expressed in my "concluding scientific postscript."

References

Bechtel, William 2006. *Discovering Cell Mechanisms*. Cambridge: Cambridge University Press.

Cartwright, Nancy 1999. *The Dappled World*. Cambridge: Cambridge University Press.

—— 2004. From Causation to Explanation and Back. In B. Leiter, ed., *The Future for Philosophy*, 230–245. Oxford: Oxford University Press.

Chang, Hasok 2004. *Inventing Temperature*. Oxford: Oxford University Press.

De Caro, Mario, and MacArthur, David 2004. *Naturalism in Question*. Cambridge: Harvard University Press.

Fine, Arthur 1986. *The Shaky Game*. Chicago: University of Chicago Press.

Giere, Ronald 1988. *Explaining Science*. Chicago: University of Chicago Press.

—— 1999. *Science Without Laws*. Chicago: University of Chicago Press.

Haugeland, John 1998. *Having Thought*. Cambridge: Harvard University Press.

Kierkegaard, Søren 1941. *Concluding Unscientific Postscript*. Tr. D. F. Swenson and W. Lowrie. Princeton: Princeton University Press.

Lange, Marc 2000. *Natural Laws in Scientific Practice*. Oxford: Oxford University Press.

Morgan, Mary and Morrison, Margaret 1999. *Models as Mediators*. Cambridge: Cambridge University Press.

Quine, W.v.O. 1953. Two Dogmas of Empiricism. In *From a Logical Point of View*, 20–46. Cambridge: Harvard University Press.

Rheinberger, Hans-Jörg 1995. From Microsomes to Ribosomes: 'Strategies' of 'Representation', 1935–55. *Journal of the History of Biology* 48:49–89.

Rouse, Joseph 2002. *How Scientific Practices Matter*. Chicago: University of Chicago Press.

—— 2006. Practice Theory. In S. Turner and M. Risjord, ed., *Handbook of the Philosophy of Science. Volume 15: Philosophy of Anthropology and Sociology*. Dordrecht: Elsevier, in press.

Searle, John 1983. *Intentionality*. Cambridge: Cambridge University Press.

Williams, Bernard 1985. *Ethics and the Limits of Philosophy*. Cambridge: Harvard University Press.

Wilson, Mark 2005. *Wandering Significance*. Oxford: Oxford University Press.

Danielle Macbeth

Naturalism in the Philosophy of Mathematics

Haverford College
dmacbeth@haverford.edu

Mathematicians distinguish in practice between those consistent systems, structures, and concepts that are of mathematical interest and those that are not; and this is problem for the would-be naturalist.[1] If, as the practice of mathematicians suggests, mathematics has its own subject matter, it is one that is abstract, that is, platonistic, but Platonism is anathema to the naturalist because and insofar as it cannot be made scientifically respectable. Unfortunately, the naturalist also cannot reject the idea that mathematics has its own subject matter because that would be inappropriately to legislate to mathematics; the naturalist philosopher has no authority to determine what is, or is not, mathematics.[2] And if the naturalist focuses not on what mathematicians do, on the distinctions they draw in practice, but instead on what mathematicians say, namely, that mathematically speaking any consistent system, structure, or concept is as good as any other, that the differences that are discernable in their practice are due only to personal preference or aesthetic considerations,[3] then a quite different but equally serious difficulty arises. If the distinctions that mathematicians draw in practice between "real" mathematics and everything else are to

---

1   For purposes here a naturalist is someone who rejects superstitious appeals to anything super- or non-natural, and rejects the conclusions of philosophical arguments when those conclusions conflict with what, on other grounds, it clearly appears rational to acknowledge. What our naturalist is not committed to is the thesis that there are no distinctively philosophical problems or distinctively philosophical means of addressing them. I take the topic of this essay to be a distinctively philosophical problem, one that is addressed here in a distinctively philosophical way.

2   Both Penelope Maddy and John Burgess, although they are largely Quinean in their naturalism, take Quine to task for legislating to mathematics. See Penelope Maddy, *Naturalism in Mathematics* (Oxford: Clarendon Press, 1997), as well as her "Three Forms of Naturalism" in *The Oxford Handbook of Philosophy of Mathematics and Logic*, ed. Stewart Shapiro (New York: Oxford University Press, 2005), which discusses both her views and Burgess's in relation to Quine's naturalism.

3   As Davis and Hersh report, "most writers on the subject seem to agree that the typical working mathematician is a Platonist on weekdays and a formalist on Sundays. That is, when he is doing mathematics he is convinced that he is dealing with an objective reality whose properties he is attempting to determine. But then, when challenged to give a philosophical account of this reality, he finds it easiest to pretend that he does not believe in it after all." P. J. Davis and R. Hersh, *The Mathematical Experience* (New York: Penguin Books, 1983), p. 321.

be explained not by appeal to objective mathematical facts but instead by appeal to subjective considerations such as the aesthetic or other preferences of mathematicians, then as Steiner has argued, the extraordinary successfulness of applications of mathematics in the natural sciences is explicable only on anthropocentric grounds. But anthropocentrism, like Platonism, is inconsistent with naturalism; there is no good reason to hold that, as Steiner puts it, "the human race is in some way privileged, central to the scheme of things".[4] Is it, then, simply impossible to be a naturalist about the practice of mathematics?

Mathematics appears to have its own proper content, its own distinctively mathematical subject matter. Mathematicians in their work tend to take this at face value, and it is corroborated by their mathematical experience.[5] Philosophers tend to treat this as a mere appearance; mathematics, they tend to think, has no subject matter, no objects, of its own. (Interestingly, at the turn of the last century the roles were reversed: the mathematicians were the formalists, the philosophers the realists. We will return to this.) Either way, naturalism in the philosophy of mathematics seems to be fatally compromised. We can, however, put aside, at least for the moment, the issues raised by the application of mathematics in the natural sciences (on the assumption that mathematics has no content of its own) and focus on the dilemma: either mathematics has no content of its own and really is nothing more than a kind of a formal game with symbols, or naturalism, at least in the philosophy of mathematics, is false. More specifically, we need to consider the assumption that underlies this dilemma, the idea that mathematical content is incompatible with naturalism. Obviously, if that assumption is false then the application problem is solved as well.

Although it can seem to us manifest that the idea of a distinctively mathematical subject matter is incompatible with naturalism, it is worth making explicit just why these two notions seem to be so deeply in tension with one another. Benacerraf's discussion in "Mathematical Truth", although not directed at precisely this issue, suggests an explanation.[6] His interest is in two conflicting accounts of mathematical truth: what he calls the standard view according to which mathematical truth is to be conceived Tarski-style, in terms of reference and satisfaction, that is, by appeal to abstract objects, and "combinatoric"

---

4   Mark Steiner, *The Applicability of Mathematics as a Philosophical Problem* (Cambridge, Mass.: Harvard University Press, 1998), p. 55.

5   Mathematicians regularly report that thinking about a problem in mathematics often involves imagining mathematical objects, and indeed imagining them doing things, that is, changing in various ways. See, for example, Reuben Hersh's description in "Wings, not Foundations!", in *Essays on the Foundations of Mathematics and Logic*, ed. G. Sica (Monza, Italy: Polimetrica International Scientific Publisher, 2005).

6   Paul Benacerraf, "Mathematical Truth", originally in the *Journal of Philosophy* 70 (1973): 661–680, reprinted in *Philosophy of Mathematics: Selected Readings* (2nd edn.), ed. Paul Benacerraf and Hilary Putnam (Cambridge: Cambridge University Press, 1983).

views that aim to explain mathematical truth in terms of formal derivability from axioms, that is, syntax. Benacerraf's main point is that standard views, although providing a very plausible account of mathematical truths, face an apparently insurmountable hurdle when it comes to accounting for how such truths are known, and combinatoric views, conversely, although providing a very plausible account of mathematical knowledge in terms of proof, face an apparently insurmountable hurdle when it comes to explaining why what has been derived from a set of axioms should be thought of as thereby true. It is furthermore clear that for Benacerraf the pivot on which the argument turns is the conception of language due to Tarski. Either we understand truth, following Tarski, by appeal to reference and satisfaction, but then have no adequate epistemology of mathematics, or we focus instead on derivability in a system, but then have no adequate conception of truth in mathematics precisely because "truth and reference go hand in hand".[7] Because truth depends on reference and satisfaction, truth in mathematics depends on the existence of abstract mathematical objects—but then, again, it is hard to imagine what our cognitive access to such objects might be or more generally how such objects might fit into our overall picture of reality. And so we recoil to formalism, that is, combinatorial views that "avoid ... the necessary route to an account of truth: through the subject matter of the proposition whose truth is being clarified"—and then we have no account of truth in mathematics.

Benacerraf appeals to Tarski's conception of truth in order to motivate what he calls the standard view; problems with the standard view in turn motivate the combinatoric view that he considers. But in fact, it was combinatorial views in mathematics that were largely responsible for the model-theoretic conception of language that is made explicit in Tarski. It was not Tarski's theory of truth that (indirectly) gave rise to combinatoric views as suggested by Benacerraf's narrative, but instead combinatoric views that gave rise to Tarski's theory of truth. Mathematicians such as Pasch in the nineteenth century and Hilbert at the turn of the twentieth took the combinatoric view to be a fundamental advance in mathematics, one that philosophers of mathematics, most notably Russell and Frege (though for very different reasons), at first strenuously resisted, but which eventually became mainstream in philosophy as well[8]—though Frege, it should be noted, never converted. But if that is right then the dichotomy of logical form or syntax, on the one hand, and semantic

---

7   Benacerraf, "Mathematical Truth", p. 419, and also for the quote to follow.
8   See especially Ernest Nagel, "The Formation of Modern Conceptions of Formal Logic in the Development of Geometry" (1939), reprinted in his *Teleology Revisited and Other Essays in the Philosophy and History of Science* (New York: Columbia University Press, 1979); but also William Demopoulos "Frege, Hilbert, and the Conceptual Structure of Model Theory", *History and Philosophy of Logic* 15 (1994): 211–225, and Stewart Shapiro, *Philosophy of Mathematics: Structure and Ontology* (New York: Oxford, 1997), Chapter 5.

content through relation to an object or objects, on the other, that Benacerraf relies on to construct his dilemma runs much deeper than it might at first appear. In fact, I want to suggest, it originates with Kant as a consequence of his discovery of the logical distinction between intuitions through which objects are given in sense experience and concepts through which such given objects are thought, a discovery that may have been motivated in turn by Kant's reflections on the mathematics of his day.[9]

Before Kant, two quite different ways to think about mathematics were suggested by the use of two very different sorts of signs in mathematics. Whereas a collection of, for example, four strokes can be taken to be an instance of a number (conceived as a collection of units), the corresponding Arabic numeral '4' would seem instead to be a symbol that only stands in for or is representative of the number, one that is enormously useful in calculations but nonetheless is not an instance of the thing itself. (Although the Arabic numeration system, with its paper and pencil algorithms for the basic arithmetical operations, was introduced into Europe around the tenth century and came to be widely used in calculations, even shopkeepers continued to record the results of their paper and pencil calculations in Roman numerals until well into the sixteenth century. Arabic numeration, however useful in calculations, was not at first read as a language within which to express and record truths; unlike Roman numerals, Arabic numerals were not seen as giving the numbers themselves.) Even more obviously, a drawn circle can be seen as an instance, however imperfect, of a geometrical circle, as an instance of that which is only represented by the equation '$x^2 + y^2 = r^2$' of elementary algebra.

There is, however, an essential difference between our two pairs of examples. Whereas the Arabic numeration system can be treated merely as a convenient shorthand by means of which to solve arithmetical problems, the rules of elementary algebra permit transformations that are, from the ancient and medieval perspective, sheer nonsense. If numbers are collections of units, and if the signs of Arabic numeration are merely representatives of the numbers, then it will seem manifest that many (apparent) problems in arithmetic can have no solution and so are not really arithmetical problems at all: although '$3 + x = 5$' is a perfectly good arithmetical problem, '$5 + x = 3$' is not because there is nothing that one might add to five (things) to yield three (things). From the perspective of the rules of elementary algebra, among which is the rule that if $a + x = b$, then $x = b - a$, the two cases are exactly the same: the solution in the first case is $x = 5 - 3$, and in the second

---

9   The discussion to follow of Kant's philosophy of mathematics and its demise in the nineteenth century owes a great deal to my "Logic and the Foundations of Mathematics", forthcoming in *The Oxford Handbook of American Philosophy*, ed. Cheryl Misak (New York: Oxford University Press).

$x = 3 - 5$. The language of algebra introduces in this way something essentially new.[10] Whereas basic arithmetic is, originally, bounded by our intuitions regarding what makes sense, the rules of algebra seem to enable us somehow to transcend those bounds, to find a new kind of meaning in the rule-governed manipulation of signs.

Arithmetic and algebra use systems of signs governed by algorithms; Euclidean geometry instead uses diagrams that involve (so it seems) instances of geometrical figures to demonstrate the truth of theorems and the solutions of problems. "Pebble arithmetic", similarly, involves instances of numbers conceived as collections of units. These seem, then, to be quite different sorts of systems, and they give rise in turn to quite different conceptions of rigor and of proof. A Euclidean demonstration would seem to be a course of pictorial reasoning, one that reveals connections to an attentive audience. It does not *require* assent but to one attentive to what is being claimed and to what is depicted in the diagram, the chain of reasoning shows the truth of the conclusion. The rigor of the demonstration thus crucially depends on intuition and meaning. From the perspective of this case, the often merely mechanical manipulation of signs according to rules in algebra can seem anything but rigorous, leading as it apparently does to the "obscurity and paradox" of, for instance, numbers that are less than nothing, or worse the roots of numbers that are less than nothing.[11] But in a different sense *only* a calculation in arithmetic or algebra is properly rigorous because only such a calculation *requires* assent by anyone who knows the rules governing the use of the signs involved. From this perspective, rigor crucially depends on ignoring intuition and meaning because they are, or at least can be, a source of error and prejudice. Lambert championed this conception of rigor and proof arguing that a proof should "never appeal to the thing itself ... but be conducted entirely symbolically", that it should treat its premises "like so many algebraic equations that one has ready before him and from which one extracts x, y, z, etc. without looking back to the object itself".[12]

A Euclidean demonstration enables one to see why a conclusion holds by literally showing the connections that are the ground of its truth, but does so at the expense of rigor in our second sense. An argument that proceeds by means

---

10   In "Viète, Descartes, and the Emergence of Modern Mathematics", *Graduate Faculty Philosophy Journal* 25 (2004): 87–117, I explore in detail just what it is that is new with the introduction of the symbolic language of algebra, and also argue that Descartes, not Viète, ought to be seen as the first truly modern mathematician.

11   The description is John Playfair's in "On the Arithmetic of Impossible Equations" (1778), quoted in Ernest Nagel, " 'Impossible Numbers': A Chapter in the History of Modern Logic" (1935), reprinted in *Teleology Revisited*, p. 173.

12   "Theorie der Parallellinien" (1786), quoted in Michael Detlefson, "Formalism" in *The Oxford Handbook of Philosophy of Mathematics and Logic*, p. 250.

of the manipulation of symbols according to strict algorithms, by contrast, definitively establishes a truth, but it does so at the expense of understanding. It does not show, with all the intuitive clarity of a Euclidean demonstration, why the conclusion should be as it is. How extraordinary, then, that Kant should claim in the first *Critique* that *all* of mathematics functions in the same way, namely, through constructions in pure intuition that enable one to see, and so to understand, the necessity of the conclusion drawn. How *could* this be given that in geometry one focuses on the things themselves whereas in arithmetic and algebra one focuses not on the things but instead on arbitrary (rule governed) signs?

Already in the "Inquiry" (1764), Kant suggests that the signs and marks employed in mathematics "show in their composition the constituent concepts of which the whole idea ... consists".[13] The Arabic numeral '278', for example, shows (on this reading) that the number designated consists of two hundreds, seven tens, and eight units. A drawn triangle similarly is manifestly a three-sided closed plane figure; like the numeral '278', it is a whole of simple parts. These complexes are then further combined to show "in their combinations the relations of the ... thoughts to each other".[14] In mathematics, one combines the wholes that are formed out of simples into larger wholes that exhibit relations among them. The systems of signs thus have three levels of articulation: first the primitive signs; then the wholes formed out of those primitives, wholes that constitute the subject matter of the relevant part of mathematics (the numbers of arithmetic, say, or the figures of Euclidean geometry); and finally the largest wholes, for example, a Euclidean diagram or a calculation in Arabic numeration, that are wholes of the (intermediate) wholes of the primitive parts. In the *Critique*, by which time Kant had discovered the logical and metaphysical distinction between intuitions and concepts, Kant further indicates that it is precisely because it is possible to reconceptualize at the second level, to see a collection of marks now this way and now that, possible, that is, to synthesize the given manifold of marks under different concepts, that one can come in the course of one's reasoning to see that the predicate of the judgment in question belongs necessarily to the concept of the subject despite not being contained in it.

Consider a demonstration in Euclid. Such a demonstration comprises a diagram constructed out of the primitives of the system (points, lines, angles, and

---

13   Immanuel Kant, "Inquiry Concerning the Distinctness of the Principles of Natural Theology
      and Morality" (1764), in *Theoretical Philosophy, 1755–1770*, trans. and ed. David Walford
      with Ralf Meerbote (Cambridge: Cambridge University Press, 1992), p. 251.
14   *Ibid.* Kant is in this passage in fact describing what the words of natural language that are
      used in philosophy cannot do. It is clear that he means indirectly to say what the signs and
      marks in mathematics can do.

areas) together with a commentary that, among other things, instructs one how to conceive various aspects of the diagram, a given line, for instance, now as a radius of a circle and now as a side of a triangle. What Kant saw is that such reconceptualizations are critical to the cogency of the demonstrations—as the very first proposition in Euclid's *Elements* illustrates. The problem is to construct an equilateral triangle on a given finite straight line. To demonstrate the solution, one first constructs a circle with one endpoint of the given line as center and the line itself as radius, and then another circle with the other endpoint as center and the line as radius. Then, from one of the two points of intersection of the two circles, one draws two lines, one to each of the endpoints of the original line. Now one reasons on the basis of the drawn diagram: two of the three lines are radii of one circle and so must be equal in length, and one of those radii along with the third line are radii of the other circle, so must be equal in length. But if the two lines in each of the two pairs are equal in length, and there is one line that is in both pairs, then all three lines must be equal in length. Those very same lines, however, can also be conceived as the sides of a triangle. Because they can, we know that the triangle so constructed is equilateral. A Euclidean demonstration works because the diagram has three levels of articulation that enable one to reconfigure at the second level, to see primitive signs now as parts of this figure and now as parts of that. The demonstration is ampliative, an extension of knowledge, for just this reason.

One can similarly demonstrate a simple fact of arithmetic through the successive reconceptualizing of the units of a number. One begins, for instance, with a collection of seven strokes and a collection of five strokes. Again, there are three levels of articulation: the primitives (the individual strokes), the two collections of those primitives, and the whole array. Because the two collections are given in the array, it is possible to reconceive a unit of one collection as instead a unit of the other and in this way to "add the units ... previously taken together in order to constitute the number 5 one after another to the number 7, and thus see the number 12 arise".[15]

Calculations in Arabic numeration are more complex, but as Kant teaches us to see, the basic principle is the same. Suppose that the problem is to determine the product of twenty-seven and forty-four. One begins by writing the signs for the two numbers in a particular array, namely, one directly beneath the other. Obviously, here again the three levels can be discerned, and here again it is this that enables one to do one's mathematical work. Suppose that one has written '44' beneath '27'. The calculation begins with a reconfiguration at the second level of articulation: the rightmost '4' in '44' is considered instead with the '7' in '27'. Multiplying the two elements in this new whole

---

15   Immanuel Kant, *Critique of Pure Reason* (1781/1787), trans. and ed. Paul Guyer and Allen W. Wood (Cambridge: Cambridge University Press, 1998), B16.

yields twenty-eight, so an '8' goes under the rightmost column and a '2' above the left. Next one takes the same sign '4' and considers it together with the '2' in '27', and so on in a familiar series of steps to yield, finally, in the last (fifth) row, the product that is wanted. The fifth row is, of course, arrived at by the stepwise addition of the numbers given in the columns at the third and fourth row; it is by reading down that one understands why just those signs appear in the bottom row. But it is by reading across, by conceptualizing the signs in the last row as a numeral, that one knows the answer that is wanted.

Exactly the same point applies in algebra; even in algebra, there is "a characteristic construction, in which one displays by signs in intuition the concepts, especially of relations of quantities" (A734/B762). In every case, through the reconfiguration of parts of wholes (made possible, on the one hand, by the fact that those wholes are themselves parts of wholes, and on the other, by the Kantian dichotomy of intuition and concept), one comes in the course of one's reasoning to see something new arise, and thereby to extend one's knowledge. Because the relevant intuitions are pure rather than empirical, the results are necessary, that is, a priori; and because the whole process is made possible by space and time as the forms of sensibility, the results are obviously and immediately applicable in the natural sciences.

Before Kant there seemed to be two incompatible ways to think about mathematical practice. One way was bottom-up: beginning with concrete sensible objects such as drawn geometrical figures or "actual" numbers, that is, collections of things, the mathematician learns to abstract from these concrete cases and to reason about mathematical entities that are only imperfectly depicted in a Euclidean demonstration or collection of strokes on a page. From this perspective, the manipulation of symbols according to algorithms in arithmetic and algebra must be understood instrumentally; such systems of signs are useful but not meaningful in their own right. The second way is top-down beginning with the symbolic language of algebra and by extension that of arithmetic. On this view the meanings of the signs are exhausted by the rules governing their use; our capacity to imagine the results of computations, for example, that of taking a larger from a smaller number, is irrelevant. Euclidean geometry, dependent as it is on drawn figures rather than on rule-governed signs, is to be replaced by "analytic geometry", that is to say, algebra. Kant overcomes this either/or. According to him, all mathematics—whether a Euclidean demonstration, a calculation in arithmetic, or a computation in algebra—functions in the same way, through the construction of concepts in pure intuition. It follows that both earlier accounts were wrong: Euclidean geometry does not function by picturing, however imperfectly, geometrical objects as the first, bottom-up account would have it; and the symbolic language of arithmetic and algebra is not merely symbolic, its meaning exhausted by the rules governing the use of its signs, as the second, top-down account would have it. Both sorts of systems of signs function to *encode information* in a way that enables rigorous reasoning in the system of signs, reasoning that is revelatory of new and substantive mathematical truths.

Unfortunately, even as Kant was working all this out mathematicians were coming more and more to eschew the sorts of constructive, usually algebraic, problem-solving techniques that Kant focuses on in favor of a more conceptual approach. A new mathematical practice was emerging, and it did so, over the course of the nineteenth century, in roughly three, not strictly chronological, stages. First, mathematicians began to introduce new mathematical objects that could not be constructed in any intuition, for example, the projective geometer's points at infinity (where parallel lines meet). Second, the focus was shifting more generally from algebraic representations of objects to descriptions of them using concepts. In the case of limit operations, for example, instead of trying to compute, that is, to construct, the limit as Leibniz had done, Cauchy, Bolzano, and Weierstrass instead aimed to describe what must be true of it. Riemann similarly did not require, as Euler had, that a function be given algebraic expression; it was enough to describe its behavior. And finally, a new sort of algebra was emerging, one that concerned not any particular mathematical objects and functions but instead the kinds of structures they can be seen to exhibit, that is, groups, rings, fields, and so on. In each case, the focus was on reasoning from concepts; no construction of concepts in intuition was needed, and intuition itself was coming to be seen as a 'foreign' element to be expelled from mathematics.[16]

But if mathematics does not involve constructions in pure intuition, there would seem to be only two options: either mathematical judgments are independent of intuition altogether and so are empty of all content, that is, merely formal, or they are contentful truths because a posteriori. That is, as the point would come to be put, either mathematics is pure, uninterpreted, necessary, and without (empirical) content, or it is applied, interpreted, contingent, and contentful—in Einstein's famous dictum (1921): "insofar as mathematical theorems refer to reality, they are not certain, and insofar as they are certain,

---

16   See Howard Stein, "*Logos*, Logic, and *Logistiké*: Some Philosophical Remarks on Nineteenth Century Transformation of Mathematics", in *History and Philosophy of Modern Mathematics, Minnesota Studies in the Philosophy of Science*, vol. XI., ed. William Aspray and Philip Kitcher (Minneapolis, Minn.: University of Minnesota Press, 1988); Nagel, "The Formation of Modern Conceptions of Formal Logic"; Mark Wilson "Frege: The Royal Road from Geometry", in *Frege's Philosophy of Mathematics*, ed. William Demopoulos (Cambridge, Mass.: Harvard University Press); and Jeremy Gray, "The Nineteenth Century Revolution in Mathematical Ontology" in *Revolutions in Mathematics*, ed. Donald Gillies (Oxford: Clarendon Press, 1992). Stein describes this transformation of mathematics in the nineteenth century as "so profound that it is not too much to call it a second birth of the subject—its first birth having occurred among the ancient Greeks" (p. 238). This is misleading insofar as it ignores Descartes' transformation of mathematics in the seventeenth century, the transformation without which modern science would have been impossible. See my "Viète, Descartes, and the Emergence of Modern Mathematics".

they do not refer to reality ... The progress entailed by axiomatics consists in the sharp separation of the logical form and the realistic and intuitive contents."[17] One can have deductive rigor by focusing on the signs and the rules governing their use, Benacerraf's combinatoric view, or one can have meaning and truth by focusing on that for which the signs stand, their semantic values, an empiricism version of what Benacerraf calls the standard view. What one cannot have is both at once—as Benacerraf laments.

Objects given in intuitions are thought through concepts; because they are, as we have seen, they can be variously conceived in ways that combine intuitive clarity and deductive rigor. The same cannot be said of concepts themselves. Although it is possible to take a bottom-up view of concepts by appeal to the objects that exemplify them and also possible to take a top-down view of concepts by appeal to inferential relations among them as stipulated in an axiomatization, it is impossible to do both at once. Deductive rigor, which requires fixing in advance the logical relations among one's primitive concepts in axioms and definitions, thus requires a kind of formalism, and thereby the loss of the sort of intuitive or contentful rigor that, if Kant is right, is displayed both in a Euclidean demonstration and in an arithmetic calculation. This (exclusive) either/or, either deductive rigor or content and meaning, which emerged first in geometry, in Pasch and in Hilbert, eventually, and inevitably, surfaced in logic as well, and is now the standard, model-theoretic view.[18] Frege long ago suggested an alternative. Rejecting the Hilbertian pure/applied distinction, the dichotomy of logical form and empirical content, Frege held that formal rigor is not incompatible with content, that form and content are combined in his logical language *Begriffsschrift*.[19] We need to understand, at least in outline, how this was to work.[20]

---

17   From his lecture "Geometrie und Erfahrung"; quoted in Hans Freudenthal, "The Main Trends in the Foundations of Geometry in the 19th Century", in *Logic, Methodology and Philosophy of Science: Proceedings of the 1960 International Congress* (Stanford, Cal.: Stanford University Press, 1962), p. 619.

18   See Freudenthal, "The Main Trends in the Foundations"; also Nagel, "The Formation of Modern Conceptions"; Demopoulos, "Frege, Hilbert and the Conceptual Structure"; Jean Van Heijenoort, "Logic as Calculus and Logic as Language", *Synthese* 17 (1967): 324–330; and Warren Goldfarb, "Logic in the Twenties: The Nature of the Quantifier", *The Journal of Symbolic Logic* 44 (1979): 351–368.

19   See, for example, his exchange of letters with Hilbert in Gottlob Frege, *Philosophical and Mathematical Correspondence*, trans. Hans Kaal and ed. G. Gabriel, H. Hermes, F. Kambartel, C. Thiel, and A. Veraart (Chicago: University of Chicago Press, 1980), and Frege's early essay "On the Aim of the 'Conceptual Notation' ", in *Conceptual Notation and Related Articles*, trans. and ed. T. W. Bynum (Oxford: Clarendon Press, 1972).

20   The account of Frege's understanding of his logical language *Begriffsschrift* to follow is explained and defended in much greater detail in my *Frege's Logic* (Cambridge, Mass.: Harvard University Press, 2005).

Although not always recognized as such, Kant's distinction between intuitions and concepts is (among other things) a properly logical advance.[21] Ancient logic is a term logic in which no logical distinction is drawn between terms that can be applied only to one thing and terms that can be applied to many. Any individual, Socrates, say, can be called many things (that is, by many names): Socrates, pale, man, snub-nosed, wise, mortal, and so on. In effect, the terms in a classical term logic combine both a 'referential' and a 'predicative' aspect—which is why it is valid in such a logic to infer from the fact that all S is P that some S is P. (If there is nothing to call an S then there is nothing to be said about the Ss.) Later rationalists and empiricists would emphasize, respectively, the predicative or the referential aspects of terms, or of their cognitive correlates, but it is only with Kant that a clean break is made. Intuitions are referential; they give objects. Concepts are predicative; they are ways the objects given in intuitions can be thought (correctly or incorrectly). What Frege realized by the early 1890s is that this Kantian distinction of two logically different sorts of representations *similarly involves a conflation*, this time of two logically different logical distinctions, that of *Sinn* and *Bedeutung* with that of concept and object: 'it is easy to become unclear ... by confounding the division into concepts and objects with the distinction between sense and meaning so that we run together sense and concept on the one hand and meaning and object on the other'.[22] Once having made this distinction between these two different distinctions we can begin, at least, to understand the nature of a properly logical language *within which* to reason discursively, that is, from concepts alone, and thereby how again to combine intuitive with deductive rigor in the practice of mathematics.

Concepts, on Frege's mature view, are laws of correlation, objects to truth-values in the case of first-level concepts, and lower level concepts to truth-values in the case of higher level concepts. A concept is thus something in its own right, something objective that can serve as an argument for a function in a judgment. One can, for example, judge of two concepts that one is subordinate to the other, that is, that the second-level relation of subordination is correctly applied to them.

21 Manley Thompson, in "Singular Terms and Intuitions in Kant's Epistemology", *Review of Metaphysics* 26 (1972–3): 314–343, makes the point that Kant has a monadic predicate calculus, that is, the calculus that Russell once described as "the first serious advance in real logic since the time of the Greeks" (Bertrand Russell, *Our Knowledge of the External World* (London: George Allen and Unwin, 1914), p. 50)—which Russell himself thought was discovered first by Peano, and independently, Frege. As Russell himself notes (see *Dear Russell—Dear Jourdain*, ed. and trans. I. Grattan-Guinness (New York: Columbia University Press, 1977), the extension of the monadic predicate calculus to the full logic of relations is a merely technical advance.

22 Gottlob Frege, "Comments on Sense and Meaning" (1892–5), *Posthumous Writings*, trans. Peter Long and Roger White, ed. H. Hermes, F. Kambartel, and F. Kaulbach (Chicago: University of Chicago Press, 1979), p. 118.

That second-level relation of subordination, similarly, is something objective about which to judge, correctly or incorrectly. It is, for instance, a transitive relation; *subordination* has the property of being transitive. There is, then, for Frege a natural division of "levels" of knowledge. First there are facts about the everyday objects of which we have sensory experience. Such facts are one and all a posteriori and contingent (setting aside instances of laws of logic or of a special science); in *Begriffsschrift*, Frege's formula language of pure thought, these facts are expressed using object names and first-level concept words. One level up are facts about first-level concepts, for example, the fact that *cat* is subordinate to *mammal*, that is, that being a cat entails being a mammal (from which it follows that any particular cat is necessarily a mammal). Such a law can be expressed in *Begriffsschrift* using the conditional stroke and Latin italic letters lending generality of content, or using the conditional stroke together with the concavity and German letter.[23] In the latter case, we have (at least on one function/argument analysis of the sentence) a sign for the second-level relation of subordination, one that is formed from the conditional stroke together with the concavity. To move up a level again, to consideration of second-level concepts such as subordination is to move from the domain of the special sciences to the domain of the science of logic. The subject matter of logic is the second-level properties and relations that hold of the first-level concepts that constitute in turn the subject matter of the special sciences—including mathematics if logicism is wrong.

In *Begriffsschrift*, Frege's formula language of pure thought, concept words, which are given relative to a function/argument analysis of a whole *Begriffsschrift* sentence, designate concepts—or at least they purport to. They also express senses. Indeed, a *Begriffsschrift* expression most immediately maps or traces a sense; it shows in its composition the sense through which something objective is, or at least purports to be, grasped. Consider, for example, the concept of continuity (of a function at a point). This concept takes mathematical functions and points as arguments to yield truth-values as values. But our grasp of that concept is mediated by a sense, one that we can have more or less clearly in mind. By the time Frege was writing, the content of this concept, that is, the sense through which it is grasped, had been clarified, and Frege shows just how that sense is expressed in a complex two-dimensional array in *Begriffsschrift*.[24] Such an expression, formed from the primitives of *Begriffsschrift* together with

---

23   True accidental generalities can also be expressed these ways in Frege's logic. (Because inferences can be drawn only from acknowledged truths in Frege's logic, this does not introduce any difficulties into the logic.) The basic case, however, is that of a relationship among concepts that is not grounded in contingent facts about objects but applies immediately to concepts. See my *Frege's Logic*.

24   In "Boole's Logical Calculus and the Concept Script" (1880/81), *Posthumous Writings*, p. 24, Frege shows how to depict the content of this concept in *Begriffsschrift*, and also how to depict the contents of many other mathematically significant concepts.

some signs from arithmetic, *designates* the concept of continuity; it is a *name* for that concept. But this two-dimensional array of signs also expresses a sense, that is, the inferentially articulated content that is grasped by anyone who clearly understands what it means for a function to be continuous at a point.

In a *Begriffsschrift* sentence, then, at least as it is conceived here, three levels of articulation are discernable. First, there are the primitive signs out of which everything is composed; then there are the concept words, the function and argument, that are given relative to an analysis of the sentence; and finally there is the whole sentence, which expresses a thought and designates, or ought to designate, a truth-value, either the True or the False. As may be evident, the primitives of the language so conceived cannot be taken to designate independent of a context of use. Only in the context of a sentence, and, relative to an analysis into function and argument, can we speak of the designation of a subsentential expression. What one grasps when one grasps the meaning of a primitive of the language is the sense expressed, and thereby the contribution that primitive makes to the thought expressed by a sentence containing it, and relative, to some assumed analysis in which the primitive occurs as a designating expression, the designation. But that primitive expression can equally well appear as a component of a complex expression that designates something quite different. Frege's concavity, for example, which taken alone functions rather like a quantifier, also occurs in a wide range of expressions for other higher level concepts such as the second-level relation of subordination, or that of the continuity of a function at a point. Again, it is only relative to a function/argument analysis that subsentential expressions of *Begriffsschrift*, whether simple or complex, can be said to designate. (Needless to say, such a conception of language is essentially late; only someone already able to read and write could devise or learn such a language.)

As it is understood here, a *Begriffsschrift* sentence is rather like a Euclidean diagram in that it can be regarded in various ways, that is, given now one function/argument analysis and now another. A sentence containing Frege's (complex) sign for the concept of continuity can, for instance, be analyzed so as to yield that concept word, but it can also be analyzed in other ways, in ways that effectively cut across the boundaries of this concept word, and it may need to be so analyzed for the purposes of proof. It is precisely because concept words in *Begriffsschrift* are at once wholes of primitive parts and themselves parts of larger wholes, namely, sentences, that a *Begriffsschrift* proof can be fruitful, an extension of our knowledge. Given what the concepts involved mean, the senses through which they are given, one can come to see, in the course of the proof, how aspects of those senses can be figured and refigured to yield something new.[25] Already Kant taught us to

---

25   In "The Role of *Begriffsschrift* in the Striving for Truth", forthcoming in *Grazer Philosophische Studien*, I work through some examples of proofs in Frege's formula language of thought, examples illustrating just this point.

see the course of a demonstration in Euclid as realizing the figure that is wanted, and the course of a calculation in Arabic numeration as realizing the product (say) that is wanted; Frege similarly can teach us to see the course of a proof as realizing the conclusion that is wanted. So conceived the proof does not merely establish the truth of the conclusion (assuming the truth of the premises); it shows *how* the conclusion follows from the premises, how the conclusion is contained in the premises "as plants are contained in their seeds, not as beams are contained in a house".[26] One reasons *in* the symbolic language (so conceived) in a way that is at once deductively rigorous and intuitively rigorous, in a way that one can follow and understand; and one can do this because a sentence in the language, in *Begriffsschrift*, puts a thought before one's eyes. Frege's logical language is in this way an utterly different sort of logical language from any we are familiar with. As the point might be put, it is not a *mathematical* logic at all; it is not an algebra of thought that reveals valid patterns or structures. It is instead a *philosophical* logic within which to express thoughts, and thereby to discover truths. As Kant taught us to read calculations in arithmetic and algebra not as merely mechanical manipulations of signs but as constructions revelatory of truth, so Frege teaches us to read a proof in symbolic logic not as a merely formal, deductively valid derivation but as a fully meaningful inference to a conclusion that is thereby revelatory of truth.

But of course not all contentful chains of reasoning are revelatory of their conclusions. As Lakatos has emphasized, the practice of mathematics in fact proceeds by way of a process of proof and refutation, that is, dialectically in a way that involves both modus ponens, inference from acknowledged truths to other truths that are entailed by them, and also modus tollens, inference from the acknowledged falsity of some putative conclusion to the falsity of what had mistakenly been taken to be true.[27] But if that is right then an axiomatization of some domain of knowledge should be seen not so much as providing a foundation for that domain as serving as a vehicle for the discovery of truths in that domain. Quite simply, by making one's conceptions explicit in axioms and definitions, one can then test their adequacy "experimentally", by deriving theorems. If a manifest falsehood, for example, a contradiction, is derived, then one knows that one's conceptions are faulty, that one has not achieved adequate grasp of some concept, or has mistakenly thought that there is any concept there to be grasped at all. This is, of course, precisely what happened to Frege. His Basic Law V, which made explicit the notion of a course of values as Frege understood it, was shown by Russell to be flawed. But whereas for Russell—who, by his own admission, wanted certainty the way others want religious faith—that discovery was a disastrous

---

26   Gottlob Frege, *The Foundations of Arithmetic*, trans. J. L. Austin (Evanston, Ill.: Northwestern University Press, 1980), §88.
27   Imre Lakatos, *Proofs and Refutations: The Logic of Mathematical Discovery* (Cambridge: Cambridge University Press, 1976).

blow to the very foundations of arithmetic, for Frege, a mathematician concerned with understanding, it was a crucial step forward, one that, as Frege writes to Russell, "may perhaps lead to a great advance in logic, undesirable as it may seem at first".[28] For it is only through such a discovery that we can recognize the flaws in our understanding and on that basis formulate better conceptions. In fact, Frege came to think, the notion of a course of values cannot be salvaged; the logicist thesis must be jettisoned. But as Frege was well aware, his logic and the language he devised for it remained intact.[29]

We began with a dilemma: either mathematics has a subject matter of its own and naturalism is false, or naturalism is true and mathematics is without content of its own, merely a kind of formal game with symbols. The dilemma arises, we can now see, out of a Kantian assumption about content, the assumption that (in Kant's own words) "without intuition all of our cognition would lack objects, *and therefore remain completely empty*" (A62/B87; emphasis added). If content lies wholly in relation to objects then there would seem to be only three options for the case of mathematics, assuming that it is contentful at all. Either mathematics is in some way about ordinary empirical objects (in which case it would seem not to be necessary), or it is about platonic abstract objects (though it is unclear what such objects could have to do with us, or indeed with anything else in the world), or, following Kant, it concerns the spatiotemporal form of ordinary empirical objects. This last option aims, of course, to have it both ways, mathematics as providing knowledge about empirical objects without itself being empirical knowledge. Our Tarskian, model-theoretic, conception of language embodies just this assumption about content; it merely transfers the Kantian dichotomy of logical form and empirical content from the cognitive realm to that of language. And having given up the notion of pure intuition, we are then left with only Platonism and empiricism, or formalism; and assuming that mathematics has content, as it seems to, Platonism seems the only option. Mathematics, on the Kantian and Tarskian view, needs objects if it is to have any content but those objects cannot be ordinary empirical objects because mathematics is not an empirical science. We are left, then, with our dilemma, either Platonism and contentful mathematics or naturalism, but not both.

But if, now, we follow Frege in distinguishing between concept and object, on the one hand, and *Sinn* and *Bedeutung*, on the other—that is, in seeing that the Kantian distinction of concept and intuition rests on a conflation of two different distinctions—we can recognize content that does not depend on relation to any object, that is, properly conceptual content. The subject matter

28   Frege to Russell 22 June 1902, in *Philosophical and Mathematical Correspondence*, p. 192.
29   See my *Frege's Logic*, Chapter 5, for an account of why Frege came to accept Basic Law V and also why it was nonetheless flawed.

of mathematics can be seen to be not objects but instead properly mathematical concepts, concepts that can be applied to empirical objects but are fully contentful in their own right. Mathematics, on this view, has no objects of its own; the only objects there are are those we find in the natural world.[30] But not everything we know is knowledge about objects. We also have knowledge about concepts. Indeed, on the Fregean view, a great deal of knowledge that we tend to think of as knowledge about objects is in fact knowledge about concepts. Consider, for instance, the mathematical fact that there are infinitely many primes. A Tarskian reading of this claim interprets it as a claim about numbers, either all of them or all of the primes (thereby directly giving rise to familiar intuitionistic concerns). On a Fregean reading that same claim is, on one particular function/argument analysis, a claim about the concept *prime number*, that it has the second-level property of being (to appropriate a phrase of Dummett's) indefinitely extensible. Objects do not come into it at all. And this is just as it should be. We do not discover that there are infinitely many prime numbers by examining cases; we *infer* it from concepts, that is, on the basis of what it is to be a prime number. The proof establishes a true about a concept.[31]

But why is realism about mathematical concepts not just as problematic as realism about abstract objects? No adequate answer can be give here, but the basic idea is roughly this. Our cognitive access to objects is sensory, and it is where we start. Our cognitive access to mathematical concepts is instead by reason; and this latter sort of access can be made intelligible only as the very late fruit of a process of intellectual evolution that has been going on for thousands of years.[32] In the case of mathematics in particular, we need to recognize

---

30 Of course Frege thought that there are, in addition to mathematical concepts, also mathematical objects. In fact none are needed to account for the practice of mathematics. That there are only mathematical concepts, and not also mathematical objects, is furthermore compatible with the experience mathematicians have of imagining objects in the course of their reflections. It may well be that, as a matter of psychological fact, we find it easiest to think about the implications of a concept when we imagine that concept to be instantiated in an arbitrary object. It does not follow that such imagined objects exist.

31 Similarly, when mathematicians and philosophers of mathematics talk of introducing or creating new mathematical objects what they in fact are talking about, according to our Fregean view, is the introduction of new mathematical concepts, for instance, that of a group of a certain kind or of a sheaf. The concepts themselves are not created but discovered; they are fully objective entities. But the senses through which they are grasped must be clarified by us. We are responsible for the language we use though not for what it allows us to discover and know.

32 I would furthermore argue that our ability to evolve intellectually is possible only in light of our having evolved socially in particular ways, a course of evolution that is dependent in turn on the emergence of a certain sort of biologically evolved creature. (See my "The Coin of the Intentional Realm", *Journal for the Theory of Social Behavior* 24 (1994): 143–166.) Naturalists who recognize only biological evolution inevitably underestimate the differences between us and other animals. Social and intellectual evolution are also fully natural, at least for creatures like us, and are furthermore essential to any intellectually respectable naturalism.

three distinct stages, each with its characteristic mathematical practice, ancient Euclidean geometry, early modern algebra, and the contemporary mathematical practice of reasoning from concepts. I have argued elsewhere[33] that Descartes' geometry is possible only through a metamorphosis of ancient mathematical practice; and I would contend that contemporary mathematical practice is dependent in turn on early modern mathematical practice. But if that is right then what is needed to show that our ability to achieve substantial knowledge by reasoning from concepts alone is consistent with naturalism is an account of our historical development as rational beings.[34]

---

33   In "Viète, Descartes, and the Emergence of Modern Mathematics".
34   In *The Metaphysics of Judgment: Truth and Knowledge in the Exact Sciences*, in progress, I aim to provide such an account.

Chienkuo Mi

What Is Naturalized Epistemology?
The Quinean Project

Soochow University, Taiwan

1. Foreword

Since the publication of Quine's "Epistemology Naturalized" in 1969, naturalized epistemology has become one of the most promising programs for pursuing epistemological issues. But almost forty years later, many philosophers still wonder what exactly Quine's naturalized epistemology is all about. Some philosophers may still doubt whether naturalized epistemology should be called epistemology at all. And if it is indeed a kind of epistemology, what kind of epistemology is it? What is the main subject matter for naturalized epistemology? What is its appropriate methodology? With respect to these questions, let's see how Quine might have responded.

> "But I think at this point it may be more useful to say rather that epistemology still goes on, though in *a new setting* and *a clarified status*. Epistemology, or something like it, simply falls into place as a chapter of psychology and hence of natural science. It studies a natural phenomenon, viz., a physical human subject. This human subject is accorded a certain experimentally controlled input—certain patterns of irradiation in assorted frequencies, for instance—and in the fullness of time the subject delivers as output a description of the three-dimensional external world and its history. *The relation between the meager input and the torrential output* is a relation that we are prompted to study for somewhat the same reasons that always prompted epistemology; namely, in order to see *how evidence related to theory*, and in what ways one's theory of nature transcends any available evidence." (Quine, 1969: 82–3)

> "Epistemology is best looked upon, then, as an enterprise within natural science. Cartesian doubt is not the way to begin. Retaining our present beliefs about nature, we can still ask how we can have arrived at them. Science tells us that our only source of information about the external world is through the impact of light rays and molecules upon our sensory surfaces. Stimulated in these ways, we somehow evolve an elaborate and useful science. How do we do this, and why does the resulting science work so well? These are genuine questions, and no feigning of doubt is needed to appreciate them. They are scientific questions about a species of primates, and they are open to investigation in natural science, the very science whose acquisition is being investigated." (Quine, 1975: 68)

If we consider these two passages as Quine's brief responses to the questions raised above, we can clearly see that naturalized epistemology, at least for Quine, can still be called epistemology. Yes, Quine's project should be understood as epistemology which studies a "natural phenomenon". The subject matter of this kind of epistemology is the study of a physical human subject who has knowledge (or science) and can use language. But more specifically, it is mainly concerned with "the relation between the meager input and the torrential output". The relation concerned here can be seen as a psychological-causal relation between the impact of light rays and molecules upon our sensory surfaces (the meager input) and the resulting scientific theories about the external world (the torrential output). However the relation can also be approached from a language-learning process from learning observation sentences (the meager input) to acquiring a whole theoretical language (the torrential output). Actually the channels by which, having learned observation sentences, we acquire theoretical language, are the very channels by which observation lends evidence to scientific theory. Both in the cases of psychological-causal relation and language-learning process, further investigation will eventually shed light on a more epistemological issue as to how evidence is related to scientific theory.

Now if naturalized epistemology is really to be seen as a kind of epistemology and it is as claimed in *a new setting* and *a clarified status*, we need to know what the new setting for naturalized epistemology is supposed to be and what clarified status it has as well. In order to know these, we need to scrutinize both positive and negative claims and proposals involved in Quine's naturalized epistemology against the traditional epistemology.

Descartes' famous words, "I think, therefore I am", signaled the beginning of the epistemological turn of modern philosophy. Not only did the concept of 'knowledge' and related philosophical issues become the main focus of philosophers continuing Descartes' work, but epistemology replaced traditional metaphysics to become what has since been called "the first philosophy".

Descartes' important contribution to modern philosophy (or to narrow our scope, to questions related to 'knowledge'), comes from the "Meditation One" of his *Meditations on First Philosophy*, in which the main question he addressed was "What should we believe?". After much reflection and application of "methodological doubt", Descartes raised a fundamental and important question both for himself and for philosophers of the following centuries: What are the foundations of our knowledge about this world? Descartes' philosophical or epistemological objective can be stated as pursuing the certainty of our human knowledge by establishing a clear and distinct foundation for our knowledge of the natural world.

Three hundred and thirty years after the publication of Descartes' *Meditations*, Quine published one of his most important works in the field of epistemology, *Epistemology Naturalized*; this was to be the fundamental resource of all subsequent research in so-called "naturalized epistemology". At the beginning of this paper Quine made reference to Descartes' question about the foundations of knowledge, and affirmed that "Epistemology is concerned with the foundations of science". Ironically, some believe that Quine's naturalism is fundamentally opposed to the idea that "Epistemology discusses any issues about the foundations of natural science"[1]. There are also some who believe that Quine is not completely opposed to the belief that "Epistemology discusses the foundations of science" but merely rejects some of the tenets of traditional epistemology in order to address certain issues related to the foundations of science, and attempts to find a way of addressing these problems from a naturalistic standpoint[2]. Clarifying our positions and opinions as to whether epistemology should (or indeed can) discuss "the foundations of science", "the foundations of knowledge about this world" and related questions, will help us grasp more firmly the precise distinction between naturalized epistemology and traditional epistemology, as well as gaining us a clearer understanding of the exact value and true meaning of naturalized epistemology.

If epistemology is a field of study concerned with the foundations of science, then naturalized epistemology should be viewed as a theory of knowledge which is used as evidence to refute dogmatic claims of a clear distinction between *a priori* and empirical knowledge. A natural conclusion of this theory is that we should abandon all attempts to build science upon the foundation offered by the so-called first philosophy, speculative metaphysics, or transcendental epistemology. Another natural conclusion is that it encourages a naturalistic approach to research in epistemology; this approach focuses on the relationship between evidence and theory, as well as on precisely how science actually develops and is learned through language. I shall attempt to show that a naturalistic theory of knowledge not only has to merge with psychology but also with linguistics; that is, we not only need to make use of research in psychology or cognitive science in order to understand precisely how mankind is able to develop his plethora of scientific theories from such scant evidence, but also apply research results from linguistics or semantics (in particular meaning holism) to understand the development process of scientific theory and language. I also aim to show precisely what the focus of Quine's naturalized epistemology is supposed to be. Hilary Kornblith and Jaegwon Kim's standard interpretation is that Quine's naturalized epistemology replaces the justification theory of knowledge, widely accepted throughout the 20th century, with a kind of descriptive psychology. My thesis is that Kornblith and Kim fundamentally misinterpreted Quine's naturalized epistemology; Quine's theory simply does not have justification as its central theme, nor does it seek to replace a justification-focused theory of knowledge.

---

1   R. Fogelin, in his "Aspects of Quine's Naturalized Epistemology", claims that Quine begins his essay declaring that epistemology is concerned with the foundations of science, but this opening claim naturally suggests a project quite the opposite of the one Quine is about to endorse.

2   This is a position and proposal I will defend in this article.

Rather, as I said earlier, naturalized epistemology is a theory of knowledge which is used to refute those who assert there is a clear distinction between *a priori* and empirical knowledge. In other words, I believe that the focus of naturalized epistemology should be understood as the refutation of *a priori* knowledge which was traditionally deemed to have some special privilege and normative force, and that the issues of different levels of epistemology and the descriptive/normative distinction are merely problems encountered in the process of refuting *a priori* knowledge and the traditional first philosophy. Building on his holistic approach towards linguistic meaning and his naturalistic standpoint of epistemology, Quine comprehensively argues against there being a clear distinction between *a priori* and empirical knowledge on metaphysical, epistemological, psychological, and linguistic levels.

2. The Problems of Traditional Epistemology: Quine's Negative Claims

At the beginning of the 20th century, advocates and supporters of logicism made both conceptual and doctrinal studies in an attempt to solve the problem of the foundation of mathematics. Conceptually, logicists hoped to use the language of logic to clarify or define the language of mathematics; doctrinally, they wished to express mathematical truth as logical truth. While the logicist plans for mathematics were ultimately doomed to failure, Quine applied the distinction between conceptual and doctrinal studies to the analogous epistemological problem of the foundations of science. Quine believed that conceptual studies are a study of meaning which, if successful, would give us a firmer grasp of the meaning of scientific language as well as a better understanding of scientific concepts. Such studies clarify concepts and define expressions; doctrinal studies on the other hand are a study of truth which aim to use clear and well defined scientific rules and truths to prove or deduce less clear and less intuitive rules and truths in natural science. These studies aim to provide the certainty for scientific theories and reveal the self-evidence of scientific truth.

Faced with the human knowledge about everything contained in the natural world (which we shall henceforth call natural knowledge), the epistemology of classical empiricism was built upon our sense experience or flux of raw sense data. If we bring our distinction between conceptual and doctrinal studies into the argument, the conceptual studies of classical empiricist epistemology use the raw sense data of concepts and impressions to explain physical objects and ideas, while the doctrinal studies use the most fundamental simple concepts and impressions to justify our knowledge of natural science. Later on logical positivists (in particular R. Carnap) and B. Russell continued to research in this area, and attempted to apply the latest logical and set-theoretical ideas and methods to express natural knowledge as observable data and to reduce theoretical language to observational expressions.

In this development process of traditional epistemology, Quine emphasized in particular the contribution of David Hume to conceptual and doctrinal studies: Hume's approach to the conceptual studies is very simple and direct, he explains external physical objects by appealing to sense impressions; his attitude to the doctrinal studies on the other hand is basically negative and reserved, as Quine has pointed out: "What then of the doctrinal side, the justification of our knowledge of truths about nature? Here, Hume despaired. By his identification of bodies with impressions he did succeed in construing some singular statements about bodies as indubitable truths, yes; as truths about impressions, directly known. But general statements, also singular statements about the future, gained no increment of certainty by being construed as about impressions." (Quine, 1968: 71–72). Quine further concludes, "On the doctrinal side, I do not see that we are farther along today than where Hume left us. The Humean predicament is the human predicament." (ibid.). Here Quine almost shares Hume's skepticism regarding induction[3], hence believes the doctrinal studies of traditional epistemology are at least to be doubted and may even be hopeless; that is, traditional philosophers' dreams of using epistemology to justify and validate natural knowledge have been swept away by Humean skepticism.

Although the development of epistemology has reached a bottleneck regarding the doctrinal studies, the conceptual studies have taken some clear steps forward. In order to see precisely what these steps forward are, as well as to see how in the course of taking them traditional epistemology has moved towards a trend of naturalism, I think it is necessary to mention Quine's "Five Milestones of Empiricism". The five milestones characterized by Quine are: firstly a change of focus from concepts and impressions to words and phrases; secondly a change from words and phrases towards sentences; thirdly from sentences towards systems of sentences; fourthly towards methodological monism; and finally the rise of naturalized epistemology. These five milestones can be seen as the course of development from classical empiricism towards Quine's idealized new empiricism (empiricism without "the two dogmas"), and also as the process of moving from traditional epistemology to naturalized epistemology. The connections between

---

3   Hume, in his *Enquiry Concerning Human Understanding*, offered the following argument: "All inference from experience suppose as their foundation, that the future will resemble the past. ... If there be any suspicion that the course of nature may change, and that the past may be no rule for the future, all experience becomes useless, and can give rise to no inference or conclusion. It is impossible, therefore, that any arguments from experience can prove this resemblance of the past to the future; since all these argument are founded on the supposition of that resemblance." (Hume, 1739: 37–38) This argument seems to be directed towards criticizing the principle of resemblance, but this type of argument can also be used to criticize the acceptability of induction.

these five milestones, however, are not all the same, because the first to third milestones are a process of continual replacement—that is, they can be seen as a linguistic turn, evident from the beginning of the 20th century, from the study of a thinking subject's concepts and impressions to the study of a speaker's use of language. The fourth milestone on the other hand is a consequence of the appearance of the third, placing importance on the holism of language, bringing with it the rejection of a clear distinction between analytic and synthetic statements, at the same time refuting reductionism[4], so in terms of methodology, the methods of philosophy or empiricism are precisely those of science; this methodological monism naturally leads to the aim of abandoning of the first philosophy, which is the background to the fifth milestone—the way to naturalism.

I mentioned above that the move from first to third milestones is a process of continual replacement; in fact we can also view it as the advancement of the conceptual studies of traditional epistemology, the most important point of which is that when we explain a scientific expression, we do not in fact need to directly handle every object referenced by this expression, whether they be external physical objects or internal abstract concepts. A benefit of the second milestone is that by using sentences as the fundamental units of semantics and making use of contextual definition, we can explain a scientific expression using the sentence by which it is defined. Hence even if in the doctrinal studies we are unable to obtain a valid foundation for the certainty of naturalized epistemology, in the conceptual studies we can continually provide sense evidence, as well as continually explicate this evidence, hoping to achieve clarity of our naturalized epistemology as well as a deeper understanding of it. However, the progress of traditional epistemology in the area of the conceptual studies cannot hide its inherent failings and inadequacies; what Quine expressed in his third, fourth, and fifth milestones are in fact precisely the key problems empiricism (from the classical era to the first half of twentieth century) has with handling the foundations of natural knowledge. These problems can be summarized as follows:

1. The problem of reductionism: Traditionally, empiricists have always hoped to be able to reduce natural knowledge to a kind of direct sense experience, be it simple concepts, impressions, sense data, or some kind of observable direct experience. If such an attempt were successful, it would mean successfully translating or defining rigorously scientific knowledge or expressions in terms of observable experience or expressions; this is the best way for the empiricist to give natural knowledge a clear foundation. In the twentieth century, Carnap was the most accomplished advocate of this position; his main aim was to use sense expressions together with the concepts of logic and

---

4   Quine's arguments against the two dogmas are nicely presented in his famous article "Two Dogmas of Empiricism".

mathematics, to give definitions and explanations for scientific concepts, and to find a conceptual solution to the problem of the foundations of science. But as Quine's long-held criticism of Carnap (also a criticism of traditional empiricism) stated, behind this reductionism is hidden Carnap and other empiricists common mistake: they have failed to notice that a sentence of any scientific theory does not have a fund of experiential implications it can call its own, and so neither does it have a meaning it can call its own. Quine's basis for his argument with respect to this problem is meaning holism or epistemic holism as mentioned in his third milestone.

2. The problem of *a priori* knowledge: Traditionally, philosophers have tended to believe that aside from empirical knowledge of the world, people also possess a kind of so-called a priori knowledge; at least since Descartes and the birth of rationalism, influenced by the admirable achievements of mathematics and geometry in the course of mankind's development, philosophers hoped to find an empirical foundation for the certainty of natural knowledge; Descartes' "I am thinking" was a product of this search. Empiricists base themselves on an anti-rationalist standpoint; although they do not directly establish the certainty of natural knowledge upon a priori knowledge, they hope to use strong definitions or synonymous translation to find a clear foundation for science; behind this is hidden a distinction between analytic truth and synthetic truth—sentences which express analytic truth play the role of organizing or governing the rules of natural knowledge, while sentences which express synthetic truth contain natural knowledge's particular experience content. For both of them, not only mathematicians and logicians, but philosophers too have a special kind of prerogative of access to the sentences of analytic truth and can make further progress in establishing foundations for natural knowledge (or the entire corpus of fact encompassed by scientific theory). Quine's argument against the distinction between analytic and synthetic was a watershed of 20th century philosophy; support of holism made this thesis even more effective. Quine's fourth milestone of empiricism is a case for methodological monism, which is that the role played by analytic sentences is in fact a feature shared by all sentences, and particular empirical content possessed by individual synthetic propositions can be allocated across the entire system of sentences. Once the distinctions between *a priori* and empirical knowledge, and analytic and synthetic truth have lost their absolute standard and necessity of existence, philosophers faced with the problem of natural knowledge have lost their prerogative, and in terms of methodology, the methods of philosophy seem to be no different to those of scientific practice.

3. The problem of first philosophy: The objective of first philosophy is to find an infallible and incorrigible foundation for natural knowledge or scientific theory; this has been viewed as the origin of certainty. In pursuit of this objective, some philosophers have employed *a priori* knowledge which is over and

beyond empirical knowledge in the hope of deducing all natural knowledge; others have used non-empirical or unobservable principles in an effort to give the foundations of natural knowledge a set of standard normative rules. In the drive towards this objective, traditional philosophers seem to see themselves as providing ultimate arbitration or highest standards. But as we have seen in the two problems above, the objective of first philosophy is already far out of reach, and the appearance of naturalism in negative terms, is to disclaim the objective of first philosophy; here naturalism's emphasis is not only on abandoning first philosophy's prerogative of access to a priori knowledge, but also abandoning philosophy's special normative role, because to the naturalist, philosophy is a part of the whole of natural knowledge, and the methods of philosophy are in no way different to those of any special area of science. On the positive side, Quine's naturalism argues for a "scientific empiricism", that is to say that the work of philosophy originally was part of science, "… whatever evidence there is for science is sensory evidence. … all inculcation of meanings of words must rest ultimately on sensory evidence." (Quine, 1968: 75).

From the point of view of the doctrinal studies, or the conceptual studies, regarding the problem of the foundations of natural knowledge traditional epistemology must either face up to Hume's predicament or to its own internal difficulties. In either case, with the approach of traditional epistemology appearing to have reached an impasse, and its methods facing collapse, does this mean that Descartes' question has no answer at all? Does it make no sense at all? Or is it not worth answering? When Quine supports naturalism and abandons so-called traditional first philosophy, how does he face and answer these questions and puzzles?

3. What is Quine's Naturalized Epistemology? The Positive Proposals

Firstly, Quine's support of naturalism does not mean he completely rejects epistemology; rather, when the Vienna Circle dismissed traditional metaphysics as a meaningless subject, and when Wittgenstein and the Oxford school viewed traditional epistemology as a delusion, Quine still saw epistemology as a continuing enterprise nonetheless—"epistemology still goes on, though in *a new setting* and *a clarified status*". Briefly speaking, for Quine the continuation of epistemology is only of value in the context of naturalism, and only in this context can it free itself from the constraints and mistakes of the past to gain its new meaning—this new approach toward epistemology is naturalized epistemology. However, exactly what are naturalism's new status and state of development?

Secondly, and most importantly, what exactly is naturalized epistemology (in particular Quine's naturalism)? How does it differ to traditional epistemology? On this point there seem to be many different views and explanations, the most widely received view at present being that presented by H. Kornblith and J. Kim[5]. The Kornblith/Kim interpretation starts from the distinction between normative and descriptive questions, they view the difference between traditional epistemology and Quine's naturalized epistemology as the difference between regard for normative and naturalistic epistemology; finally they directly view traditional epistemology and naturalized epistemology as epistemological and psychological enterprises. The traditional normative problems of epistemology include: "How should we compose or justify our beliefs?", "What is the standard of a justified belief?", "How should we compose a good inference (the process from evidence to theory)?", and the questions which naturalized epistemology aims to answer are of expressions of fact: "How do we compose or justify our beliefs?", "How can we develop scientific theories from limited experiential evidence?" The Kornblith/Kim interpretation views naturalized epistemology as a replacement theory, that is it replaces normative questions with descriptive questions, and replaces the normative theory of justification with factual descriptive science of cognition, and for Kim even more so replaces epistemology with psychology.

The Kornblith/Kim interpretation is understandably a direct or superficial understanding of Quine's naturalized epistemology, because Quine apparently emphasized on more than one occasion his view that psychology replaces traditional epistemology: "Naturalism does not repudiate epistemology, but assimilates it to empirical psychology." (Quine, 1981: 72). Furthermore, he asserts: "Epistemology, or something like it, simply falls into place as a chapter of psychology and hence of natural science. It studies a phenomenon, viz., a physical human subject. This human subject is accorded a certain experimentally controlled input—certain patterns of irradiation in assorted frequencies, for instance—and in the fullness of time the subject delivers as output a description of the three-dimensional world and its history. The relation between the meager input and the torrential output is a relation that we are prompted to study for somewhat the same reasons that always prompted epistemology; namely, in order to see how evidence relates to theory, and in what ways one's theory of nature transcends any available evidence." (Quine, 1968: 82–83). This passage not only points out that epistemology is part of natural science, but also how we can use psychology to

---

5   The received view about their interpretation comes from Kornblith's "Introduction: What Is Naturalized Epistemology?" and "Beyond Foundationalism and the Coherence Theory", and from Kim's "What Is "Naturalized Epistemology"?". All three articles (including some important discussions and influential articles on this topic) are collected in the edition edited by Kornblith himself *Naturalizing Epistemology* (2nd edition, 1994).

carry out epistemological research; no wonder these days most people mentioning naturalized epistemology always connect it to psychology, this seemed to be unassailable. However, I shall argue that the Kornblith/Kim interpretation (if not very misleading) is at most partial and incomplete. My reasons for this are as follows:

1. The initial distinction between normative and descriptive questions involved in the Kornblith/Kim interpretation is actually a justification-oriented distinction. The question concerning what should be seen as a justified belief was undeniably the most important question in the 20th century debates about epistemology—there are even those who view the 20th century theory of knowledge simply as the theory of justification. With this in mind, regarding the question of exactly what is naturalized epistemology, we are suddenly forced to contemplate whether epistemology should or should not answer the question "What is justified belief?". If it should, then we need to look at this problem from both normative and descriptive standpoints. Thus when we finally answer what is naturalized epistemology, using the practical descriptive method of psychology is almost a foregone conclusion. But there is a question worthy of doubt here: Is Quine's naturalism, or naturalized epistemology, primarily concerned with addressing the issue of "justification"? The reason for doubt is that, as those who are familiar with Quine's philosophy are well aware, in none of his philosophical publications has he been so concerned with such issues. Furthermore, in his key work "Epistemology Naturalized" Quine immediately made clear that "Epistemology is concerned with the foundations of science"; from our understanding of this work we can determine that the epistemological issue Quine is most concerned with is: "Precisely what are the foundations of our knowledge about the natural world?", or more specifically, the question he wished to answer is "How can we produce our scientific knowledge and theories about the world from such limited amounts of empirical observations and sensory evidence?". In this context we can at most say that justification may be a related (or connected) issue, we cannot say it is the heart of the matter. In particular, when Quine mentions that the traditional research on this matter can be split between "the doctrinal studies" and "the conceptual studies", the issue of justification can at most be said to be a constituent part of "the doctrinal studies", and as far as Quine is concerned there has been no significant progress in this area since Hume, whereas the conceptual studies have been making gradual steady progress. This is why it is still worth continuing the discussion and development of epistemology.

2. In the Kornblith/Kim interpretation, Kim in particular takes the whole focus of development of naturalized epistemology in "Quine's arguments" (Kim, 1994: 36–40) to be an attack on justification-centered epistemology, aiming to replace it with a pure descriptive, causal-nomological science of human cognition. Here, Kim again quotes Quine to support his interpretation: "Why not

see how the construction of theory from observation actually proceeds? Why not settle for psychology?", "Better to discover how science is in fact developed and learned than ..." (Quine, 1970: 75–83). Thus Kim sees naturalized epistemology as replacing the rational constructive methodology of normative epistemology with a constructive methodology of practical psychology, and ultimately to replace normative justification epistemology with descriptive empirical psychology. From this conclusion, Kim's criticism of Quine naturally leads to the conclusion that an epistemology with neither justification nor the ability to explain the concept of knowledge, simply cannot be called an epistemology. Kim's conclusion is actually dissatisfaction that development of naturalized epistemology will cause epistemology to become a part of psychology and will disappear into psychological research. This worry is superfluous; we need only understand, in Quine's terms, that not only is epistemology contained in natural science, but natural science is also contained in epistemology. We need only appreciate that epistemology and natural science have this relation of reciprocal containment, and Kim's worry will naturally recede. In addition, Quine has never denounced the normative aspects of epistemology, what he really wants to reject is the normative authority endorsed by the traditional epistemologists.

3. The Kornblith/Kim interpretation contains another problem (one which is often overlooked when understanding Quine's naturalized epistemology), which is that naturalized epistemology aims not only to unite epistemology with psychology, but also attempts to closely link epistemology with linguistics. The Kornblith/Kim interpretation almost completely overlooks Quine's discussion of language learning and meaning in the course of constructing naturalized epistemology. This can be seen not only in the latter half of Quine's "Epistemology Naturalized", but even more so as a key feature of his work *The Roots of Reference* which can be seen as the most direct application of naturalized epistemology[6]; "The Nature of Natural Knowledge" again emphasizes the important contribution of the research in the theory of language to the theory of knowledge[7]. On this point I can use Quine's own words to directly support my claim; when Quine has finished discussing the Vienna

---

6   As Quine himself wrote on the back-page of this book: "Our only channel of information about the world is the impact of external forces on our sensory surfaces. So says science itself. There is no clairvoyance. How, then, can we have parlayed this meager sensory input into a full-blown scientific theory of world? This is itself a scientific question. The pursuit of it, with free use of scientific theory, is what I call naturalized epistemology. *The Roots of Reference* falls within that domain."

7   This article can be seen as a short version of Quine's *The Roots of Reference*. In this article, we see once again that the vital role the theory of language or linguistics plays in the naturalistic approach toward epistemology.

circle's debate on the concept of observation, and argues why he continues
to argue that observation sentences play a key role in scientific research,
Quine concludes: "It is no shock to the preconceptions of old Vienna to say
that epistemology now becomes semantics. For epistemology remains centered
as always on verification; and evidence is verification. What is likelier to
shock preconceptions is that meaning, once we get beyond observation
sentences, ceases in general to have any clear applicability to single sentences; also that epistemology merges with psychology, as well as linguistics."
(Quine, 1968: 89–90). In this passage we can clearly see that for Quine,
epistemology should be merged with both psychology and linguistics; some
people perhaps believe the merging of epistemology with linguistics is a tenet
of old Vienna, and Quine's naturalism is an attempt to transcend and replace
this idea by directly merging epistemology into psychology. My stance on
this issue is that "epistemology merging with psychology" does not completely
cover "epistemology merging with linguistics or semantics", rather the emphasis is on a process of gradual progress, in which epistemology should merge
not only with linguistics but also with psychology. Just as the final three
empirical milestones, the appearance of naturalism is the latest development
brought about by gradual developments in holism and methodological
monism. An important reason for this analogy is that the development of
naturalized epistemology must also emphasize holism (the linguistic feature)
and methodological monism (the scientific feature), and even more so for
the "linguistic turn" in the 20th century.

In order to understand Quine's naturalized epistemology more correctly and
completely, I propose a discussion starting from the question, "What are the
foundations of natural knowledge and science", with reference to the distinction
between the doctrinal and conceptual studies (rather than emphasizing the distinction between normative and descriptive), examining in detail the development
and difficulties of traditional epistemology in these two areas, then examining
naturalism's reflections on and modifications to this question. After comparing
and contrasting these, we should be able to see the real differences between
traditional epistemology and naturalized epistemology, and be better able to
grasp the spirit of Quine's naturalized epistemology. In the course of his criticism
of traditional epistemology (be it the doctrinal studies or the conceptual studies),
Quine did not offer a satisfactory answer to this question, but neither did he
abandon his aim of providing one. He abandoned only the traditional objective
of first philosophy (the Cartesian dream), then with the spirit of scientific
empiricism reconstructed the original question, aiming to answer "How can
mankind use limited information (experience, stimulus, observation, or evidence)
to create or produce our natural knowledge or science?" Science itself tells us
that our information about the world is limited to surface stimuli, and in reality

we do possess knowledge about the world and we can use our language to talk about the world as well; how these surface stimuli lead to our possession of natural knowledge and to our acquisition of theoretical language is a question we require natural science (in particular cognitive psychology and linguistics) to answer for us. This is a new scenario which modern epistemology must face, and it is also the reason why epistemology has become a part of natural science. Some people think that using scientific methods to study the foundations of science will lead us into an endless circle, but Quine believes that once we have abandoned our dream of reducing science to sense data directly, it will be easy to see that our understanding of science itself is of a natural sequence of events occurring in the natural world, and so can of course itself become an object of scientific research. The object of research in epistemology (viewed as a branch of science) is then precisely the understanding of this natural science (viewed as a sequence of events occurring in the natural world) itself, this is the reason that epistemology and science are reciprocally contained. Traditional epistemology attempted to avoid this reciprocity by searching for a method of research superior to (or transcendental to) science; Quine's new scientific empiricism has already woken us from this philosophical dream of a bygone age, and it is in this context that naturalized epistemology has arisen.

4. The Genetic Approach toward Quine's Naturalized Epistemology—Psychological-Linguistic Epistemology

Exactly what is Quine's Naturalized Epistemology? If it is a type of epistemology, then what is its subject matter? In answering this, we must once again refer to Quine's own words: "(Naturalized Epistemology) studies a natural phenomenon, viz., a physical human subject. This human subject is accorded a certain experimentally controlled input—certain patterns of irradiation in assorted frequencies, for instance—and in the fullness of time the subject delivers as output a description of the three-dimensional external world and its history. The relation between the meager input and the torrential output is a relation that we are prompted to study for somewhat the same reasons that always prompted epistemology; namely, in order to see how evidence relates to theory, and in what ways one's theory of nature transcends any available evidence." (Quine, 1969: 82–83)

From this passage we can clearly see that in Quine's study of epistemology, the key topic is "the relation between the meager input and the torrential output", which is in fact also "the relation between observational evidence and scientific theory". Quine himself actively suggested a research method (and strategy):

"We see, then, a strategy for investigating the relation of evidential support, between observation and scientific theory. We can adopt a genetic approach, studying how theoretical language is learned. For the evidential relation is virtually enacted, it would seem, in the learning. This genetic strategy is attractive because the learning of language goes on in the world and is open to scientific study. It is a strategy for the scientific study of scientific method and evidence. We have here a good reason to regard the theory of language as vital to the theory of knowledge." (Quine, 1975: 74–75)

As was mentioned in section 3, as far as Quine is concerned, epistemology not only needs to be combined with psychology, but also with linguistics, and from the above passage we can see once again that Quine believes the theory of language is central and indispensable to epistemological research. Here we face some important questions which must be answered: precisely what is this close connection between epistemology and linguistics (or between the theory of knowledge and the theory of language)? Why must epistemology be combined with linguistics (or why is the theory of language essential for the theory of knowledge)? What exactly does Quine mean here when he says linguistics or theory of language? And what is Quine's suggestion of a genetic approach to language learning? The discussion below will focus on these questions; as we find answers to them so we shall gain a clearer understanding of the true meaning of Quine's Naturalized Epistemology.

If, for Quine, the key issue of epistemology is "the relation between observational evidence and scientific theory", then it is not difficult to see why for him at least linguistics and epistemology are closely linked. For Quine always maintains that the evidential relation from observational evidence to scientific theory and the semantic relation from observational evidence to scientific language have the same extension. In Quine's writings he espouses the epistemic/semantic dichotomy, by which the relationship between scientific theory and the observations used to support it can be revealed from two aspects: that of epistemology, and that of semantics (Quine, 1974, p. 37). The epistemological aspect reveals the relation through which our epistemic beliefs justified in the theory gain their support. The semantical aspect reveals the relation through which our linguistic statements expressed in theory gain their meaning. With respect to these double aspects, 'observation' takes on two different roles. On the one hand, 'observations' are related to the epistemological aspect of theory by way of the 'evidential relation'; in this relation, 'observations' play the part of evidence in support of a theory. On the other hand, 'observations' are related to the semantical aspect of theory by way of the 'semantic relation'; here the role of 'observation' is as the basis of empirical content and the learning of scientific language. The evidential and semantic relationships between observations and science also have the same extension; we can go so far as to say, these two aspects of science ultimately arrive at the same focal point: 'observation' (or experiences of the world).

The construction and expression of scientific theory can never be separated from our language (scientific theory can only be expressed using some kind of linguistic expression), nor can the formation and appearance of scientific theory be divorced from our beliefs (scientific theory can only be developed upon some basis of belief). Science must on the one hand establish a semantic relationship with our linguistic system, and on the other hand must establish an epistemological relationship with our epistemic system. Furthermore, our linguistic and epistemic systems rely upon each other; for Quine, empiricist verification theory is the best bridge connecting these two systems. Finally, the evidential and semantic relationships between observation and scientific theory, be they in their most basic forms or with complex additions, always share the property of having a common extension. Hence there is a close relationship between (in terms of epistemology) the establishment of a system of knowledge and beliefs, and (in terms of linguistics) the foundation of a linguistic system. Of particular note is that Quine's so-called linguistics mainly refers to semantics established within the linguistic system. Through the relationship between scientific theory and observation experiences, we can clearly see the reciprocal connection between epistemology and linguistics. Thus when Quine states that epistemology must merge with linguistics, he surely means that epistemology and linguistics can both take the relationship between observation experience and theory as the subject matter and focus of their research.

Science is generally characterized by Quine as a linguistic structure that is keyed to observation at some points (Quine, 1975: 72–74). An issue we can pursue here is to see how this "linguistic structure" is acquired and how it is connected to observation. To be sure, the linguistic components have to be mastered and practiced in an appropriate way in order to learn and operate the scientific theories correctly. Studying how theoretical language is acquired, then, seems to be a reasonable strategy for investigating the relation of evidential support between observation and scientific theory. In other words, the semantic aspect of scientific theory is somehow needed for understanding the evidential aspect of scientific theory. Therefore, a genetic approach of studying how theoretic language is learned is adopted by Quine for understanding the relation between scientific theory and the observation sentences. The learning of language, for Quine, is a matter of fact which is accessible to empirical science. By exploring the process of language-learning, Quine believes that "science can in effect explore the evidential relation between science itself and its supporting observations." (Quine, 1974: 37)

The genetic approach of studying how our children learn their language will show the following concerns: When a child learns his language from his elders, what does he have to go on? How can he be engaged in mastering a complete language, including the language of scientific theories? Why is the holistic picture of language an inevitable result, even if an observation sentence plays such an important role in the process of language learning? And, finally, how can we produce science that works so well for human beings just based on the meager inputs?

Quine's genetic study as to how language is learned is intimately connected to his naturalistic-behavioral approach towards the linguistic phenomena, since he persistently insists that "language is a social art which we call acquire in the evidence solely of other people's overt behavior under publicly recognizable circumstances." (Quine, 1968: 26) Infant learning is a bright domain, and the mystery of mental states should be reduced to a minimum here. Given Quine's behavioristic standpoint, presuppositions, either of preprogrammed human language or of *a priori* ideas, are not to be assumed in the speculations concerning language learning. And the first few sentences learned by the child, for Quine, should bear a very important relation to concurrent observable circumstances. Quine presumes that most of us learn our language by observing and imitating other people's verbal behavior and also having our own verbal behavior observed and corrected. This interactive learning process, especially at the early stage, should depend largely on overt behavior in observable situations; and presumably it is done via our nervous system by habituation to a pattern.

When the question regarding how our children start learning their first a few sentences or words arises, the observation sentences or observation terms serve nicely to play a role as an entering wedge because, as defined by Quine, not only can they be learned ostensively, they are also required to be intersubjectively observed and checked. The child learns some brief sentences (either some one-word sentences or some shorter sentences as unstructured wholes) by learning them from adults in the appropriate observable circumstances, while on the other hand he is expected and encouraged to show his own (verbal or nonverbal) behavior. Therefore, ostensive learning—a simple matter of learning to associate the heard sentence as a whole with situations simultaneously observed—is fundamental to our language acquisition, and it is even the initial method for the whole learning process. The part of language that the child learns first without depending on other language-learning has to be learned ostensively. Ostensive learning requires intersubjectively observable immediacy. By ostension we learn to use and react to observation sentences in the holophrastic sense. This approach of learning observation sentences holophrastically shows why observation sentences are the gateway to language-learning.

An observation sentence is often and always acquired by direct conditioning. This learning process could also be described as simple induction because a child's success in learning an observation sentence, say "Red", consists in his being trained by successive reinforcement to say "Red" on the right occasions and those only. The child's learning by simple induction is a process of habit formation in which he is in effect determining the range of situation in which the adult will assent to the query "Red", or to approve his utterance of "Red". The linguistic mechanism of this learning depends on substantial agreement between his subjective similarity standards and those of the adult.

However, the method of ostensive learning alone is notoriously incapable of carrying us very far in our learning process, and simple induction does not suffice for the acquisition of language generally either. We all know observation sentences do not exhaust all parts of language. There are a large number of non-observation sentences in our resources of language which include occasional sentences that are however non-observational sentences (e.g. "John is a bachelor"), eternal sentences ("A dog is an animal"), as well as scientific sentences ("Every electron is negatively charged"). We also know that most sentences consist of more than one word; and the right arrangements of those component words have to be mastered in order to produce the right kinds (in the grammatical and semantic senses) of sentences. If ostensive learning or simple induction can only account for our acquisition of a modest part of language, what else do we need in order to be engaged in mastering a more complete language?

By ostension we learn some observation sentences as wholes by a direct conditioning of them to appropriate non-verbal stimulations. But it is not the case that all or most sentences of our language are learned as wholes, it is rather that most sentences are built up from parts of other learned sentences by the way of analogy. In *Word and Object* Quine describes this way of learning as "analogical synthesis" (Quine, 1960: 9); and in *The Web of Belief* he attributes this major source of learning language to be an elaborate process of abstraction and generalization (Quine & Ullian, 1970: 27). According to Quine, we all start learning a simple sentence as a whole, and then we project a component word of it by analogy into the construction of another sentence. We produce further sentences partly from imitating the use of sentences we have previously learned by ostension, partly from guessing the force of one sentence by noting its use in relation to other sentences, and partly from grasping the use of a word by abstraction from sentences in which it occurs.

To cite the only example of analogical synthesis used by Quine, he says: "Having been directly conditioned to the appropriate use of 'Foot' (or 'This is my foot') as a sentence, and 'Hand' likewise, and 'My foot hurts' as a whole, the child might conceivably utter 'My hand hurts' on an appropriate occasion, though unaided by previous experience with that actual sentence." (Quine, 1960: 9) This example reveals how the child could have learned to inferentially apply a new sentence ('My hand hurts') on an appropriate occasion based on those previously learned sentences ('Foot', 'Hand', 'My foot hurts', and maybe more.) It also shows the initial stage in which an observation sentence can be analytically associated with other sentences (and the word in the observation sentence 'Hand' can recur in the occasion sentence 'My hand hurts'). Although it seems to be a giant step when we are skilled in using this method in the whole process of language learning, this simple example cannot really explain how the acquisition of the higher reach of language is achieved and how observation sentences are correlated with the more complicated structure of scientific language.

And if our total language-learning is confined in such limiting ways, the whole language would be strikingly like bare reporting of our sense experiences only.

As Quine puts it, "we cannot rest with a running conceptualization of the unsullied stream of experience; what we need is a sullying of the stream. Association of sentences is wanted not just with non-verbal stimulation, but with other sentences, if we are to exploit finished conceptualizations and not just repeat them" (ibid.: 10). So, according to what Quine has mentioned here, we still have to know how our children can properly associate all learned sentences and form a workable conceptualization in which all further verbal and non-verbal stimulations can be responded (or a working system which can meet our social standards).

When we move from observation sentences on to grammatical constructions, to past and future tenses, to conditionals and conjecturals and metaphors, and to theoretical and abstract terms, the learning process will become more complicated and elaborate. In order to account for the learning of language that lies beyond the range of ostensive learning and simple analogical learning, Quine concentrates on a speculative inquiry into the linguistic mechanism of objective reference which could be seen as representing a major leap from the learning of primitive language towards the learning of theoretic language. After all, to learn a scientific theory is to learn a theory of the world (in one aspect or another). To learn a theory of the world, in some sense, is to learn a theory of what there is in the world. And what a theory says there is in the world is closely related to a matter of reference. This referential aspect of learning is the acquisition of an apparatus for speaking of (concrete or abstract) objects, and it is an important aspect of learning theoretic language.

What is the referential apparatus? And when can we say a child has learned to refer to the color "red", for example? A child may be said to have mastered the use of the term "red" or one word sentence "Red" when he has learned to respond correctly in various situations according as red is conspicuously present, but this is not enough for what Quine has called the apparatus of objective reference. At this point we might say the child has the ability to *discriminate* the color red or to *recognize* the color red, but the apparatus of reference involves more than the simple ability to acknowledge a presence.

According to Quine, the referential apparatus should include a cluster of interrelated grammatical particles and constructions. He specifically mentions pronouns, plural endings, and copulas (Quine, 1974: 84–123). Following his speculations, a speaker could be said to have acquired the ability of objective reference only when he has learned all the grammatical apparatus of particles and constructions that go to implement objective reference: the apparatus of pronominal cross reference, of identity and distinctness, and of counting (Quine, 1977: 159). For example, a child would not be credited to have fully mastered the term "apple" in its referential use, if he has not realized the scheme of enduring

and recurrent physical objects, i.e., if he has not been able to engage in sophisticated discourse of "that apple", "not that apple", "an apple", "some apple",
"another apple", "these apples", and so on. An object, such as an apple in our
case, as referred by a term is usually conceived as retained its identity over
time between its different appearances.

Now, the question as to whether the apple we see today is the same one
tomorrow, or only another similar one like it, is not to be settled just by simple
induction. The referential part of language learning, which could probably be
the initial stage of learning process that involves a considerable part of linguistic
mechanism as to how we take advantage of other learned sentences and terms,
how we utilize analogical synthesis, and how we associate sentences with one
another in multifarious ways (logical or causal connection, just to name a few).
We learn to use a term referentially by inference from a network of hypotheses,
while those hypotheses owe their plausibility to our having inferred other consequences from them. The contextual learning of these interrelated linguistic
apparati seems to go on simultaneously, according to Quine, "so that they are
gradually adjusted to one another and a coherent pattern of usage is evolved
matching that of society." (Quine, 1960: 93) Language learning at this level
has been beyond the reach of simple induction. And the method governing this
stage of learning process should be settled, according to Quine, "by inference
from *a network of hypotheses* that we have [habitually] internalized little by little
in the course of acquiring the *non-observational superstructure of our language*"
(Quine, 1977: 159; *my emphasis*). It is the continuing method of science—the
hypothetical-deductive method—that is dominating our acquisition of higher
reach of language. It is this method and at this point that our language is doomed
to work as a whole—as a man-made fabric of sentences variously connected to one
another and to non-verbal stimuli by the mechanism of conditioned response.

The following passage, quoted from Quine's "Reply to Robert Nozick",
indicates very clearly how holism sets in within the speculative process of language learning:

> "Turning to holism, he [Nozick] asks whether a non-Duhemian language would be impossible
> for us. Let me say that the observation sentences, in my behaviorally defined sense, constitute
> already a rudimentary language of the kind. It admits of non-Duhemian enlargement, moreover,
> without clear limits. ... But I see no hope of a [language of] science comparable in power to
> our own that would not be subject to holism, at least of my moderate sort. *Holism sets in when
> simple induction develops into the full hypothetico-deductive method*." (1986: 364; *my emphasis*)

There are at least two points to be mentioned here. First, we have to be very
careful about why Quine seems to allow the non-holistic (or non-Duhemian)
picture of language here. This picture seems plausible only to the extent that the
whole range of language comprises only observation sentences and the method
of language learning is confined to simple induction. Within this so-called
rudimentary language, observation sentences have their individual empirical

meaning—i.e., stimulus meaning—due to the way they are acquired holophras-tically (as it has been described above). However the development of our human language does not stop at this very primitive level. As a matter of fact, our language has been developing to a very complicated system in which we can establish a global view about this world, we can describe various aspects of human concerns, and we can even predict the future outlook of the whole nature and human society. All those developments have gone far beyond the control of observational situations and inductive expectation. A language endowed with such a powerful scientific background, as we shall see in the kernel of the next point, will be inevitably subject to holism.

Second, nonetheless, the holistic picture of language is still an inevitable result when the non-observational part of language emerges and the method of language learning develops into the hypothetico-deductive method. But why does the non-observational part of language learning have to be associated with the hypothetico-deductive method? Why is holism a necessary result when the process of learning develops into the hypothetico-deductive method?

To answer the question, we have to characterize first what the non-observational superstructure of our language is like. The non-observational superstructure of language mentioned by Quine here is nothing more than the "Two Dogmas" model of language—language as a man-made fabric which impinges on observations only along the edges. Observation sentences are the exterior edge of language, where our language contacts with experiences, and where our speech is condi-tioned to stimulations. Our learning of the primitive vocabulary of observation sentences consists in our learning of associating it with the appropriate sensory stimulations. However, language will naturally grow as a fabric of sentences, because somehow the child learns to carry his observation terms over into the-oretical contexts, variously embedded; and somehow he learns to connect his observation sentences to non-observational sentences (especially standing or scientific ones) in multifarious ways. Here, we start to pass through the observa-tional edge of language and work our way into the discursive interior where scientific theory can begin to be expressed.

The interior structure of language is fabricated of theoretical terms linked by fabricated hypotheses, and only "indirectly" is this labyrinthine superstructure keyed to observation at some points. Of course, the point here is to see how this non-observational superstructure indirectly comes in contact with observation. The interior part of language, including scientific and non-scientific standing sentences or hypotheses, imbibes the empirical meaning by virtue of the way that hypotheses support each other and ultimately the way that hypotheses cor-relate with observation sentences. Sometimes, hypotheses (or hypothetical statements) are made to posit bodies, events, or hypothetical particles. Sometimes, hypotheses are used to predict the behaviors of (macro- or micro-) physical objects or fictional objects. However, most of those hypothetical formulations involved in the scientific theories or located in the interior realm of language are not directly conditioned to stimulation or observation. Then, how do we test the acceptability of those hypotheses? How can those theoretical formulations be empirically justified or falsified? And how does science (or the theoretical part of language) stay responsive to sensory stimulation?

There is an infinite number of possible observations that we try to capture in a finite formulations within our superstructure of language. To accomplish this complex work, we have to apply generalization, to exercise the logical method, and even to install the whole facility of our ontological commitment. A universal standing sentence like "All swans are white" has been a sentence which cannot be directly associated with observation and justified by limited evidence. And for the most part a hypothesis of scientific theory has to join forces with other sentences in order to imply observable consequences. We cannot hope to correlate hypotheses or standing sentences generally with observations, because the empirical meaning of single scientific sentences has largely defied isolation. A multiplicity of standing sentences will interlock as an inclusive theory to be capable of predicting observational events and having empirical implications. The relationship between a scientific theory or a hypothetical formulation and its empirical implications involves a procedure of logical inference which is normally deductive: it depicts the line that under appropriate observable conditions, the hypothetical formulation that we are testing logically implies such and such observable results. Or to put it in Quine's own terminology, "the observation categoricals implied by a theory formulation constitute, we may say, its empirical content." (Quine, 1981: 28)

"Observation categorical" is a term designed by Quine to epitomize the experimental situation as well as to solve the problem of linking theory logically to observation (Quine, 1992: 9–11; 1981: 24–30). An observation categorical is a generality that is compounded of observables in the form—"Whenever X, Y"—where X and Y are both observation sentences. This design tries to capture the observational results (an implied generality) from the test of a hypothesis involved in scientific experiment in which a backlog of accepted theory tells our scientist that if the hypothesis under consideration is true, then, whenever a certain observable situation (represented by X) is set up, a certain effect (represented by Y) should be observed.

So, according to Quine's suggestion, the empirical significance of a scientific theory or a hypothetical formulation consists of its observation categoricals which are to combine observation sentences two by two and to provide empirical checkpoints of science. The test of a scientific hypothesis hinges on the logical relation of implication between a backlog of accepted theory plus the hypothesis and the observational categorical. Observation categoricals are the deductive empirical output of the inclusive theory. Therefore when a predicted event fails to present, or an observation is in conflict with our theory, it is the language of inclusive theory in question rather than any sentence in particular that needs to be accommodated. This result shows how holism sets in our picture of learning a language. Observation sentences enter the process of language learning holophrastically, with no regard to internal structure beyond what may go into the logical links of implication between theory formulations and observation categoricals. It is only when observation sentences are analytically connected to the rest of language and logically implied by scientific hypotheses that the holistic structure stands up and governs the working process of language.

Children's progressive process of language learning, or the evolution of human language, from ordinary observation sentences to scientific sentences, "is not a continuous derivation, which, followed backward, would enable us to reduce scientific theory to sheer observation. It is a progress rather by short leaps of analogy." (Quine, 1975: 77–78) Quine himself expresses a great interest in knowing how it is learned and how it came about. This would address the question as to how we can have projected our scientific theory of the whole world from our meager contacts with it. But Quine's answer seems to be simple. "Each man is given a scientific heritage plus a continuing barrage of sensory stimulation." (Quine, 1951: 46) The ability to learn language is a product of natural selection with its survival value. The hypothetico-deductive method, like the animal's simple induction over innate similarities, is also a biological device for anticipating experience and owes its origins to natural selection. So man's ascent to language and to science is a history of the survival of happy accidents.

The discussion, so far, is by no means a complete survey of Quine's speculations concerning the psychogenesis of language learning. But it suffices as an indication to the process of how one might begin with ostensive learning, which is ultimately concerned with the observational edge of language, and work one's way toward the higher reaches of language learning. Quine's genetic approach appears to be a plausible theory in explaining how it is possible to initiate the whole process of language acquisition and language growth, and, meanwhile, characterizing how a full-blown scientific language works as a whole. Furthermore, we get a sense of what epistemology aims to study—i.e., how a human subject as a natural phenomenon learns his scientific language from observation sentences and arrives at his scientific knowledge based on his sensory stimulations.

References

Descartes, R. (1986). *Meditations on First Philosophy*. John Cottingham (ed.), Cambridge University Press.

Fogelin, R. (2004). "Aspects of Quine's Naturalized Epistemology." In R. Gibson's (2004).

Gibson, R. (2004). *The Cambridge Companion to Quine*. Cambridge University Press.

Guttenplan, S. (1975). *Mind and Language*. Clarendon Press, Oxford.

Hahn, L. E. and Schilpp, P. A. (1986). *The Philosophy of W. V. Quine*. Open Court, La Salle, Illinois.

Hume, D. (1739). An *Enquiry Concerning Human Understanding*. Charles, W. (ed.), Hendel.

Kim, J. (1994). "What Is 'Naturalized Epistemology'?". In Kornblith, (1994), pp. 33–56.

Kornblith, H. (1994). *Naturalized Epistemology*, 2nd edition. MIT Press Mass.

———— (1994a). "Introduction: What Is Naturalized Epistemology?" In Kornblith, (1994), pp. 1–14.

———— (1994b). "Beyond Foundationalism and the Coherence Theory." In Kornblith, (1994), pp. 131–46.

Quine, W. V. (1951). "Two Dogmas of Empiricism." In Quine, (1953).

———— (1953). *From a Logical Point of View*. Harvard University Press, Cambridge, Mass.

———— (1960). *Word and Object*. M.I.T. Press, Cambridge, Mass.

———— (1966). *The Way of Paradox and Other Essays*. Harvard University Press, Cambridge, Mass.

———— (1968). "Ontological Relativity." In Quine, (1969a).

———— (1969). "Epistemology Naturalized." In Quine, (1969a).

———— (1969a). *Ontological Relativity and Other Essays*. Columbia University Press, New York.

———— (1970). *Philosophy of Logic*. Harvard University Press, Cambridge, Mass.

———— (1974). *The Roots of Reference*. Open Court, La Salle, Illinois.

———— (1975). "The Nature of Natural Knowledge." In S. Guttenplan, (1975).

———— (1977). "Facts of the Matter." In R. Shahan and C. Swoyer, (1979).

———— (1981). "Five Milestones of Empiricism." In Quine, (1981a).

———— (1981a). *Theories and Things*. Harvard University Press, Cambridge Mass.

———— (1986). "Reply to Robert Nozick." In Hahn and Schilpp, (1986).

———— (1992). *Pursuit of Truth*. Revised Edition. Harvard University Press, Cambridge, Mass.

———— (1995). *From Stimulus To Science*. Harvard University Press, Cambridge, Mass.

Quine, W. V. and Ullian, J. S. (1970). *The Web of Belief*. Random House, New York.

Shahan, R. and Swoyer, C. (1979). *Essays on the Philosophy of W. V. Quine*. University of Oklahoma Press, Norman.

Ruey-Lin Chen

The Structure of Experimentation and the Replication Degree—Reconsidering the Replication of Hertz's Cathode Ray Experiment

Soochow University & National Chung-Cheng University
rueylin@scu.edu.tw

Abstract

Over ten years ago Buchwald (1995a) discussed Jean Perrin and J. J. Thomson's attempt to replicate Hertz's cathode ray experiment. He concluded that both failed to achieve their purpose. Mattingly (2001) thought that Buchwald made a mistake in focusing on Hertz's experimental instruments and suggested that we should focus instead on Hertz's experimental goal. He concluded that Thomson did in fact replicate Hertz's experiment, while Perrin did not. I propose we should tackle the general problem of an experiment's replication by considering ends and means together. So the *aim* of the present paper can be laid out by the following points. *First*, I shall build a theoretical scheme to analyze the structure of experimentation in virtue of the means-end relation. *Second*, I shall propose a general theory, based on the notion of the degree of replication. *Third*, I shall claim that Thomson did replicate Hertz's experiment *to a higher degree* than did Perrin by means of an analysis different from Mattingly's.

Keywords: Replication, Experimentation, Experimental model, Replication Degree

1. Introduction: Replicating Hertz's Experiment

Over ten years ago Buchwald (1995a) discussed Jean Perrin and J. J. Thomson's attempt to replicate Henrich Hertz's cathode ray experiment in his article, "Why Hertz was right about cathode rays." The title revealed Buchwald's commitment to reversing the received view that Hertz's experiment had been replicated and his result refuted by Perrin and Thomson.

By 1883, there existed two rival hypotheses about the nature of cathode rays. One claimed that cathode rays in nature are ethereal waves; and the other that they are electrified particles. While supporting the former, Hertz decided to pursue the truth by means of experimentation. He designed an experimental device and made it work in 1883 (see the third section below). Using this device, he performed a series of experiments. One of them tried to catch the charge of the cathode-rays, supposing they were really electrified particles. It was known as the charge-catching experiment. Another tried to deflect the cathode-rays from their normal path by interpolating electrified plates along side the cathode rays. It was called the ray-deflection experiment. Hertz observed no charge was caught and no deflection of the rays occurred and so concluded cathode rays were unlikely to be electrified particles. Thus, the summary result of his experiments confirmed his belief. Nevertheless, Perrin in 1895 and Thomson in 1897, respectively, reproduced Hertz's experiments using a somewhat different device from Hertz's and got the contrary result (see the third section below).

Most scientists and historians of science accepted the view that Perrin and Thomson had replicated Hertz's experiment and confirmed that his experimental result was wrong. They all agree that Perrin's and Thomson's experiments had at the same time falsified the ethereal wave hypothesis supported by Hertz's result. (Harré, 2002; Thomson, Sir George, 1969; Whittaker, 1989). Their inference is that unless Hertz's experiments have been replicated with a contrary result, we cannot claim that the ethereal wave hypothesis is falsified. According to the same mode of inference, it's plausible to say that Buchwald argued that, since Perrin's and Thomson's experiments failed to replicate Hertz's, they also failed to falsify Hertz's hypothesis about cathode rays by means of their unsuccessful replication.

Relying on Hans Radder's (1995) notion of "the reproduction of an experiment under a fixed theoretical interpretation," which means the original experiment and the replicated are interpreted under a common theoretical hypothesis in question, Buchwald evaluated Perrin's and Thomson's attempted replication of Hertz's experiment and drew up a pair of tables, the first for the charge-catching experiment (table 1), and the other for ray-deflection (Buchwald, 1995a, 164, 165). The items in each column represent each scientist's requirements for his own experiment.

Based on the data summarized in table 1, Buchwald said,

> From the table for charge-catching experiments, we see that Hertz and Thomson each deems irrelevant one of the other's requirements. Perrin deems both of their stipulations to be unimportant. Though all three consider the anode-cathode relationship to be significant, Perrin's setting differs from Hertz's and Thomson's, which do not differ from one another. Each experimenter consequently had critical requirements that the other experiments failed to satisfy. (Buchwald, 1995a: 164)

This assessment implies that both Perrin and Thomson failed to replicate Hertz's charge-catching experiment. Similarly, in the case of the ray-deflection

Table 1

Hertz	Perrin	Thomson
Result: Rays do not carry charge	Result: Rays carry charge	Result: Rays carry charge
1. Anode close to cathode	1. Anode far from cathode	1. Anode close to cathode
2. Current trapped past anode	2. Irrelevant	2. Irrelevant
3. Irrelevant	3. Irrelevant	3. Charge-catcher not on cathode-anode axis

experiment, both Hertz and Thomson failed to satisfy each other's demands. Buchwald concluded, "Using Radder's terminology, we can say that Thomson did not replicate Hertz's experiment under a fixed theoretical interpretation." (165) Buchwald went on to write, "... despite the wrong direction of time's arrow, it perhaps makes better sense to say that Hertz did not reproduce Thomson's experiment." (165)

Mattingly(2001) rejected Buchwald's judgment in his article entitled "The replication of Hertz's cathode ray experiments" arguing that Thomson did in fact replicate Hertz's experiment. After a reexamination of the history of replication and a careful review of Buchwald's historical analysis, Mattingly argued that Buchwald's mistake was to focus on Hertz's experimental resources, namely, the wire gauze he had used in his experiment, because what is important is not the experimental instruments but rather the experimental goal, from which he derived all of his requirements. So, if Thomson could achieve Hertz's goal, that is, satisfy all of Hertz's requirements, then he would successfully replicate Hertz's experiments, no matter how he arranged his resources or instruments. Mattingly therefore suggested that we "should focus instead on what Hertz wanted to achieve, his experimental goal," and then:

> .... adopting the perspective of experimental goals forces us to cast a broader net. We focus our attention first on the requirements of the experiments itself. What is necessary for the production of the effect? For measuring the effect? For eliminating unwanted background influences? Only when we have answered these questions can we move on to the question of relevant replication. Rather than asking if Thomson utilized Hertz's mesh, we ask if Hertz's answers to the above experimental questions are suitably represented in Thomson's experiment. (Mattingly 2001, p. 73)

Following this line of analysis, Mattingly made a new historical and philosophical analysis of the replication of the cathode ray experiment and a new comparison (table 2) of Hertz's and Thomson's experiment. In that table, the *irrelevant* points in Buchwald's table 1 are now attributed to the same category, namely, the category of eliminating unwanted electrostatic interference. Mattingly supported

Table 2

Hertz	Thomson
Result: Rays do not carry charge	Result: Rays carry charge
1. Anode close to cathode	1. Anode close to cathode
2. Faraday cage around entire apparatus	2. Charge catcher not on cathode axis

his interpretation by pointing out that "Hertz hides his detector from electrostatic fields while Thomson removes his detector to a region where these fields provide no more than a background effect." (Mattingly, 2001, p. 72).

The comparison allowed Mattingly to conclude that Thomson did satisfy all requirements of Hertz's goal, and then replicate Hertz's charge-catching experiment. But Mattingly also wrote, "I will not attempt to argue that Perrin's experiment would fully satisfy Hertz." (Mattingly 2001, 70).

Mattingly's criticism of Buchwald's view reveals that, while Buchwald paid attention to the "means" of experimentation, Mattingly himself emphasized the "end". Why don't we integrate the two different focuses by considering ends and means together? I think this idea indicates an available approach which can give us a better understanding of the replication of experiments. Taking this approach, a question immediately arises: how should we integrate ends and means of experimentation? I suggest that we can start analyzing the structure of experimentation by considering the relations among means and ends, which are interpreted as abstract parts of the structure of experimentation. Since we can break down an experiment into interrelated parts, we can compare two experiments by looking at the similarities between the corresponding parts. The result gives us the degree of replication. Two different attempts to replicate an original experiment can be assigned different scores, as their constituent parts resemble those of the original to varying degrees. This approach lends support to Mattingly's claim that Perrin's experiment would not have fully satisfied Hertz's requirements and Thomson's would have, although Mattingly didn't provide a sufficient analysis of Perrin's experiment.

In sum, I hope to use Buchwald's and Mattingly's investigations of cathode ray experiments, and those of others, to provide a structuralist account of the replication problem. My aim can be laid out in the following points. *First*, I shall build a theoretical scheme to analyze the structure of experimentation in terms of the means-end relation. *Second*, I shall propose a general theory of replication based on the notion of the degree of replication. *Third*, I shall claim that Thomson did replicate Hertz's experiment to *a high degree* by means of an analysis different from Mattingly's.

2. Characterizing the structure of experimentation

First of all let me provide an intuitive description of how an experiment is built. From the scientific history, we know that every experiment takes place against a certain scientific background, which includes the academic climate of a community, the competition of hypotheses, and the constraints of technological and material resources. Against that background, a scientist would form her own ideas of important questions or problems, the possible answers or solutions, and how to justify her answer or solution, etc. So let's call those ideas background ideas. In solving her problem and justifying her solution, the scientist would form a conception of how to do an experiment using her background ideas. In general, the conception includes what goal the experiment is intended to achieve, what object the experiment is intended to operate on, how to combine the available resources or apparatuses, how to make the apparatuses operate, and what consequence would be anticipated. Then the scientist has to design an experimental model from the primary conception. The model provides a blueprint according to which she can build the experimental apparatus and make it operate. This step we call the material realization of experimentation.

Now I'll begin to articulate the intuitive description into a theoretical construction. It's obvious that every experiment can be treated according to the means-end relation, which gives an inner structure to every performance of experimentation. Thus, we can formally characterize the typical structure of experimentation as consisting of three interrelated parts: the experiment's background ideas (realizing the background is the end of the experiment), the experimental model (as the means of the experiment), and the material realization of experimentation (as the actual consequence of the experiment). The implication of each part needs be explained as follows. The background ideas, drawn from a specific scientific background, are the most basic units the experimenter works with in constructing the experiment, which in turn can only be realized through a complex device with a material apparatus that is assembled in a specific fashion. The inner structure of this device is what we call the experimental model.

Let me say a few more words about background ideas. These are a variety of antecedent beliefs, the selected hypothesis for solving a problem, and the theories presupposed in the experiment. Not all background ideas can be described as theoretical, because an experiment may be designed according to a primary belief or image which cannot be defined as a theory, as those described in Hacking's *Representing and Intervening* (Hacking, 1983, ch. 9). However, the background ideas of many experiments contain at least a theoretical hypothesis.

Hans Radder (1995, 58–62) proposed a division of the experimental process into two parts: theoretical hypothesis and material realization. The theoretical

hypothesis provides a description of experimentation or a theoretical interpretation of experimental object, apparatus and consequences. He said,

> Both object and apparatus may be of various kinds. Now, the experimental process involves
> the *material realization* and the *theoretical description or interpretation* of a number of
> manipulations of, and their consequences for, the object and the apparatus, which have been
> brought into mutual interaction. (Radder 1995, 58)

In my opinion, not making a clear distinction between the description of the
experiment and the theoretical interpretation is a defect of Radder's schema.
Description and interpretation are quite different things. As we have seen, I suggest a distinction between the experimental model and the background ideas. The
former is used to correspond to and substitute for the description of the experiment, and the latter similarly regarding the theoretical interpretation. Moreover,
I claim two functions of the background ideas should be identified: shaping the
design of the experimental model and interpreting the process of experimentation
and its results. Since the background ideas usually involve a theoretical hypothesis, I need to make a brief account of the meaning of "theory" I adopt. I see a theory as a set or population of models containing an inner hierarchy, a view of the
structure of theories derived from Ronald Giere's works (Giere, 1988, 62–91;
1999, 97–117). If a theoretical hypothesis is applied in designing an experimental
model, then it implies a realizable model that is at the lowest-level in a hierarchy
of theoretical models. In other words, the realizable model plays an intermediate
role linking theoretical hypothesis (a relatively abstract higher-level model) with
the experimental model that is closer to the concrete apparatus.[1]

Why should we distinguish between the background ideas and the experimental model? The reason is that two experiments with a similar model may be
designed according to two quite different, or even opposing, theoretical hypotheses. Furthermore, the predicted outcomes of the two experiments may be utterly
divergent. By contrast, a single theoretical hypothesis can be presupposed in two
different experimental models; two different experiments can yield the same
experimental result. Thus the theoretical hypothesis or background ideas and the
experimental model can be two distinct parts of one and the same experiment.
Moreover, the goal of the experimental model is to realize the background ideas.

The experimental model accounts for the structure of manipulations of the
experimental apparatuses. It connects the theoretical hypothesis (and background

---

1   A realizable model, by definition, has a similar structure to that of the explained phenome-
     non. In an explanatory situation, we derive a realizable model from a higher-level theoreti-
     cal model to explain the intended phenomenon. Similarly, in an experimental situation, we
     derive a realizable model from a theoretical hypothesis to design an experimental model.
     And then we try to realize the experimental model by a material apparatus. For a detailed
     description of the concept of realizable model, see Chen (2004).

ideas) with the material realization and plays the "means" role in experimentation. This model assigns a specific function and identity to an experiment or an experiment-type; to put it simply, different experimental models define different experiments. In our consideration of replication, the experimental model is of crucial importance: the degree of replication is determined by the degree of similarity between the model of the replica and that of the original experiment.

How then can one analyze an experiment to determine the degree of similarity between experimental models? The answer lies in the structure of the experimental model.

Let me apply again the relation of means and end to analyze the experimental model. An experimental model can be viewed as a means-end system with a series of means-end relations. First of all an experimental model is structured by (a) the experimental objective, (b) the experimental means, and (c) the anticipated consequences. Moreover, each constituent element consists of two or three sub-items, allowing the structure of an experimental model to be characterized as an action system with seven sub-items: *Goals, Objects, Apparatus, Operation, Control, Collection, and Prediction*. Why these? Because every experimental model is required to give answers to the following seven questions. They are: (1) What *goals* the experiment is intended to achieve? (2) On what *objects* the experiment is intended to operate? (3) How to combine various instrumental parts into an entire *apparatus*? (4) How to *control* the operation in order to avoid unwanted interferences? (5) How to make the apparatus *operate*? (6) How to *collect* the output of the experiment? (7) What possible consequences would be yielded? These sub-items merit a detailed explication.

(a1) Every experimenter sets up a goal for his or her experiment. The goal may be to test a single hypothesis, to evaluate two competing hypotheses, to test the consequences of an antecedent experiment, to test the operation of an experimental apparatus, and so on. Clearly testing a theoretical hypothesis is not the only goal of scientific experiments, although it has absorbed the attention of most philosophers of science. Some experiments may even have multiple goals. (a2) Every experiment must have its own experimental object, in other words, the physical objects or materials under experimentation. In a fluid boiling experiment, for example, the experimental object is the fluid. In a cathode ray experiment, the experimental object is the cathode ray.

(b3) Material equipment is always used to perform a concrete experiment. In a fluid boiling experiment, for example, the container containing the fluid, the equipment that heats the fluid, and the instrument that measures the temperature of the fluid are the indispensable parts. In addition, the successful outcome of the experiment depends on the appropriate assemblage and combination of the apparatus' parts. Taking the fluid boiling experiment as an example again, if the heater could not supply enough energy the value of the experiment would be nil. (b4) If the experiment is to be performed successfully the experimental apparatus has to interact with the objects under experimentation. For example, in order to transfer heat energy from a heater to fluid, the vessel containing the fluid must not be made of adiabatic material, that is, material that cannot undergo changes in temperature. In the interaction between the apparatus and the experimental objects, all potential interference must to be minimized. Considering again the fluid boiling experiment, all reactions between the container and the fluid must be reduced to a bare minimum. (b5) Of course, the experimenter has to work out a series of operative steps.

(c6) All experiments must involve the observation and measurement of phenomena that result from the interaction between the apparatus and the objects. This means that, in designing the experiment, these phenomena must be approached as readable or interpretable data. Though the equipment that collects and processes data is not a subject of the experimental apparatus proper, it is an indispensable element of all experiments: just imagine our fluid boiling experiment without a thermometer! (c7) Predictions are also crucial: they are a "theoretical consequence" naturally derived from the experimental goal and the operation of the apparatus. In order to obtain foreseen results, the experimenter designs an experiment in accordance with a working hypothesis. The performance of the experiment may, of course, yield results utterly different from those anticipated. It is important to note here that the actual result belongs to the material realization of experiment and is not a part of the experimental model.

In keeping with the foregoing discussion, the typical structure of experimentation can be pictured as follows.

Roughly, the background ideas guide the design of the experimental model, especially the apparatus, the operation, and the control and collection involved in an experiment; the experimental model in turn dominates the experiment's material realization.

In most situations of replicating an experiment, the aim of reproducing an experiment is to test the original experiment. This implies that there may be flaws or something wrong in the original experiment; or the experimenter might

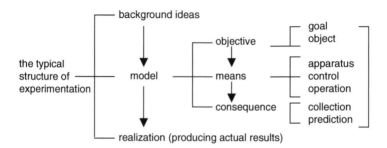

Fig. 3.   Diagram of the typical structure of experimentation.

doubt the result of the original, especially when she supports a rival hypothesis. So she always attempts to do a better job of reproducing an experiment. She cannot but modify the equipment, since she thinks the original is suspicious. In addition, she obviously has background ideas different from those of the original experimenter. Under the conditions of different background ideas and different equipment, the experimenter has to manage to replicate the structure of the original experimental model to a high degree; the reproducing experiment is thus *a valid replication*. If an experimenter uses the same equipment and the same experimental model as that of the original to repeat the experiment and obtain the same results under the same background ideas, then she replicates the original in a quite trivial sense. Let's call this *a trivial replication*; it has no testing power.[2]

I am proposing a solution to the replication problem that relies on the typical structure of experimentation and in particular the specification of experimental models, by gauging the degree of replication in terms of the sub-items described above. It's a matter of comparison. We decide which of two or more validly replicated experiments has a higher degree of replication by comparing their sub-items to those of the original experimental model. To be precise, the comparison involves the *comparative values* of all sub-items. Let's construct a three-value system of comparison by defining those values as *whole similarity, partial similarity, and dissimilarity*. By determining which sub-items of the replicated experiment are wholly similar, partially similar, or dissimilar to those of the original, we can decide the summary similarity of the replicated experiment to the original and then the degree of replication. The comparison of the degree of replication is thus reduced to the computation of the comparative values. We can now define the degree of replication.

> An experiment R replicates an original experiment O to a higher degree than does experiment R' if the experimental model of R possesses a higher degree of congruity in sub-units than does the experimental model of R'. This congruity is to be measured first in terms of the total number of *wholly similar values* assigned in a comparison of sub-units and, in case of an inconclusive result, then in terms of the total number of *partially similar values*.

According to this definition, the degree of replication depends on the comparative evaluation of sub-units. In other words, an experiment's degree of

---

2   Making an important point, Ian Hacking (1983, 231) said, "No one ever repeats an experiment." He had in mind the improbability of using the same equipment employed in the past to replicate an experiment. "There are cases," he noted, "from time to time when people simply do not believe an experimental result and skeptics try again" (231). But the motive did not involve inductive confirmation and this was not a *trivial replication*. "Typically serious repetitions of an experiment are attempts to do the same thing better— to produce a more stable, less noisy version of the phenomenon. A repetition of an experiment usually uses different kinds of equipment" (ibid.). Hacking's observations on the history of scientific experiments show that working scientists hardly ever bother with *trivial replications*.

replication is a combined function of the goals, means, and consequences of its experimental model.

Two questions may arise. Why is a three-value system of comparison proposed, but not a two-value or a four- or even more-value one? What happens when we have to look at the results of real experiments?

My answer to the first question is that a two-value system is not complete enough to fit our needs. Imagine the case that when an experimenter thinks the apparatuses or any sub-items of two experiments are not dissimilar, but she is reluctant to assign a "similar value" to them as well. The dilemma cannot be solved by a two-value system. If she uses a three-value system, she can conveniently assign a "partial similarity" to the compared sub-items. As to the four-value or more-value system, they may be too complex to satisfy the criteria of applicability and relative simplicity. So a three-value system of comparison is the best one for determining the degree of similarity and replication. The further justification will be shown by way of the application of those comparative values. This brings us back to my second question, about applying these values in the context of real experiments. I propose to answer it with the case study that follows.

3. A Reappraisal of Several Experiments on Cathode Rays

Buchwald (1995a, 1995b) has provided detailed investigations of Hertz's experimental physics and I encourage those interested in the subject to consult these excellent studies. I won't consider all of Hertz's experiments. My subject is those experiments exploring the nature of cathode rays. Those experiments were designed to test two rival hypotheses, namely, the ethereal wave hypothesis and the electrified particle hypothesis. I shall begin with the births of the two hypotheses.

Julius Plücker, a German scientist, carried out a series of experiments in 1858 to explore various properties of low-pressure discharge, which means a discharge produced by a cathode in a closed space that is gas-exhausted or near to a vacuum. He observed that the glow surrounding the negative electrode in a vacuum chamber was deflected when a magnet was brought near to it. When he reduced the negative electrode to a single point he saw that the glow became concentrated along the line of magnetic force passing through this point. When he employed a cathode made of platinum, Plücker observed that small particles were torn off of it and deposited on the wall of the glass bulb (Whittaker 1989: 350–351). All of those experimental results urged scientists who were interested in the subject to believe that that the cathode ray was a stream of electrified particles. In spite of these discoveries, Plücker seems to have been more interested in the beauty of the novel glow than anything else (Harré 2002, 173–174).

In 1869, Plücker's pupil Johann W. Hittorf placed a solid body between a point-cathode and a phosphorescent light and found that a sharp shadow was cast (Hittorf 1969, 563). In his own experiments, Eugen Goldstein found that distinct shadows were cast when the cathode had an extended surface. This clearly showed that the cathode surface emitted rays that traveled in a single direction. Goldstein dubbed the rays emitted from the negative electrode *cathode rays* (Whittaker 1989, 351). The shadow-casting phenomenon suggested that the cathode rays might be a new form of radiation. With the advent of Maxwell's electromagnetic wave theory, the idea that the cathode rays were a form of ethereal wave could not be resisted.

In 1879 Goldstein proposed that the cathode rays were ethereal waves agitated by a species of open current. He spoke of an "intermittent discharge," hypothesizing a special current that transferred no charge from the end of one ray to the beginning of the next one. As the current passed through the ether contained in the gas-exhausted tube, it collided with residual atoms to impart motion to the ether (Buchwald 1995a, 153; 1995b, 136–137). This explained both why a shadow would be produced when the path of the cathode ray was barred and why the cathode rays would be deflected when a magnetic field was introduced. German scientists embraced Goldstein's hypothesis.

In England such ideas enjoyed little favor. Sir William Crookes was a leading critic of the ethereal wave hypothesis. He and others viewed cathode rays as a species of "molecular current" and drew analogies between the cathode's discharge and glow and the electrolysis process.[3] Crookes explained the process by supposing that "the molecules of the residual gas, coming into contact with the cathode, acquire from it a resinous charge, and immediately fly off normally to the surface, by reason of the mutual repulsion exerted by similarly electrified bodies" (Whittaker 1989, 352). To support his hypothesis, Crookes pointed out that the dark space in the middle of the tube (known as Crookes' dark space) enlarged along with the rarefaction of the gas. By 1879 he had carried out a series of experiments to explore the properties of the "molecular current," investigating the projection of molecular shadows, the mechanical action of projected molecular shadows, and the magnetic deflection of lines of molecular force (Crookes 1969).

When he encountered the debate in the 1880s, Hertz was a laboratory colleague of Goldstein and naturally took his side. He was struck by the ability of the cathode rays to penetrate a metal film impervious to ordinary light. In fact, the penetrative power of cathode rays constituted the chief obstacle to the electrified particle hypothesis. But why were the cathode rays deflected by a magnetic or electrostatic field if they were ethereal waves? This was the biggest problem with the ethereal wave hypothesis (Whittaker 1989, 354). It was

---

3   In an electrolysis experiment, the experimenter puts the electrodes into a chemical solution and connects the electrodes with a power source. He would observe that a flow of current passes through the electrometer. Scientists in 19th century believed the phenomenon resulted from the many electrified (ionized) particles were produced in the electrolyte and "swimming" through the solution.

against this background that Hertz began to design his experiment for probing the nature of cathode rays.

Hertz began from a premise more radical than Goldstein's: he believed that the cathode rays were something new, entities *sui generis* that had nothing to do with electricity (Buchwald 1995a, 153). Even if Hertz were correct, all of the phenomena associated with cathode rays had to be produced by low-pressure discharge. Since an electric current (Buchwald calls it a "tube current") would necessarily be generated in the tube when discharges were produced between two poles, Hertz felt that cathode rays in the tube were always "contaminated" by this current—this explained why they exhibited various properties of electric currents. Hertz concluded that the nature of cathode rays could only be understood by separating them from tube current (Buchwald spoke of the production of "purified cathode rays"): only then could the electromagnetic and electrostatic properties of cathode rays be truly understood.

Was such a parsing possible? Hertz did perform several experiments intended to purify cathode rays: my case study is based on the experiment he did to explore the electrostatic properties of cathode rays, the same experiment that Perrin and Thomson tried to replicate later.

To perform this experiment, Hertz designed and built an apparatus (fig. 4), which Buchwald has described in detail:

> In Hertz's device a brass-tube anode closely surrounds the cathode. The rays flow from the cathode through a perforation in the brass, which is in metallic connection with a very important, cylindrical piece of wire gauze or mesh that hangs below it, as well as with an external mantle that surrounds the tube. The mantle in turn connects to a pole of the induction coil. The space between the enclosed cathode and the anode fills with intermixed current and rays as the coil works. The rays stream perpendicularly toward the perforation; the current presumably follows a broad path to the cylindrical anode. Just past the perforation the space therefore contains primarily rays, but also some polluting tube current that has leaked through. The gauze or mesh captures this last bit of current, so that "the cathode rays are to be regarded as pure after they have passed through the opening in the metal cylinder and the wire-gauze beyond it." The space past the gauze is bathed in the current-free rays. (Buchwald 1995a, 157)

By means of the cylindrical anode, the perforation in the anode, the wire gauze, and other devices, Hertz hoped to purify the cathode rays. When he activated his apparatus, he observed no reaction in the electrometer. To him, this implied that the purified rays no longer carried a charge. He believed that he had falsified the electrified particles hypothesis and proven the rival ethereal wave hypothesis.

Let's reconstruct the structure of Hertz's experimental model from the above descriptions.

(Ha1) *Goal*: to test the ethereal wave hypothesis and the rival electrified particles hypothesis by exploring the electrostatic properties of cathode rays.
(Ha2) *Object*: cathode rays.

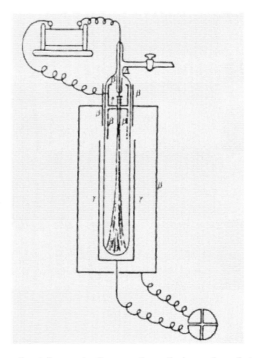

Fig. 4. Hertz's experimental apparatus for separating cathode rays from electrical current. Reproduced from Mattingly 2001, 60.

(Hb3 & Hb4) *Apparatus & Control*: a gas-exhausted discharge-tube with a cathode α surrounded by a cylindrical anode β, a power source, a system for controlling interfering factors (that is, wire gauze β-β in the tube), a system for detecting electric charges (an electrometer connected to the metal case γ γ and mantle). All parts are assembled into the apparatus illustrated as fig. 4.

(Hb5) *Operation*: to arrange the parts in such a way that the cathode rays can be separated from tube current. By placing the anode tightly around the cathode and making the rays pass through the anode, the discharge tube is divided into a "current section" and a "cathode ray section." The detecting system must be placed entirely outside the discharge tube and there must be no contact between the metal case and the cathode rays.

(Hc6) *Collection*: to detect the electrical charge on cathode rays by creating an electric induction between the metal case γ γ and the rays. An electrometer is used to detect the induction.

(Hc7) *Prediction*: Hertz actually predicted that the electrometer would not react. (Based on the prediction, Hertz's inference is: If the electrometer fails to react, then the cathode rays carry no charge, substantiating the ethereal wave hypothesis. If the electrometer does react, the cathode rays do carry charges and the ethereal wave hypothesis is disproved.)

When he looked at his electrometer and saw that the needle did not budge, Hertz inferred that the electrified particles hypothesis was falsified.

In 1895 the French physicist Jean Perrin designed and performed an experiment that he hoped would vitiate Hertz's. Two years later the English physicist J. J. Thomson performed a series of experiments similar to Perrin's. While the results of these experiments were seen as falsifying the ethereal wave hypothesis and corroborating the electrified particles hypothesis, they should be recognized as such only if the experiments indeed replicated Hertz's. We will examine this issue below.

For now, let's consider Perrin's and Thomson's experiments by reconstructing the structure of their experimental models. By comparison, we can assign comparative values to them in order to show their degree of replication of Hertz's experiment. Taking Perrin's experiment first (fig. 5; see also Perrin 1969, 581):

(Pa1) *Goal*: wholly similar to (Ha1).

(Pa2) *Object*: cathode rays; wholly similar to (Ha2).

(Pb3 & Pb4) *Apparatus & Control*: a gas-exhausted discharge tube with an anode-chamber EFGH and a cathode plate N, a power source, and a detection system (an electroscope connected to the chamber's metal case, ABCD). All parts are assembled into the apparatus as illustrated in fig. 5.

(Pb5) *Operation*: to arrange the parts so that the cathode rays can be separated from the tube current. The anode is far from the cathode. The detection case is placed entirely inside the anode so that the cathode rays will strike the case.

(Pc6) *Collection*: the detection case captures the cathode rays directly; an electroscope is used to detect electrical charges on the cathode rays.

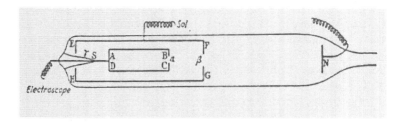

Fig. 5. Perrin's experimental apparatus. Reproduced from Perrin, 1969, 581.

(Pc7) *Prediction*: Perrin actually predicted the electroscope would react. (If the electroscope reacts, then the cathode rays carry charges, implying that the electrified particles hypothesis is true. If the electroscope doesn't react, then the cathode rays carry no charge.)

A little reflection shows that in designing his experimental model Perrin had in mind a very different hypothesis from Hertz. Although Perrin took Hertz's line of thought to separate the cathode rays from the tube current, he designed the apparatus under the belief that the cathode rays were electrified particles: this is why he placed the detection case in the direct path of the rays. Finally, the material realization of Perrin's experimental model confirmed his assumption.

Did Perrin's experiment replicate Hertz's? Let's imagine a historian at the end of the 19th century and review Perrin's experiment in terms of a fair consideration of Hertz's perspective. Extant descriptions of Hertz's experimental model and Perrin's suggest that many of the sub-items differed significantly from each other. For example, a comparison of (Hb3) and (Hb4) to (Pb3) and (Pb4) shows that Perrin's experimental model paid no attention to interfering factors (i.e., there was nothing corresponding to Hertz's wire gauze). To take another example, a comparison of (Hb5) and (Pb5), Perrin's experiment did not purify the cathode rays. If a tube current was produced by ionized gases at very low pressure (as is the case with electrolytes), then it is not possible to rule out the possibility of a tube current inside of the anode chamber EFGH. Moreover, Perrin surrounded the detection case ABCD with the anode chamber, which necessarily brings the tube current into contact with the detection case. Therefore, Perrin didn't purify the cathode rays at all. Additionally, if we compare (Hc6) and (Pc6) we find that Hertz and Perrin employed divergent approaches to the detection of electrical charges, the former insisting that the detection system cannot be put inside the tube without contamination and the latter insisting that because electricity was particulate it had to be measured directly.

Thomson's experimental model can be described as follows (fig. 6; see Thomson 1969, 584–85):

(Ta1) *Goal*: wholly similar to (Ha1).
(Ta2) *Object*: cathode rays; wholly similar to (Ha2).
(Tb3 & Tb4) *Apparatus & Control*: a gas-exhausted discharge tube with a cathode A and an anode B+, a power source, a system for controlling interfering factors, and a detection system (a cylindrical detector C with an opening is connected to an electrometer and surrounded by a grounded coaxial cylinder). All parts are assembled into the apparatus as illustrated in fig. 6.
(Tb5) *Operation*: to arrange the parts so that the cathode rays can be separated from the tube current. The anode is placed a short distance from the cathode and the rays are induced to pass through the anode. The discharge tube can be divided into a "current section" and a "cathode ray section."

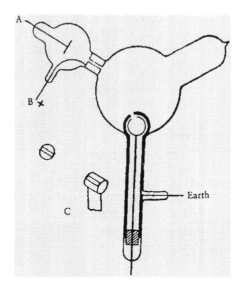

Fig. 6. Thomson's experimental apparatus. Reproduced from Thomson 1969, 584.

The detection system is placed entirely inside the cathode ray section under the assumption that the cathode rays passing through the anode will be captured by the detector.

(Tc6) *Collection*: the detector placed inside the ray tube collects the cathode rays and an electrometer detects the electrical charge of the cathode rays.

(Tc7) *Prediction*: Thomson actually predicted the electrometer would react. (If the electroscope reacts, then the cathode rays carry charges, implying that the electrified particles hypothesis is true. If the electroscope doesn't react, then the cathode rays carry no charge.)

Viewed from the supposed historian's perspective, Thomson's experiment replicated Hertz's to a higher degree than did Perrin's. Like Perrin, Thomson didn't use wire gauze to absorb any current that might leak out, but since the point of the gauze was to control any potentially interfering factors, it is significant that Thomson utilized the grounded cylinder for that very purpose. In other words, when we view the sub-items of Thomson's experimental model we find that they partially match Hertz's.

Furthermore, while Perrin's design called for catching the cathode rays directly, Thomson utilized a magnetic field to deflect them. Thomson's design supports the electrified particles hypothesis because only electrified particles would be deflected by a magnetic field. Thomson also made a sharp distinction between the current section and the ray section, placing the detector far from

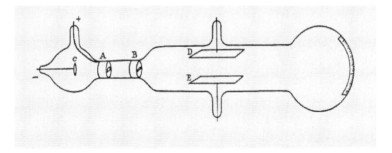

Fig. 7. Thomson's experimental apparatus. Reproduced from Thomson 1969, 586.

the current section to avoid contamination. In short, where Perrin's experimental model deviated from Hertz's, Thomson's approximated it. As to the third difference, the method used to detect the electricity of cathode rays, Thomson worked from the same premise as Perrin and produced a similar design—there he parted company from Hertz.

Later, in 1897, Thomson designed a new type of apparatus to perform a deflection experiment (fig. 7). The experiment he then performed, which was remarkably close to one of Hertz's, was subsequently viewed as a fatal blow to Hertz's ideas and the ethereal wave hypothesis in general. Hertz had performed a deflection experiment by placing two plates inside or outside a discharge tube and generating an electrostatic field between them, but when he introduced a stream of cathode rays he observed no deflection from their normal path (Buchwald, 1995a, 165). The model of Hertz's deflection experiment can be described as follows.

(H'a1) *Goal*: to explore the deflection of cathode rays in an electrostatic field.
(H'a2) *Object*: cathode rays.
(H'b3 & H'b4) *Apparatus & Control*: a gas-exhausted discharge tube with a cathode α surrounded by a cylindrical anode β, a power source, a system for controlling interfering factors (that is, wire gauze β-β in the tube), a pair of plates with a electrostatic field placed inside or outside the tube.
(H'b5) *Operation*: to arrange the parts in such a way that the cathode rays can be separated from tube current. By placing the anode tightly around the cathode and making the rays pass through the anode, the discharge tube is divided into a "current section" and a "cathode ray section," allowing only the "purified" rays pass through between the plates.
(H'c6) *Collection*: to observe if there is any deflection of cathode rays or not.
(H'c7) *Prediction*: Hertz actually predicted that no deflection would be observed. (If no deflection is observed, then the cathodes rays carry no charges. The ethereal wave hypothesis is true.)

In Thomson's "improved" experiment he did observe the deflection. He went further, defining a scale for measuring the degree of deflection so that he could compute the mass-charge ratio of the electron through the magnitude of the electrostatic field. Thomson's revised experimental model (1969, 586–87) looked like this:

(T'a1) *Goal*: to explore the deflection of cathode rays in an electrostatic field.
(T'a2) *Object*: cathode rays; wholly similar to (Ha2).
(T'b3) *Apparatus*: a gas-exhausted discharge tube with a cathode C and an anode A with an opening, a power source, a system for controlling interfering factors (the metal cylinder B with an opening in fig. 7, used to filter tube current from the cathode rays), and a detection system (to deflect the rays by two parallel plates D and E with an electrostatic field). All parts are assembled into the apparatus illustrated as fig. 7.
(T'b4) *Control*: The rays are induced to pass through section AB and the electrostatic field DE so as to strike the sphere at the end of the tube. Rarefying gases and reducing the pressure in the tube as much as possible in order to assure that there is no current between the two plates.
(T'b5) *Operation*: to arrange the parts so that the cathode rays can be separated from tube current. The anode is placed a short distance from the cathode and the rays are induced to pass through the anode. The discharge tube can be divided into a "current section" and a "cathode ray section." The electrostatic plates are placed inside the cathode ray section so that the cathode rays traveling between the two plates will be deflected.
(T'c6) *Collection*: to observe where the cathode rays strike on the scale.
(T'c7) *Prediction*: Thomson actually predicted the rays would be deflected. (Here the inference is: If the cathode rays are deflected by the electrostatic plates, then they carry charges, meaning that the electrified particle hypothesis is true.)

A comparison of Thomson's experimental model with Hertz's reveals a high degree of replication—not to mention that Thomson's deflection experiment has been viewed as the moment of the discovery of the electron, since he devised the means for measuring the ratio of elementary electric charge to mass. In reviewing Thomson's and Hertz's experiments, one may have a question: why did Hertz not observe the deflection of the cathode rays? Thomson attempted to answer this question by suggesting that the gas pressure in the tube had remained too high in Hertz's experiment, producing a current between the two plates perpendicular to the path of the cathode rays that weakened the effect of the electrostatic field. For lack of a stronger electrical force, the cathode rays didn't deflect. Thomson said,

Hertz made the rays travel between two parallel plates of metal placed inside the discharge-tube, but found that they were not deflected when the plates were connected with a battery of storage-cell; on repeating this experiment I at first got the same result, but subsequent experiments showed that the absence of deflexion is due to the conductivity conferred on the rarefied gas by the cathode rays. On measuring this conductivity it was found that it diminished very rapidly as the exhaustion increased; it seemed then that on trying Hertz's experiment at very high exhaustions there might be a chance of detecting the deflexion of the cathode rays by an electrostatic force. (Thomson, 1968, 586)

Let's construct a comparative table to show the degree of replication achieved by Perrin and Thomson. The comparative values are abbreviated as WS (whole similarity), PS (partial similarity), and DS (dissimilarity).

Experiments Scheme		Hertz (charge-catching)	Perrin (charge-catching)	Thomson (charge-catching)	Hertz (deflection) H'	Thomson (deflection) T'
End	Goal	Ha1	WS	WS	H'a1	WS
	Object	Ha2	WS	WS	H'a2	WS
Means	Apparatus	Hb3	PS	WS	H'b3	WS
	Control	Hb4	DS	PS	H'b4	PS
	Operation	Hb5	PS	PS	H'b5	WS
Consequence	Collection	Hc6	DS	DS	H'c6	WS
	Prediction	Hc7	DS	DS	H'c7	DS

The table shows that Thomson's charge-catching experiment achieved a higher degree of replication than Perrin's and that Thomson's deflection experiment came closer to reproducing Hertz's than any of the other replication experiments. Thomson's experiments jointly provide a strong rejection of Hertz's hypothesis.

4. Conclusion

Radder (1995) distinguished three types of replication: replication under a fixed theoretical interpretation, replication of material realization, and replication of experimental results.[4] In Buchwald's estimate, Perrin's and Thomson's

---

4   Radder (1995, 64–67) interpreted his three types of replication as follows. The type of reproducibility of the material realization of an experiment obtains when the same material realization can be reproduced under different interpretations, such as p→q, p'→q', p'→q, or p→q', in which p and p' represent theoretical interpretations and q and q' represent material realizations. The type of reproducibility of an experiment under a fixed theoretical interpretation p•q implies a repeatability of the experiment from the point of view of the theoretical interpretation in question. The type of reproducibility of the result q of an experiment applies when it is possible to obtain the same experimental result by means of a set of different experimental processes.

experiments were not "replications under a fixed theoretical interpretation." The other types of replication were never the ends which Perrin and Thomson wanted to achieve. But if Perrin and Thomson had background ideas different from Hertz's, then their experiments cannot be compared with Hertz's by being subjected to the type of "replication under a fixed theoretical interpretation". My proposal suggests that we can make a comparison under different theoretical interpretations and without distinguishing different types of replication. To assess whether an experiment replicates successfully an original or not from the perspective of types of replication is a kind of "absolute assessment". But it is more useful to provide a relative assessment of replication and working from such a perspective it is accurate to say that that Perrin and Thomson replicated Hertz's experiment *to differing degrees* by considering the similarity of the experimental models. Since the replication of an experiment whose goal is to test hypotheses is always related to the problem of falsification, I would like to close with a few words on that thorny subject. The view that replication of experiments is a matter of degree suggests that falsification may be also a matter of degree. How to talk about falsification in terms of degrees? This is a very complicated problem that I leave for the future.

Acknowledgments

The original version of this paper was first presented at the 6th East Asia STS conference, which was held at Northeastern University, Shengyang City in China in September 2005. After that conference, I modified its content and sent it to Sam Gilbert for revision. Sam made every endeavor to revise many sentences of the original version and provided many good opinions about the content and arguments. Using the revised version, I gave a talk at the department of Philosophy in National Chung-Cheng University in 2006 April. Professors Hahn Hsu, Shiu-Ching Wu, Ser-Min Shei, Tsung-Wen Shi, and other teachers and graduates eagerly asked me many questions and in particular Professor Wen-Fang Wang gave me a valuable suggestion. I revised my paper again and presented the third version at the 2006 Soochow University International Conference on Naturalized Epistemology and Philosophy of Science. Professors Ron Giere, Joseph Rouse and other participants made very deep comments on my paper. After that conference, Professor Rouse wrote a longer comment to me by email. Professor Giere even took time off to read my paper carefully, revise many sentences, and provide good suggestions again. A final version was accomplished. Here I express my deep gratitude to everyone mentioned in the above. I am especially thankful to Sam Gilbert and Professor Giere, who gave the greatest help to my paper. Without them, this paper cannot be published in its present version. Lastly, I want to express my regards to my colleague and good friend, Professor Chienkuo Mi. His efforts in organizing the 2006 "Naturalized" Conference, and his work on editing this volume, are greatly appreciated.

References

Buchwald, J. Z. (1995a). Why Hertz was right about cathode rays. In J. Z. Buchwald (Ed.), *Scientific practice: Theories and stories of doing physics*. Chicago: The University of Chicago Press (pp. 151–169).

Buchwald, J. Z. (1995b). *The creation of scientific effects*. Chicago: the University of Chicago Press.

Chen, R.-L. (2004). Testing through realizable models, *National Taiwan University Philosophical Review*, 27, 67–117.

Crookes, S. W. (1969). The cathode discharge. In E. Madden (Ed.) *Source books in the history of science*. Cambridge, Mass.: Harvard University Press (pp. 564–575).

Giere, Ronald (1988). *Explaining science*. Chicago: The University of Chicago.

Giere, Ronald (1999). *Science without laws*. Chicago: The University of Chicago.

Hacking, Ian (1983). *Representing and intervening*. Cambridge: Cambridge University Press.

Harré, Ron (2002). *Great scientific experiments: Twenty experiments that changed our view of the world*. New York: Dover Publications, Inc.

Hittorf, Johann, W. (1969). The cathode discharge. In E. Madden (Ed.), *Source books in the history of science*. Cambridge, Mass.: Harvard University Press (pp. 561–563).

Mattingly, James (2001). The Replication of Hertz's Cathode Ray Experiments. *Studies in History and Philosophy of Science*, 32A, 53–75.

Perrin, Jean (1969). The negative charges in the cathode discharge. In E. Madden (Ed.). *Source books in the history of science*. Cambridge, Mass.: Harvard University Press (pp. 580–583).

Radder, H. (1995). Experimenting in the natural sciences: A philosophical approach. In J. Z. Buchwald (Ed.). *Scientific practice: Theories and stories of doing physics*. Chicago: The University of Chicago Press.

Thomson, J. J. (1969). The electron. In E. Madden (Ed.), *Source books in the history of science*. Cambridge, Mass.: Harvard University Press (pp. 583–597).

Whittaker, Sir E. (1989). *A history of aether and electricity*. New York: Dover Publications.

Patrick Hawley

Skepticism and the Value of Knowledge

Hong Kong University, Hong Kong

1. Introduction

The main claim of this essay is that knowledge is no more valuable than lasting true belief. This claim is surprising. Doesn't knowledge have a unique and special value? If the main claim is correct and if, as it seems, knowledge is not lasting true belief, then knowledge does not have a unique value: in whatever way knowledge is valuable, lasting true belief is just as valuable. As will become clear, this result does not show that knowledge is worthless, nor does it undermine our knowledge gathering practices. There is, rather, a positive philosophical payoff: skepticism about knowledge is defused. Assuming one can have lasting true belief, then even if one cannot have knowledge, one can have something just as valuable.

1.1 The main claim motivated and clarified

1.1.1 The main claim motivated

In the Meno, Plato raises a question about the value of knowledge. [14, 97A-98A] If, wonders Plato, a man knows which road leads to Larissa, he can surely get there. And if a man does not know, but has a true belief about which road leads to Larissa, he can get there all the same. Why then is it better for him to know which road leads to Larissa? Why is knowledge more valuable than mere true belief? Plato's answer is that knowledge is more valuable than mere true belief because mere true belief can be easily lost; knowledge, however, is "fastened" by an explanation and thus more difficult to lose.

An example will help explain the Platonic thought:

> Restaurant reviewers Joe and Renata are dining in a fancy new trattoria. Joe knows that the unusual mushroom on Renata's plate is poisonous. Renata does not know that the unusual mushroom on her plate is poisonous, although she has a true belief that the unusual mushroom is poisonous. Renata concluded this from her false belief that the chef, bitter at her negative reviews, is trying to poison her. The chef, in fact, holds no grudge; he has simply made a mistake. The chef comes out and clearly does not recognize Renata. So she gives up her belief that the mushroom is poisonous, and starts to eat it. Renata is in danger because her true belief was

easily dislodged by new evidence. Luckily for Re-nata, Joe's knowledge is not so easily dislodged; Joe, who knows, stops her in time.[1]

The example about Joe and Renata supports two Platonic theses:

(1) Knowledge is more valuable than mere true belief,

and

(2) Knowledge is more valuable than mere true belief because knowledge is more stable.

Indeed, the example suggests, more boldly, that

(3) Knowledge is more valuable than mere true belief only because knowledge is more stable.

However, none of (1), (2) and (3) is particularly clear. What is stability, for example? Why does stability help make knowledge valuable? How are we to compare the value of such very different things as knowledge and mere true belief?[2]

When interpreted in a certain way, (3) is very close to the main claim. Suppose that to be stable is to be likely to last longer. Then (3) says that knowledge is more valuable than mere true belief only because knowledge is likely to last longer. But what about a lasting true belief, a true belief which will last as long as knowledge? That sort of true belief, arguably, is just as valuable as knowledge. That is the main claim.

1.1.2 The main claim clarified

Spelled out in more detail, the main claim is that a state s of knowing that p is no more valuable than a state of having a true belief that p which will last at least as long as s.

---

1   Williamson gives a similar example. [20, 87]

2   In recent literature, (1) is presented as an obviously true premise ready for deployment in philosophical argument. Zagzebski [21] argues that reliabilist accounts of epistemic justification are incompatible with (1), and, since (1) is obviously true, reliabilism should be rejected. Jones [6] argues, more generally, that any account of epistemic justification which sees epistemic justification as valuable only as a means to gaining true beliefs and avoiding false beliefs, is incompatible with (1), and thus objectionable. Riggs [17] replies that Jones's and Zagzebski's arguments only support the weak conclusion that, in order to preserve (1), certain accounts of justification need to be supplemented. Another sort of argument is given by DePaul [2] and Riggs [18]. They conclude that gaining true beliefs and avoiding false-hoods cannot be the only epistemic values, otherwise (1) would be false. See especially Kvanvig [10] for a useful discussion of the value of knowledge and Pritchard [15] for a help-ful review of the growing literature on epistemic value.

It may seem odd that the main claim is about having a lasting true belief—having a true belief which will last at least as long. One might instead have opted for something like a true belief which is unlikely to be changed or not easily dislodged or likely to last. Isn't that what the Joe and Renata case suggested? Here I must ask the reader's patience; the reasons behind this surprising choice are best explained later.

Note some superficially similar claims which differ from the main claim. The main claim does not say that for any time t, a state s of knowing that p at t is no more valuable than any state of having a true belief that p at t. The main claim does not say that for any stretch of time T, a state s of knowing that p throughout T is no more valuable than any state of having a true belief that p throughout T. The main claim does not say that knowledge is no more valuable than true belief (when that is understood as meaning that for any state of having a true belief that p, a state of knowing that p is no more valuable than it.) Rather, according to the main claim, if a state s of knowing that p lasts from *t1* (and no earlier) to *t2* (and no longer), then s is no more valuable than any state of having a true belief that p which lasts from *t1* until at least *t2* (and possibly longer).

Instead of discussing the value of the state of knowing, I might have chosen to discuss the value of the concept of knowledge. The value of the concept of knowledge is not my topic. Indeed, the value of the concept of knowledge should be clearly distinguished from the value of the state of knowing. The concept of knowledge may be valuable even if the state of knowing is not, just as the concept of a perfect vacuum may be valuable even if perfect vacuums are not. Conversely, the state of knowing where to find his favorite toy may be valuable to a child, even if he has no need for the concept of knowledge. I will focus on the value of the state of knowing, leaving other questions about value for another occasion.

Some readers may continue to feel puzzled by the main claim that the state of knowing that p is no more valuable than the state of having a true belief that p which will last at least as long. In what respect are we to compare these two states? Their value for action? Their intrinsic value? Or what? The answer: we are to compare these two states in any important respect in which knowing is valuable. Spelled out in even more detail, then, the main claim is: in any important respect in which a state s of knowing that p is valuable, a state of having a true belief that p which will last at least as long as s, is just as valuable. Since this is rather longwinded, in the interests of brevity I will often simply abbreviate: knowledge is no more valuable than lasting true belief.

1.2 A related claim and an assumption

In the process of defending the main claim I will also evaluate a second, related claim. The related claim is that knowledge is no more valuable than a certain group of lasting true beliefs. Or, in detail: a state s of knowing that p is no more valuable than some group g of true beliefs (including a belief that p) which will last at least as long as s. Call this the group claim. While my main focus will be to defend the main claim, we shall see that the group claim is defensible too.

Finally, and importantly, one assumption required for the defense of the main claim: the states of believing discussed are states of agents who are weakly rational. An agent is weakly rational if and only if: if S notices that she has no reason in favor of some belief, S stops believing it. As we go along, the role of this assumption will become clear.

2. The main claim defended

I will now defend the main claim by surveying the principal proposals to explain why knowledge is valuable. Some of these proposals appear in the literature, some do not. For each proposal, I will argue that if knowledge has that proposed value, then lasting true belief does too.

2.1 Knowledge is useful

It is sometimes suggested that knowledge is valuable because knowledge is useful. Proposals along these lines include: knowledge enhances your chance of survival; knowledge helps you make good decisions; knowledge helps you satisfy your desires; knowledge helps you to act morally; knowledge gives you power over others.

These proposals are easily dealt with. In each case, it is easy to see that a lasting true belief is just as useful.

According to these proposals, knowledge is useful for action—useful either in deciding which action to choose or in carrying out an action. Plato has already gone down this road. In trying to explain why knowledge is more valuable than mere true belief, Plato considers why knowledge is more useful to a person performing the action of traveling to Larissa.

Unlike Plato, I am comparing the value of knowledge to the value of lasting true belief. Is knowledge more useful for action than lasting true belief? Consider a case where knowledge enhances your chances of survival. If I know there is an angry, hungry tiger behind the door, then, as long as I am trying to stay alive, I won't open it. My knowledge keeps me from life-threatening danger. If I have a lasting true belief that there is an angry, hungry tiger behind the door, then, as long as I am trying to stay alive, I won't open it either. Knowledge seems to have no advantage here.

The example suggests a general point. When deciding what to do, it is useful to have an accurate picture of the world. And when acting, it is useful to maintain an accurate picture of the world. But my picture of the world, with respect to the proposition p, is no more accurate when I know that p, than when I truly believe that p. And when maintaining an accurate picture of the world with respect to the proposition p, knowing that p, and having a lasting true belief that p, are on a par.

I hear questions about this line of thought. One objector claims that false beliefs are sometimes more useful than knowledge. A rough and ready picture of the world can be better than an accurate one. For one thing, gaining true beliefs or knowledge sometimes carries too high a cost. In response, although false beliefs may sometimes be more useful than knowledge, I am comparing the value of knowing that p to the value of having a lasting true belief that p. Whether or not it is sometimes better to have a false belief is beside the point.

A second objector notices that, in some situations, knowing that p is clearly more useful than having a mere lasting true belief that p. Suppose an evil demon will hinder my actions as long as I fail to know that p. Then I'd be better off knowing that p than having a mere lasting true belief that p. Such cases are to be expected. The presence of an instrumental value can require that certain background conditions hold. An example: a refrigerator, normally useful to keep the milk from going sour, doesn't help much during a long blackout. Although a lasting true belief may normally be useful for action, in this evil demon case, it is not. Although the second objector's point is correct, the claim here should anyway be limited to normal conditions: Knowledge is, in normal background conditions, no more useful for action than lasting true belief. With that understood, I'll now drop the reference to normal conditions.

A third objector accepts that, in having and maintaining an accurate picture of the world with respect to the proposition p, knowing that p and having a lasting true belief that p are on a par. However, the third objector claims, one who knows that p still has and maintains a more accurate picture of the world because one who knows that p has a fuller or more complete picture of the world.[3] (Perhaps one who knows that p has and maintains a more accurate picture of the world with respect to propositions other than p.) Now, this point is not specifically about whether knowledge is more useful. I will respond to this objection in a later section.

Assuming that the last objection is successfully answered, it seems fair to conclude that if the value of knowledge lies only in its usefulness for action, then knowledge is no more valuable than lasting true belief. But there are other proposals for the value of knowledge.

---

3   Thanks to an anonymous reviewer for raising this and some of the other objections I consider.

2.2 Valuable for others

Your knowledge is not only valuable for you, it is valuable for others as well. You can inform others. You can give them a stock tip, warn them of imminent danger, or just satisfy their intellectual curiosity. Could your knowing that p be more valuable for others than your having a true belief that p? This looks like a non-starter. When you know that p you can inform your friend that p. Just as easily, when you have a lasting true belief that p you can inform your friend that p.

There is more to say. E. J. Craig [1] suggests that being a good informant involves more than having a true belief. According to Craig, a good informant is recognizable as a good informant; someone trying to find out whether p needs to be able to pick a good informant out of a crowd. Craig thinks that a good informant not only has a true belief that p, she has a detectable property X which correlates well with being right about p.

Craig's broader project is curious. He suggests that thinking about our practical need to find good informants helps us to explain why our concept of knowledge is the way it is. Thus, he tries to understand the concept of knowledge by means of the concept of being a good informant. But Craig does not make the straightforward claim that to know that p is to be a good informant whether p. Instead, according to him, the concept of knowledge is a stretched and twisted version of the concept of being a good informant.

I simplify Craig's wide-ranging discussion, and extract the following thought: knowing that p is valuable to others because someone who knows that p has a detectable property which correlates well with having a true belief that p. So let us look to see if knowers do have such a detectable property, and, if they do, whether that makes knowledge more valuable than lasting true belief.

Here is one possibility: A person who knows that p can give reasons in support of his view about p. If so—if a person who knows that p can defend his view when asked—then knowing looks to have an advantage over merely having a lasting true belief. When you are looking for a good informant, you can ask your target what reasons she has. If she knows that p, she can give you some. So you can get some evidence that she knows that p.

Lasting true belief differs from knowledge in this respect. To say that a person has a lasting true belief that p is not to say that she has or lacks reasons. It is only to say that she has that belief. If knowing that p always comes with reasons, then knowing that p is, apparently, more valuable to others than having a lasting true belief that p. (Even if, more weakly, knowing that p often (but not always) comes with reasons, then knowing that p is often more valuable to others than having a lasting true belief that p.) This conflicts with the main claim.

The group claim mentioned earlier resists this objection. Rather than comparing knowing that p to having a lasting true belief that p, compare knowing that p to having a lasting group of true beliefs. Include in the lasting group of true beliefs not only a true belief that p, but some reasons in favor of p that the person can give. A person who has this lasting group of beliefs can give evidence that she has a true belief that p. Although weaker than the main claim, the group claim does not depart from its spirit—that there is nothing distinctively valuable about knowledge not found in lasting true belief. If knowing that p is often detectable because knowing that p always (or often) comes with reasons, then a lasting true belief that p (when part of an appropriate lasting group of true beliefs) is equally detectable.

However, more interesting is to defend the main claim in the face of the objection. Consider a person who is rational, and who will continue to be rational, in the following weak sense: If she notices that she has no reason in favor of some belief, she stops believing it. Thus, a weakly rational person will not, for example, hold on to some belief merely out of stubbornness after noticing that she has no reason to believe it. However, a weakly rational person believing without reasons may, insofar as she is weakly rational, continue believing as long as she doesn't notice that she lacks reasons. A completely unreflective person, who never notices whether or not she has reasons for her beliefs is weakly rational. Being weakly rational merely means that one does not both notice that one has no reasons in favor of a belief and yet continue to believe it. It seems to me intuitively plausible that the constraint of weak rationality really is weak. That, together with its usefulness in defending the main claim justifies its use here. While a stronger justification of this constraint is clearly desirable, I will leave that for another occasion.

Now, assuming we are discussing weakly rational people, the objection can be answered. A weakly rational person can give reasons in support of her view just as well as someone who knows. Suppose Bob knows that the nearest decent cup of coffee is two miles away. Suppose also that Bob will be asked about it tomorrow, and because he knows he can give reasons for his view. Compare weakly rational Ray who merely has a lasting true belief that the nearest decent cup of coffee is two miles away—weakly rational Ray has a true belief which will last as long as Bob's knowing state. It can't happen that Ray is asked it about tomorrow without reasons to give. For if Ray is asked about it tomorrow, and he has no reasons, then he will notice he has no reasons and will stop believing it. (He will notice he has no reasons because he will notice that he has no answer to give.) But that can't happen because Ray's true belief will last just as long as Bob's knowing state. So it can't happen that Ray is caught without reasons.

Thus, even if knowing that p includes the detectable property of being able to give reasons in support of p, that does not mean that knowing is more valuable than lasting true belief. For, a weakly rational believer with a lasting true belief also has reasons when asked. In short, the objection does not show that knowledge is more valuable than lasting true belief, assuming that the lasting true believer is and will continue to be weakly rational.[4]

Some readers may worry that restricting the discussion to weakly rational people brings knowledge in the back door: perhaps a weakly rational person with a lasting true belief that p, knows that p. This is clearly not the case, if knowing requires having reasons. A weakly rational person can believe that p with having any reasons, as long as he doesn't notice. So a weakly rational person can have a lasting true belief that p without knowing that p, by having no reasons for her belief but not noticing. Moreover, whatever knowing requires, a Gettier-style example shows that a weakly rational person with a lasting true belief that p need not know that p. Jed comes to truly believe that someone at the lab owns a Toyota, having often seen Smith drive around in a Toyota. Since Smith owns no car, although Jed's belief is true, Jed does not know. Suppose further that Jed's belief is also lasting; he will never run into any reason to doubt his belief. Even so, he still does not know that someone at the lab owns a Toyota. Suppose further that Jed is and will continue to be weakly rational. That means that if he has no reasons he will not notice. He still doesn't know that p. Jed is a weakly rational person with a lasting true belief that p, who fails to know that p. Restricting the discussion to weakly rational people does not bring knowledge in the back door.

This, I believe, satisfactorily dispenses with the objection that knowing that p is more valuable because a person who knows that p often has the detectable property of having reasons to believe p. Yet, knowing that p may sometimes be accompanied by some other detectable property.

I can think of only one other plausible candidate detectable property.[5] When you know that p, you know related things. When searching for a good informant as to p, I can ask you about related topics of which I am already informed. If you

---

4   S. Haslanger [4] has an interesting connected suggestion. She suggests that knowledge is valuable because knowers have and respond to reasons, and being responsive to reasons is part of what it is to be autonomous—which is a constitutive part of a flourishing life which is valuable for creatures like us. But the value that Haslanger points to can surely be present whether or not knowledge is present. One can have and respond to reasons even if all one's beliefs are false, and thus even if one has no knowledge. So Haslanger's proposed value can be present whether or not one has knowledge. Moreover, I am doubtful that knowing requires having and responding to reasons. But if having and responding to reasons is indeed valuable and present in all knowers, we may, in comparing knowledge to lasting true belief, assume that the believer has and responds to reasons. Note that this assumption would not bring knowledge in the back door as shown by Gettier-style examples like the one in the next paragraph.

5   Well-known analyses of knowledge fail to provide a plausible candidate. A true belief reliably formed [3], or the output of properly functioning cognitive equipment [13], or tracking the truth in nearby possible worlds [12], is no more detectable than a lasting true belief.

know about related topics, I have evidence that you know whether p.[6] Arguably, then, knowing that p is more valuable than a lasting true belief that p because a lasting true belief that p may stand alone, unaccompanied by true beliefs about related topics. This conclusion conflicts with the main claim.

Again, the group claim resists the objection. Talk not of a lasting true belief that p, but a group of lasting true beliefs, including beliefs about related topics. Knowing that p, even if accompanied by knowledge of related topics, is not more valuable than this group of lasting true beliefs.

Although the group claim is interesting, the bolder main claim is defensible too. Now it seems clearly false that when you know that p you always know related things. (Remember that these related known things are not supposed to be reasons you have in support of p.) You can have isolated bits of knowledge; you can know random trivia without knowing related things. For example, you can know that "George Orwell" was Eric Blair's pen name without knowing anything else about Eric Blair. (Or at least anything else that would provide evidence that you know Eric Blair's pen name.) You can know that it is sunny today without knowing anything else about the weather, or anything else about today. However, while it seems false that when you know that p you always know related things, it is plausibly true that when you know that p you often know related things. But the plausibly true claim is not strong enough to support the objection. For it is also plausibly true that when you have a lasting true belief you often know related things. That is because in normal circumstances, a person with a lasting true belief that p is surely just as likely be exposed to information about related topics than a person who knows that p. A person with a lasting true belief surely has the same opportunity to learn about related topics. So there is no reason to think that a person with a lasting true belief is often any less informed about related topics; knowing that p is not more valuable even if often accompanied by knowledge of related topics.[7]

I can see no further plausible reason to think that knowledge is more valuable to others than lasting true belief. Let's move on.

---

6   I have heard this objection mentioned in conversation. I am unsure what counts as a topic related to p. At least knowledge of these topics should provide evidence that you know that p. And presumably these related topics you know about should not include reasons you have in favor of p, or else this objection would not significantly differ from the last objection, that when you know you have the detectable property of having reasons.

7   Now I can return to the objection from the end of section 2.1 that a knower has a more accurate picture of the world than someone who merely has a lasting true belief. Assuming that the picture is more accurate either because the knower has reasons, or because the knower knows about related topics, by the argument in the present section, the earlier objection fails to show that knowledge is more valuable than lasting true belief, assuming weak rationality.

2.3 Knowledge as an achievement

One somewhat vague suggestion is that knowledge is valuable because knowledge is an achievement. Riggs [17] [18] tries to cash out this suggestion. Riggs' thought is that knowing that p is valuable (in part) because a person who knows that p deserves some epistemic credit for having reached that state:

> Being in the state of "knowing that p" entails of a person that she have a true belief for which she deserves a certain degree of epistemic credit. Believing something true by accident entails no credit of any sort to the person. This is so despite the fact that the belief is no more valuable in the former case then the latter, nor need we assume that the believers in question differ in their respective epistemic qualities. The difference that makes a value difference here is the variation in the degree to which a person's abilities, powers, and skills are causally responsible for the outcome, believing truly that p. [18, 94]

Riggs may think that he has isolated a value distinctive of knowing, as opposed to mere true believing. A Gettier-style example shows that this is not correct; mere true believers can deserve just as much epistemic credit as knowers. Suppose that Ned comes to know that someone at the lab owns a Toyota, having often seen Jones drive around in Jones' own Toyota. Jed, who works in the same lab, comes to truly believe that someone at the lab owns a Toyota, having often seen Smith drive around in Jones' Toyota. Since Smith owns no car, although Jed's belief is true, Jed does not know. Ned and Jed, we can assume, are causally responsible to just the same degree for their true beliefs. So, by Riggs' lights, they deserve the same epistemic credit for their respective true beliefs.

Perhaps Riggs' point is instead that knowers always deserve some epistemic credit, but mere true believers only sometimes do. This may be correct. But that does not mean that knowers always deserve at least as much epistemic credit as mere true believers do. In fact, knowers sometimes deserve less epistemic credit than mere true believers: Joe the policeman happens to walk by at the moment Lefty the gardener pets the dog. Joe comes to know that one of the gardeners petted the dog. Smitty the detective, after an exhaustive and careful investigation, comes to falsely believe that Righty the gardener petted the dog. Smitty concludes that one of the gardeners petted the dog. Surely Smitty is more causally responsible for his true belief than Joe. So, apparently, by Riggs' lights, Smitty deserves more epistemic credit. That means Joe, who knows, deserves less epistemic credit than Smitty, who has a mere true belief; someone who knows can deserve less epistemic credit than someone with a mere true belief. Thus Riggs' proposal does not support the conclusion that knowing is more valuable than lasting true belief.

Step back from Riggs' proposal, and return to the thought that knowledge is valuable because it is an achievement. Sometimes knowledge is an admirable achievement. But not always; sometimes knowledge comes easy. And sometimes lasting true belief is an admirable achievement. But not always; sometimes lasting true belief comes easy. Either state can be an achievement or not. So we have not yet found something distinctive of knowing which makes knowing that p more valuable than having a lasting true belief that p.

2.4 A close connection to the world

Another suggestion is that knowing involves a close connection to the world; knowing gives you a firm grip on the way things are.

More specificity is needed to evaluate this thought. Robert Nozick's tracking theory of knowledge is one way to make this close connection idea more precise. [12] Bells and whistles aside, Nozick claims that to know that p is to have a true belief that p which tracks the truth, where your belief that p tracks the truth just in case: if p were false you wouldn't believe that p, and if p were true you would believe that p. Possible worlds talk helps make the notion of truth-tracking clearer. Your belief tracks the truth just in case in nearby possible worlds where p is true, you believe it, and in nearby possible worlds where p is false, you don't. A person with a truth-tracking belief has a grip on the way things are—small changes in the way things are would not disturb his grip on the truth.

Even if (as compelling examples suggest) Nozick's conditions are neither necessary nor jointly sufficient for knowing that p, his proposal has an appeal which suggests that he may be on the right track. So it is worth asking whether a truth-tracking belief is more valuable than a lasting true belief.

Initially, it seems implausible to think that a truth-tracking belief is more valuable than a lasting true belief. Why would you care whether or not your beliefs are true in some nearby possible world? You are not in some nearby possible world; you are in the actual world. If in some nearby world you get hit by a car, come down with the measles or get a terrible toothache, too bad for you in that possible world. Luckily, you are in this world, where these things don't occur. Similarly, in some nearby world you may have some extra false beliefs, or fail to have some true ones. So what? You are in the actual world where this didn't occur.

Yet, there is reason to care whether your beliefs track the truth in nearby worlds: you don't know which world you are in. Moreover, since some of your beliefs are almost certainly false, you are almost certainly in a world that you consider to be merely possible. Thus, since you care whether or not your beliefs are true in the actual world, you should care whether or not your beliefs are true in worlds that you consider to be merely possible.

This reasoning does not show that truth-tracking beliefs are more valuable than mere lasting true beliefs. According to this reasoning you should care whether or not your beliefs are true in worlds that you consider to be merely possible because you care whether or not your beliefs are true in the actual world. But if your belief is lasting and true, then it is lasting and true in the actual world; if your belief is lasting and true then you have what you want already.

Having true beliefs (and avoiding false beliefs) in some other world does not satisfy any further want.

(A similar line of thought explains why the main claim concerns the longevity of true belief rather than some modal property a true belief might have—like stability or robustness. Ask a parallel question: why should you care whether a true belief is stable—whether a belief would be held truly in a range of non-actual situations? The answer that comes to mind is that since you don't know what situation you are in, you want to hedge your bets. So you ensure that the belief is truly held in a range of situations. But if you have a lasting true belief, you have what you want already—that the belief continue to be held and be true in the actual world. Having a stable true belief gives you nothing further that you want.)

Let's take stock. I turned to Nozick's tracking account of knowledge in developing the idea that knowing involves a close connection to the world. Then I tried and failed to find a reason to think that a truth-tracking belief is more valuable than a lasting true belief. But perhaps truth-tracking was not the right place to start. Let's try again.

One thought is that lasting true belief can be lucky in a way that knowing cannot, and in a way that weakens your connection to the world. Big Al thinks the government owes him $200. Big Al is right, but only by luck. His accountant made several errors on his tax return which cancelled each other out. Luckily for Al, his belief is lasting; he won't notice any of the errors. Al's grip on the fact that the government owes him $200 seems tenuous. Al's connection to the world seems much weaker than that of Slim, who comes to know that the government owes him $200 because his accountant, who made no mistake, tells him so.

There is a good reason to disvalue luck: as any gambler should know, you can't count on luck. Luck comes and goes. But why think that luck makes Al's state more tenuous (and thus less valuable) than Slim's? One reason is that Al is in a state that could easily be lost if his luck turns bad. However, we should not disvalue Al's state because his good luck might run out. For his luck won't run out; his state won't be lost—it is lasting.

Another reason to think that luck makes Al's state less valuable than Slim's is that Al was very lucky to have a true belief. He might easily have had a false one. His accountant could have easily made one less error. Again, however, we should not disvalue Al's state because he might easily have had a false belief. Knowing can depend on luck in just the same way: I should have mentioned earlier that Slim usually uses Al's mediocre accountant, but this year he was lucky that his cousin the excellent accountant was visiting at tax time.

This is enough, I think, to see that this is another false lead. Knowing can occur by luck, be maintained by luck, or not. Lasting true belief can be had by luck, or be maintained by luck, or not. So lasting true belief is not dependent on luck in a way that makes it less valuable than knowledge.

Here is one last reason to think that knowing brings a closer connection to the world than lasting true belief. When you know that p you have a thorough understanding which may be lacking when you have a lasting true belief that p. For example, Andrew Wiles knows that Fermat's Last Theorem is true because he proved it. He understands how FLT connects to other theorems; he understands why it is true. Silly Billy, on the other hand, believes that Fermat's Last Theorem is true on the basis of a mistaken proof he concocted in the eighth grade. Luckily for Billy, his belief is lasting. Unlike Wiles, however, Billy has no deep understanding.

This objection is familiar. We have already considered the objection that knowing is better because knowers have reasons, and the objection that knowing is better because knowers know about related topics. If to have a thorough understanding is either to have reasons or to know about related topics (or both), then this objection has already been answered. To summarize: a weakly rational person with a lasting true belief either does have reasons or he never notices that he lacks them. Either way, his state is not worse than that of a knower, even if knowing requires reasons. On the other hand, there is no reason to think that knowers always know about related topics, and even if knowers often know about related topics, lasting true believers do too. In normal circumstance they have just as much opportunity to learn about related topics.[8]

2.5 Valuable as a means

I may have missed something when arguing that truth-tracking belief is no more valuable than lasting true belief. Nozick himself posits a value for truth-tracking belief. In a section called "What's so special about knowledge?", Nozick says that evolutionary processes can't directly put true beliefs in our heads—they can only produce a capability to form true beliefs in a changing world. But the kind of capability which evolution can produce is a capability to form beliefs which track the truth. [12, 283ff]

It is difficult to evaluate evolutionary considerations at this level of detail. But Nozick's thought suggests an interesting proposal. How can you get a lasting

---

8   Suppose that to have a thorough understanding is something more or different than knowing about related topics or having reasons. Here, one notes that one was too quick to agree when you know you have a thorough understanding. You can know that Fermat's Last Theorem is true without understanding why it is true. You can know because the respected mathematician tells you so. Knowing that p does not always bring a thorough understanding. But perhaps someone who knows is more likely to have a thorough understanding—and thus a closer connection to the world—than someone who has a lasting true belief. Here I am unsure what to say in detail, because I am unsure what it is to have a thorough understanding if not to know related things. But, as before, the reply will be that a lasting true believer is no less likely to be exposed to situations in which surrounding lasting true beliefs can be acquired.

true belief? Perhaps an effective way is to get—or at least try to get—knowledge. If this is right, then knowing that p may have a value that a lasting true belief that p lacks. Maybe knowing that p is useful as a means to have a lasting true belief that p.

While knowing may indeed be useful as a means to have a lasting true belief, this does not make knowing more valuable than lasting true belief.

One way that knowing is perhaps useful as a means for having a lasting true belief is this: anyone in the state of knowing that p is also in the state of having a lasting true belief that p. But even if knowing is valuable for this reason, lasting true belief is just as valuable. Having a lasting true belief is just as useful as a means for having a lasting true belief: anyone in the state of having a lasting true belief that p, is in the state of having a lasting true belief that p.

There is another way that knowing may be thought useful as a means for having a lasting true belief: trying to know may be useful as a means to get a lasting true belief. But even if trying to know is more effective in getting a lasting true belief than trying to get a lasting true belief, that does not show that the state of knowing is more valuable than the state of having a lasting true belief. The value of trying to reach the state of knowing is one thing; the value of the state of knowing is quite another. The main claim only concerns the latter value.

2.6 Knowledge is valuable in itself

I have discussed several different kinds of value which knowledge might have. The first proposal was that knowledge is useful for action. The second proposal was that knowledge is valuable for others. Both of these two proposals see knowledge as valuable for the sake of something else. The third proposal was that knowledge is valuable because it is an achievement. The fourth proposal was that knowledge is valuable because knowing brings a close connection to the world. I have suggested that these proposals see knowledge as valuable because something other than knowledge is valuable. The fifth proposal was that knowledge is useful in getting lasting true beliefs. Again, this proposal sees knowledge as valuable for the sake of something else.[9]

Here are two distinctions in value.[10] The first distinction is between being valued for its own sake (as an end) and being valued for the sake of something else. For example, if knowledge is valued because it is useful for action, then

---

9   One last proposal is that knowledge has no value. Jonathan Kvanvig [9] makes this surprising claim, arguing that we value other things which we confuse with knowledge. Suffice it to say that if knowledge has no value, the main claim is correct. If knowledge has no value, knowledge surely has no more value than lasting true belief.

10   C. Korsgaard [8] draws similar distinctions and argues that they should not be collapsed together. I am indebted to R. Langton [11], who amends and criticizes Korsgaard's discussion. However, I ignore many of the complexities which Langton uncovers.

knowledge is valued for the sake of something else—successful action. The second distinction is between being valuable in itself and being valuable in virtue of something else. For example, if knowledge is valuable because it is an achievement, then knowledge is valuable because something else—achievement—is valuable. The first distinction is a distinction in the way we value things, as ends or for the sake of something else. The second is a distinction in the way things have value, in themselves (intrinsically) or in virtue of something else (extrinsically).

So far I have discussed every proposal I can find according to which knowledge is valued for the sake of something else. And I have discussed every proposal I can find according to which knowledge is valuable in virtue of something else. (Some of the proposals I have discussed fall into both of these categories.) I have argued that, if knowledge has that value, then lasting true belief has that value too. It seems fair to conclude that if knowledge is valuable for the sake of or in virtue of something else, then lasting true belief has that value too. But that leaves two open questions: is knowledge valued as an end? is knowledge valuable in itself?

There is evidence that it is. People talk about the value of learning for its own sake. Research projects get funded on the grounds that they might bring us new knowledge. Scholars spend years trying to answer obscure questions. But we need stronger evidence than this, if we are to conclude that knowledge is valuable in itself, or valued as an end.

A test for intrinsic value comes from G. E. Moore. To apply the isolation test to see whether X has intrinsic value, you imagine a world in which nothing exists except X, and ask whether X has value. Knowing presumably does not exist without a knower, so imagine a world in which the only existing thing is a person P1 who knows something. Since nothing exists except P1, one thing he might know about is himself. So let's suppose that he knows that he exists. Is his knowing valuable? Maybe. I am not sure. At least, I don't see any contrast with lasting true belief. If I imagine a different world in which nothing exists except P2, who has a lasting true belief that he exists, and ask whether his having a lasting true belief is valuable, I have the same reaction. This test does not clearly show that knowing has an intrinsic value which lasting true belief lacks. As far as I can tell, this test only shows that if knowledge has intrinsic value, then lasting true belief does too.

Here is a second test. To apply the choice test to see whether X is more valuable than Y , ask yourself whether you would rather choose a life in which you have X or one in which you have Y . This is not directly a test whether knowing is valuable in itself, or as an end. However, given the conclusion that knowing is no more valuable than lasting true belief in virtue of, or for the sake of something else, this test will indirectly help decide whether knowing is valuable in itself or as an end.

So here goes. Would you rather choose a life in which you know that the Federated States of Micronesia gained independence in 1989, or one in which you merely have a lasting true belief that the FSM gained independence in 1989? Again, this is not clear.

Here's a thought that may decide the question. In the life in which you merely have the lasting true belief, you may have the lasting true belief because you concluded it from a false belief, for example the false belief that all U. S. territories gained independence in 1989. But in the life in which you know, you couldn't have gained this knowledge by drawing a conclusion from this false belief. Otherwise you would not have knowledge. Choosing the life with the mere lasting true belief risks having such false beliefs. So, since false beliefs are bad, you should choose the life in which you know so as to avoid false belief.

This is not a good reason to choose the life in which you know. For you might still have this false belief—indeed you might have many, many false beliefs—in the life in which you know. You just can't gain your knowledge by drawing a conclusion from such a falsehood. And in the life in which you merely have the lasting true belief, you might, in addition, have a multitude of other lasting true beliefs, comprising a complete and comprehensive picture of the world. Thus, avoidance of false belief is not a good reason to choose the life in which you know.

So let's try again. Would you choose the life in which you know over the life in which you merely have a lasting true belief? I feel somewhat uncertain about which life I would choose; at least I do not have a definite preference for the life in which I know. For me, this test does not clearly indicate that knowledge is valuable in itself. Perhaps your reaction to this test differs. If so, unless we are to engage in a battle of intuitions, the burden is on you to say something more to defend the claim that knowledge is valuable in itself.

I believe that it is now time to give up the search for some value of knowledge over lasting true belief, and tentatively conclude that the main claim is correct: knowledge is no more valuable than lasting true belief. I will now see what conclusions follow from this claim about the value of knowledge.

3. Conclusions

3.1 Skepticism about knowledge not considered dangerous

Skepticism about knowledge is an affront to common sense. No one can know anything about the past? Ridiculous. No one can know anything about the external world? Absurd. No one can know anything at all? Crazy. According to common sense, we know many things; according to common sense, such skeptical claims are obviously false.

A difficulty arises. There are some appealing arguments leading to skeptical conclusions about knowledge. Many philosophers have faced this difficulty, strenuously laboring to find flaws in skeptical arguments about knowledge.[11] But we should pause to ask whether such effort is necessary.

After all, there is an easier way out of the difficulty. We might—to consider the extreme case—accept that no one can know anything. If the main claim of this essay is correct then we need not hesitate to accept that no one can know anything; skepticism about knowledge is not intellectually threatening. If knowledge is not lasting true belief, but knowledge is no more valuable than lasting true belief, then even if no one can have knowledge, one can have something just as valuable: lasting true beliefs.

Is this an acceptable response to skepticism about knowledge? I will now argue that it is.

3.1.1 Reasons for

The first reason that this response to skepticism should be accepted is that it fits well with the way people actually respond to skepticism about knowledge. In my experience the typical neophyte philosophy student gets convinced by skeptical arguments about knowledge; the typical student agrees that, strictly speaking she doesn't know anything. But that doesn't bother her, she says, as long as that does not mean that her ordinary beliefs about the world are unreasonable, or should be given up. The typical neophyte philosophy student is often puzzled by philosophers like Barry Stroud who get themselves worked up about skeptical conclusions about knowledge:

> The consequences of accepting Descartes's conclusion as it is meant to be understood are truly disastrous. There is no easy way of accommodating oneself to its profound negative implications. [19, 38]

I don't mean to rely too heavily on the evidence of my own personal experience, but it does seem to me that my experience is not unusual. (Perhaps one day an experimental scientist will do philosophers a favor and get some good data about how non-philosophers respond to skepticism.)

A second reason why this response to skepticism should be accepted is that it is compatible with a straightforward explanation why some skeptical arguments are compelling: some skeptical arguments about knowledge are sound. Those who try to dismantle a skeptical argument have the burden both of explaining why that argument is unsound, and why it appears sound. They try to explain both why we are almost taken in, and why we should not be taken in. The approach I am suggesting is more straightforward.

A third reason why this response to skepticism should be accepted is that other approaches are inadequate. I won't argue this point here, except to note

---

11   [7] and [16] contain recent attempts.

that no approach to skepticism about knowledge is widely accepted (if not to simply ignore skepticism and think about something else).

Further reasons make this approach to skepticism about knowledge appealing. It is simple. It is general, applying to any argument that concludes that no one can (or does) know anything about a certain subject matter. Nonetheless, it is perfectly compatible with sometimes taking the usual approach to a skeptical argument: trying to find a flaw in that argument.

3.1.2 Reasons against

There are objections to this approach to skepticism. But these objections do not show that this approach is inadequate.

One objection is that to accept skepticism about knowledge is an affront to common sense. According to common sense, skepticism about knowledge is obviously false. So it is a mistake to accept skepticism about knowledge. In reply, if this objection is not to be simple intransigence, one needs to see why common sense should carry the day. That a belief is a common sense belief is certainly not, by itself, sufficient reason to reject every argument to the contrary. So-called common sense has failed us in the past. It was once common sense that women are less rational than men. It was once common sense that slavery is morally permissible. Those common sense beliefs have, thankfully, been left in the past. This is not to deny that common sense has weight; it is where we start, after all. But rejecting this approach to skepticism merely by claiming that skepticism about knowledge conflicts with common sense is very weak.

A second objection is that it is not clear that we have lasting true beliefs. Why is it reasonable to believe that we have lasting true beliefs? This objection looks serious. If we cannot have lasting true beliefs, then my main claim leads to an uninteresting conclusion: even if we cannot have knowledge there is something else, just as valuable, that we cannot have either. In reply: we have very good evidence that at least some of our beliefs are both true and lasting. Here is just one example. I believe that I have blue eyes. Every time I look in the mirror I get more evidence that this belief is true; my memory testifies that I have had this belief for a long time.

A third objection is that accepting that you cannot know that p may rationally require you to suspend judgment about p. If, for example, you conclude that you cannot know whether Mars will be colonized in the next 100 years, then, perhaps, you ought to suspend judgment about whether Mars will be colonized in the next 100 years. But if accepting the conclusion of some skeptical argument about knowledge rationally requires you to suspend judgment about some subject matter, then, if you rationally accept that conclusion, you do not have lasting true beliefs about that subject matter. In that case, it would be a hollow victory to say that even if one cannot have knowledge one can have something of equal value—lasting true beliefs. I grant that the approach I have suggested for skepticism about knowledge would be feeble indeed if accepting that no one can have knowledge about some subject matter requires one to suspend judgment about that subject matter. But whether accepting the conclusion of certain skeptical arguments about knowledge rationally requires one to suspend judgment is not clear. I might accept that I can never know what color Stegosauruses were, and still think that I have good reason to continue believing that Stegosauruses were green.

Still, to be clear, the response to skepticism about knowledge I am presenting in this essay only succeeds in cases when accepting the conclusion of a skeptical argument is rationally compatible with having lasting true beliefs about that subject matter. In other cases, a different response to skepticism is needed.[12]

Setting skepticism aside, let me now turn to other lessons to be drawn.

3.2 Knowledge devalued?

The main claim that knowledge is no more valuable than lasting true belief is initially surprising. One might have thought that knowledge has a unique and special value, that knowledge is the worthy goal of laborious effort, that knowledge is to be cherished when attained. If the main claim is correct, then there is something just as valuable as knowledge, which is not knowledge. So there is no special value unique to knowledge alone.

However, it certainly does not follow from the main claim that knowledge is not the worthy goal of laborious effort, or that knowledge is not to be cherished when attained. Rather, if knowledge is the worthy goal of laborious effort, then lasting true belief is too. And if knowledge is to be cherished when attained, then lasting true belief is to be too. The main claim does not devalue knowledge; it reveals that there is something else which is just as valuable.

Still, to the extent that our educational practices and methods of scholarship are aimed at achieving knowledge rather than mere lasting true belief, our practices and methods may need revision. Maybe it is easier to get lasting true beliefs than knowledge; if so, we should give up our attempts to gain knowledge, and turn to lasting true belief activities.

Even so, I doubt that our practices need much revision. First, knowledge is a close cousin of lasting true belief, even if they differ. Assuming that knowledge requires true belief, both require the hard work of getting true belief. That is no mean matter. Second, as pointed out earlier, maybe a good way—perhaps even the best way—to get lasting true beliefs is to seek knowledge. If so, we have seen no reason to give up our knowledge seeking practices.

---

12   I provide such response in [5] where I argue that certain skeptical arguments can be rationally
      ignored because suspension of judgment can undermine rational action.

4. Final remarks

The main claim I have defended in this essay is that knowledge is no more valuable than lasting true belief. This defense assumed that the believer is weakly rational. I drew two conclusions from the main claim: (1) skepticism about knowledge is harmless as long as one can have lasting true beliefs; (2) knowledge is not devalued and there is no need to give up current knowledge gathering practices and methods.

Finally, some questions for further study include: Is the assumption of weak rationality indeed justified? Is knowledge valuable in itself? Is lasting true belief something we can really have even if we cannot have knowledge?

References

[1] Edward Craig. *Knowledge and the State of Nature: An Essay in Conceptual Synthesis.* Oxford University Press, Oxford, 1990.

[2] Michael R. DePaul. Value monism in epistemology. In Matthias Steup, editor, *Knowledge, Truth, and Duty*, pages 170–183. Oxford University Press, Oxford, 2001.

[3] Alvin Goldman. What is justified belief? In George S. Pappas, editor, *Justification and Knowledge*, pages 1–23. D. Reidel, Dordrecht, 1979.

[4] Sally Haslanger. What is knowledge and what ought it to be. *Philosophical Perspectives*, 13:459–480, 1999.

[5] Patrick Hawley. A practical response to skepticism. Ms., 2006.

[6] Ward E. Jones. Why do we value knowledge? *American Philosophical Quarterly*, 34(4): 423–437, 1997.

[7] Peter Klein. Skepticism. http://plato.stanford.edu/archives/fall2006/entries/skepticism/, 2005.

[8] Christine Korsgaard. Two distinctions in goodness. *Philosophical Review*, 92:169–195, 1983.

[9] Jonathan Kvanvig. Why should inquiring minds want to know? *The Monist*, 81(3):426–451, 1998.

[10] Jonathan Kvanvig. *The Value of Knowledge and the Pursuit of Understanding.* Cambridge University Press, Cambridge, 2003.

[11] Rae Langton. Values, conditioned and conferred. Ms., 2003.

[12] Robert Nozick. *Philosophical Explanations.* Harvard University Press, Cambridge, Massachusetts, 1981.

[13] Alvin Plantinga. *Warrant and Proper Function.* Oxford University Press, New York, 1993.

[14] Plato. *Meno.* W. R. M. Lamb, translator, Loeb Classical Library, volume 165, Harvard University Press, Cambridge, MA, 1924.

[15] Duncan Pritchard. Recent work on epistemic value. Ms., 2006.

[16] James Pryor. The skeptic and the dogmatist. *Noûs*, 34:517–549, 2000.

[17] Wayne D. Riggs. Beyond truth and falsehood: The real value of knowing that p. *Philosophical Studies*, 107:87–108, 2002.

[18] Wayne D. Riggs. Reliability and the value of knowledge. *Philosophy and Phenomenological Research*, 64(1):79–96, 2002.

[19] Barry Stroud. *The Significance of Philosophical Skepticism.* Oxford University Press, Oxford, 1984.

[20] Timothy Williamson. *Knowledge and its Limits.* Oxford University Press, Oxford, 2000.

[21] Linda T. Zagzebski. *Virtues of the Mind: An Inquiry into the Nature of Virtue and the Ethical Foundations of Knowledge.* Cambridge University, Cambridge, 1996.

Jeu-Jenq Yuann

A Naturalistic Approach to Scientific Methodology:
A Comparative Study of O. Neurath and P. Feyerabend

National Taiwan University, Taiwan, e-mail: jjyuann@ntu.edu.tw

1. Introduction

This paper presents an examination of the development of a naturalized philosophy of science that is both historical and methodological. Historically, I attempt to show that Feyerabend developed further the naturalistic theses of Neurath. Methodologically, I intend to present the growth of scientific knowledge in general while taking into account Feyerabend's 'pragmatic theory of observation'.

I should admit right in the beginning that naturalistic philosophy of science shares problems with naturalistic epistemology. As Philip Kitcher says, naturalistic epistemologies confront a range of traditional questions: "What is knowledge? What kinds of knowledge (if any) are possible? What methods should we use for attaining knowledge, or, at least, for improving the epistemic qualities of our beliefs? Because the sciences appear to be the shining exemplars of human knowledge, pursuit of these questions leads easily into the philosophy of science. Naturalistic philosophy of science emerges from the attempt to understand the growth of scientific knowledge."[1] The emergence of the naturalistic philosophy of science from within the naturalistic epistemology, the naturalization of knowledge in general and of scientific knowledge in particular that Kitcher discusses here, is, I argue, an outcome of a process that stems from the Vienna Circle. It originated from the debates about protocol sentences that took place during the heyday of logical positivism.

Those who know the fate of logical positivism will find this rather ironic. My historical presentation conflicts with the stereotypical image of logical positivism as being ousted by the naturalistic approach generally associated with names of post-positivists such as W. V. Quine or T. S. Kuhn. My methodological presentation conflicts with the stereotypical image of another allegedly anti-positivist, Feyerabend, known for his general theme "Against Method". I will argue that these images are misleading. They obliterate the historical links between developments then and now within and beyond logical positivism.

---

[1] P. Kitcher, "The Naturalists Return" in *The Philosophical Review*, 100: 56.

They likewise obliterate the significant methodological contribution of logical positivism that Feyerabend repeatedly claimed on their behalf.

For these reasons, an image of logical positivism beyond that of R. Carnap's *Aufbau* is presented in this paper.[2] I include the debates on 'protocol sentences' in the Vienna Circle mainly by Neurath and their continuation by Feyerabend as indispensable parts of the philosophical movement. More importantly, the movement should be characterized as a methodological trend of naturalistic philosophy of science.

2. The Resuscitation of the Vienna Circle

The history begins with the 'protocol sentence debates' in the Vienna Circle. Misunderstandings arise from the perceived and misleading view that there was a unanimous stand in the Circle. Victor Kraft, in an interview, while stressing the heterogeneity and dynamism in the Circle, says: "The Vienna Circle was so lively that it always continued its development, so much so that it cannot be reduced to one determinate doctrine".[3] The significance of Kraft's observation is echoed by many. R. Haller talks about the diversity of stands during the Circle, making the distinction between the early (consisting mainly of P. Frank, H. Hahn, and O. Neurath) and later (around M. Schlick) Vienna Circle.[4] Uebel talks about the 'right-wing' and 'left-wing' existing in the 'protocol sentence

---

2   The employment of 'logical positivism' might appear misleading as the title is used to refer to the philosophical movement flourished in Vienna in the 1920s and early 1930s. Then, the movement's epitome was Carnap's *The Logical Structure of the World*, trans. By R. A. George (Berkeley: University of California Press, 1967). According to some, the movement was soon replaced in the second half of the twentieth century by 'logical empiricism' (See W. Solmon, "Logical Empiricism" in *A Companion to the Philosophy of Science*, W. H. Newton-Smith ed. (Oxford: Blackwell, 2000), pp. 233–4.). However, we hold that, on the one hand, the distinction of 'logical positivism' and 'logical empiricism' is never a clear-cut one (sometimes these terms are even used interchangeably) and on the other, the employment of 'logical positivism' in this paper contains a purpose of demonstrating the fact that "logical positivism and the Vienna Circle are almost synonymous", says C. Ray in "Logical Positivism" in *A Companion to the Philosophy of Science*, W. H. Newton-Smith ed. (Oxford: Blackwell, 2000), p. 243). Due to this fact, we prefer the term 'logical positivism' to the other in order to fully demonstrate that an essential part of our argument lies in the historical link between the Vienna Circle and the debates derived from the then flourished 'logical positivism'.

3   V. Kraft, "Gespräch mit Viktor Kraft" in *Conceptus*, 21:17 (The English translation is an excerpt from F. Stadler, *The Vienna Circle* (Wien: Springer, 2001), p. 222).

4   R. Haller, "The First Vienna circle" in T. E. Uebel (ed.), *Rediscovering the Forgotten Vienna Circle* (Dordrecht: Kluwer, 1991), pp. 95–108.

debate' by referring respectively to Schlick and Neurath.[5] Uebel's description might follow the words of Tscha Hung, the only Chinese member of the Circle, who said in an interview:

> At that time, there were only discussions about the nature of the protocol sentences and the concept of affirmation, that is, about the foundation of knowledge, and about physicalism and unified science, etc. In these discussions it appeared to me that Schlick and Waismann stood on one side and Carnap, Neurath and Hahn on the other. Occasionally Frank came from Prague to take part in the discussions. What he contributed did not express agreement with Schlick's, even less with Waismann's views.[6]

Tscha Hung clearly categorizes all members of the 'first Circle' to a group which held opposite opinions concerning the foundation of knowledge from that of Schlick, the commonly deemed leader of the Circle. Then, he says in his "Several Problems Concerning Logical Empiricism" that: "There were two groups of opinions discussed fiercely in the Circle on the 'foundation of knowledge'. These discussions are called the 'Right wing' (represented mainly by Schlick and Waismann) and 'Left wing' (represented mainly by Neurath, Hahn, Frank, and Carnap) of the Vienna Circle."[7] Regardless of the 'political implications'[8] of the two wings in the Circle, we must remain aware of the conflicts between Neurath and Schlick in the debates. Unfortunately, the divided view of the Circle is ignored by the commonly and long cherished view that the Circle represented a rigid and predetermined view of verifiability.

This view, though popular, is wrong. Its mistakes consist not only in portraying a unanimous view, but also in undermining the significance of the above-mentioned conflict. How could a group of splendid philosophers become holders of such a dogmatic view unanimously? For the answer to this question, we must turn to A. Ayer's contribution. He was, as is well-known, the pioneer

---

5   T. E. Uebel, *Overcoming Logical Positivism from Within* (Amsterdam: Rodopi, 1992), especially chapter three, " Stage One, Stage Right: Schlick's Anti-Formalist Challenge" and chapter four, "Stage One, Stage Left: Neurath's Naturalistic Challenge".

6   Tscha Hung, "Interview mit Professor Tscha Hung" in *Conceptus* 53/54, pp. 7–17 (The English translation is an excerpt from F. Stadler, *The Vienna Circle* (Wien: Springer, 2001), p. 226).

7   Tscha Hung, "Several Problems Concerning Logical Empiricism" in *Journal of New Asian College*, 9: 1 (the paper is in Chinese and the English translation is mine).

8   It would not be an accident to consider the two wings of the Vienna Circle by referring to the political terminologies. The Circle, aside from its epistemological and methodological content, is also a political movement in line "with some of the left social movements of its time", according to Wartofsky. Whereas, Schlick "strongly disagrees with this perspective". See M. Wartofsky, "Positivism and Politics: The Vienna Circle as a Social Movement" in S. Sarkar, *The Legacy of the Vienna Circle: Modern Appraisals* (New York: Garland, 1996), pp. 53–75.

of logical positivism in England,[9] and responsible for promoting the idea of verifiability. I. Lakatos says this in this respect:

> In the Circle itself you will never get such a marvelous summary of its obviously false doctrines which received their psychological inauguration in Ayer's *Language, Truth and Logic.* For instance, Ayer dared to claim that ethical statements cannot be verified: they are meaningless, unless perhaps you think that they are poetry because they are not cognitively meaningful. All this brushing aside of all old philosophical problems as sheer meaningless nonsense you will find nowhere else but in Ayer's book (which contains his criterion of verifiability). Of course, it was very successful.[10]

Lakatos might be too harsh in blaming Ayer's promotion of the criterion of verifiability, but he would not disagree with its success. However, the 'success' would not mean much, if the criterion remained unclear. Unfortunately, this was precisely what Hacking ironically pointed out: "The success of the verification principle is amazing, for, as we shall see, no one has succeeded in stating it!"[11] We nowadays can fairly judge that 'the successful story' was a futile effort since Ayer could never clearly offer an explicit principle on the basis of which the identity between being verified and being meaningful can thus be established.

Fortunately, remarkable and intensive researches contributed to a more profound study of the Vienna Circle mainly documented in the last decade of the Twentieth Century. We thus appreciate a thriving force trying assiduously to correct and then to recover the accurate picture of the Circle.[12] It would not be

---

9   V. Kraft, *The Vienna Circle* (Westport, Connecticut: Greenwood, 1953), p. 9. Ray says this even more explicitly: "A. J. Ayer visited Vienna in 1933, revealing his excitement in a letter to I. Berlin ... Ayer returned to England to write the enormously influential *Language, Truth and Logic,* the first edition of which was published in 1936" (*op. cit.,* p. 244).

10   I. Lakatos, "Lectures on Scientific Method" in *For and Against Method,* M. Motterlini ed. (Chicago: The University of Chicago Press, 1999), p. 54.

11   I. Hacking, *Why does Language Matter to Philosophy?* (Cambridge: Cambridge University Press, 975), p. 95.

12   There are undoubtedly many crucial works on this regard. I can merely mark those available within my very limited extent of knowledge. I have in mind: Cartwright, N., Cat, J., Fleck, L. & Uebel, T. [1996]: *Otto Neurath: Philosophy between Science and Politics,* Cambridge, Cambridge University Press; S. Sarkar: [1996]: *The Legacy of the Vienna Circle: Modern Appraisals,* New York: Garland; Cirera, R. [1994]: *Carnap and the Vienna Circle,* Amsterdam/Atlanta, GA. Rodopi; Giere, R. & Richardson, A. (eds.) [1996]: *Origins of Logical Empiricism,* Minneapolis, University of Minnesota Press; Oberdan, T. [1993a]: *Protocols, Truth, Convention,* Amsterdam/Atlanta, GA., Rodopi; Rescher, N. (ed.) [1985]: *The Heritage of Logical Positivism,* Lanham, MD, University Press of America; Richardson, A. [1998]: *Carnap's Construction of the World,* Cambridge, Cambridge University Press; Rungaldier, E. [1984]: *Carnap's Early Conventionalism,* Amsterdam/Atlanta, GA. Rodopi; Salmon, W. & Wolters, G. (eds.) [1993]: *Logic, Language and the Structure of Scientific Theories,* Pittsburgh, University of Pittsburgh Press; Stadler, F. [1993]: *Scientific Philosophy: Origins and Developments, Dordrecht, Kluwer;* Uebel, T. [1991]: *Rediscovering the Forgotten Vienna Circle,* Dordrecht, Kluwer; Uebel, T. [1992a]: *Overcoming Logical Positivism from Within,* Amsterdam/Atlanta, GA., Rodopi. The most direct reaction in this regard is that of Friedman, M. [1999]: *Rediscovering Logical Positivism,* Cambridge, Cambridge University Press.

an overstatement to say that the refurbished image of the Vienna Circle has essentially a great deal to do with the 'rediscovering' of Neurath's philosophy. The 'rediscovered' image thus balances the erstwhile misleading impression and hence conveys the idea that a more accurate understanding of the Vienna Circle as well as of logical positivism would not be possible unless the balanced view (referring to the divided views in the Circle) is taken into a full account. As a matter of fact, this division and its consequences were actually commented on by Carnap himself referring to the 'protocol sentence debates' taking place in the Circle. With a reference to 'absolutism', Carnap appeared to show his sympathy with the 'minority' (mainly represented by Neurath's view) in the debates.

> There is also a residue of this idealistic absolutism in positivism; in the logical positivism of our circle—in the writings on the logic of science (theory of knowledge) of Wittgenstein, Schlick, Carnap published up to now—it takes the refined form of an absolutism of the ur-sentence ('elementary sentences', 'atomic sentences'). Neurath has been the first to turn decisively against this absolutism, in that he rejected the unrevisability of protocol sentences. From other starting points Popper succeeded a step further: in his testing procedure there is no last sentence; his system describes therefore the most radical elimination of absolutism.[13]

Carnap's words here explicitly manifest that in these debates concerning 'the foundation of knowledge', Neurath's position was fundamentally different from the 'right wing' represented then mainly by Wittgenstein, Schlick and Waismann. Once Schlick's ideas of verifiability had been successfully introduced into the English-speaking world by Ayer, we should not be surprised to learn that Schlick became well known as the 'major' representative of the Circle. At the same time, Neurath's resistant but 'less absolutistic' view was unfortunately eclipsed. Actually, the repercussions took place even during the debates as Kraft recorded Carnap's swing from the 'right' to the 'left' wing. He says,

> Schlick considered the empirical statement of an observation, an assertion, as absolutely valid. The subject of the experience is immediately aware of it as true.... Its assertion is the only statement about reality which is not hypothetical. For this reason, Schlick declared it to be the foundation of knowledge ... Neurath fought against this view. Protocol sentences are no more original than other statements; like others they can be corrected. They, too, are only *hypothetical*. Carnap later accepted Neurath's view ... Therefore there are no statements about facts which are indubitably true. There is no such thing as final verification, and therefore no absolute foundation for the knowledge of nature.[14]

Kraft's remarks delve deep into an entirely new approach to the nature of knowledge from Neurath's point of view. As a matter of fact, Neurath's opposition against Schlick is more than a conflict between two stands. We all now realize that what Neurath did at that point was something of valuable and original

---

13   R. Carnap, "On Protocol Sentences", *Noũs* 21 (1987), p. 469 (translated by R. Creath & R. Nollan from "Über Protokollsätze", Erkenntnis Bd 3, H. 2–3 (1932), pp. 215–228).

14   Kraft, V. "Popper and the Vienna Circle" in Paul A. Schilpp (ed.), *The Philosophy of Karl Popper* (La Salle, Il.: Open court, 1974), p. 193.

nature. The value amounts to nothing less than an epistemological revolution—
I am using the term in its traditional sense since the time of R. Descartes. Indeed,
this type of 'knowledge without foundation' sheds light on a 'new epistemology'
which is best described by Quine in his reputed essay on 'epistemology naturalized'.[15] This also constitutes an essential part of the reason why Neurath is
deemed to be someone who "anticipated the programme of naturalized epistemology already at the time of the Vienna Circle".[16] All this will be further
examined in the next section.

3. Neurath, the naturalistic epistemologist

Though Neurath might not have been in full awareness of the impact of his
'anti-philosophy',[17] what he actually did was open up a 'new philosophy', or
more precisely, a 'new epistemology'. Neurath talked about this 'new' trend by
cutting himself away from the tradition of epistemology dated back at least to
the very beginning of its development.

> There is no way to establish fully secured, neat protocol statements as starting points of the sci-
> ences. There is no *tabula rasa*. We are like sailors who have to rebuild their ship on the open sea,
> without ever being able to dismantle it in dry-dock and reconstruct it from the best components.
> Only metaphysics can disappear without trace. Imprecise 'verbal clusters' [*Ballungen*] are
> somehow always part of the ship. If imprecision is diminished at one place, it may well re-appear
> at another place to a stronger degree (Neurath, 1983: 92).

This is the famous metaphor of the 'raft' or 'boat' expounded in his paper
"Protocol Statements".[18] In it, Neurath deemed the traditional epistemology
something hardly different from metaphysics. By referring to this metaphor,
Neurath intentionally and cautiously kept himself from falling into metaphysics,
which, for him, is totally negative. I strongly believe that Neurath's employment
of this metaphor is not only significant but also necessary. Keeping away from
the epistemological tradition is significant, yet the employment of a metaphor
is necessary for opposing the strict requirement of accuracy and clarity pervasive
in the tradition.

Having taken stand against traditional epistemology, Neurath was probably
not in full notice of the likely consequence of his 'revolutionary measure'. It was

---

15 W. V. O. Quine, "Epistemology Naturalized" in *Ontological Relativity & Other Essays*
    (New York: Columbia University Press, 1969), pp. 69–90. Underneath abbreviated as 'EN'.
16 T. Uebel, "Neurath's Programme for Naturalistic Epistemology" in *Studies in History and
    Philosophy of Science*, **22**, p. 623. Underneath abbreviated as 'NPN'.
17 O. Neurath, *Philosophical Papers 1913–1946* (Dordrecht: D. Reidel, 1983), p. 48.
18 For details of a full exposition of Neurath's boat, please refer to Cartwright, N., Cat, J.,
    Fleck, L. & Uebel, T., "Part II: Neurath's Boat" in *Otto Neurath: Philosophy between
    Science and Politics* (Cambridge: Cambridge University Press, 1996), pp. 89–166.

only afterwards, and notably in Quine's adoption of it that Neurath's metaphor gradually turned into "an emblem of *naturalism*, the metaphilosophical view that denies the autonomy of philosophy."[19] Quine's measure, though helpful undoubtedly in making known Neurath's 'philosophy', was by all means a 'mixed blessing'.[20]

Quine argues in his paper 'Epistemology Naturalized' that Neurath contributed an 'attitude' to the formation of the naturalized epistemology (EN 84). Quine's appreciation of Neurath's contribution is limited within an 'anti-foundationalist epistemology'. To this, Quine draws a comparison between two kinds of epistemologies: 'the old epistemology' and 'its new setting' (EN 82). The distinction lies in their attitude towards natural science in general and its relationship towards sense data in particular. Quine says,

> In the old epistemological context the conscious form had priority, for we were out to justify our knowledge of the external world by rational reconstruction, and that demands awareness. Awareness ceased to be demanded when we gave up trying to justify our knowledge of the external world by rational reconstruction. What to count as observation now can be settled in terms of the stimulation of sensory receptors, let consciousness fall where it may (EN 84).

What is crucial to us is the fact that for Quine, the new epistemology no longer appeals to rational justification and hence the need for foundation dissolves too. Quine nonetheless still emphasizes: 'This attitude (the new epistemology) is indeed one that Neurath was already urging in Vienna Circle days, with his parable of the mariner who has to rebuild his boat while staying afloat in it" (EN 84). What Quine says here refers to the idea that the utterance of sense data does not need justification in order to form a 'protocol sentence'. Though the idea is by all means crucial to the formation of naturalized epistemology, the recommendation of Neurath by Quine in the formation stops here too. There is no full programme of 'naturalized epistemology' in Neurath. What Neurath did in the 'protocol sentence debates' appeared to Quine as an 'attitude' or an 'urge' leading to the realization that "there seemed to be no objective way of settling the matter: no way of making real sense of the question (EN 85)". In brief, Neurath did not offer a full programme of 'naturalized epistemology'. However, T. Uebel sees the matter all together different from Quine.

According to Uebel, Neurath's naturalistic epistemology "not only constituted a precursor, but also an alternative to Quine's [naturalized epistemology]".[21] A full exposition of Neurath's programme has a great deal to do with the two possibilities of interpreting 'Neurath's boat': one austere, the other rich. Both

---

19   Ibid, p. 90.

20   Since Quine's 'naturalizing measure' regarding Neurath, there has been a gradual unraveling of Neurath's naturalism. Among such contributions those dealing most directly with this theme are several publications of T. Uebel included in this paper.

21   T. Uebel, *Overcoming Logical Positivism from Within* (Amsterdam/Atlanta, GA.: Rodopi, 1992), p. 3.

interpretations endorse the principle that no possibility allowed to repair defi-
ciencies in the body of scientific knowledge beyond the practice of science, yet
they disagree regarding what science is. The 'austere interpretation' adopts a
restriction of the concept of science by insisting that whatever cannot meet the
individuation conditions of physical kinds must be expelled from the range of
science. However, the 'rich interpretation' includes all human endeavors serving
as replacement planks and beams to keep the ship of science afloat, provided
all assertions which are characteristics of these various human endeavors be
empirically testable. We can see that their difference can be demonstrated by
taking the difference between natural and social sciences into account as follows.

> Given the austere reading, Neurath's Boat means that natural science explains (knowledge of)
> natural science... Given the rich reading, Neurath's Boat means that natural and social science
> explains (knowledge of) natural and social science.[22]

With this distinction in mind, Uebel considers that Neurath follows a 'programme
of naturalistic epistemology' which tolerates more empirical data than that of
Quine's. Suffice to say that the idea of toleration here sheds light directly on
the idea of "knowledge as an instrument of emancipation".[23] Uebel hence attempts
to reveal that Neurath's programme is set to uphold the principle of exploring
all ideas for the pursuit of knowledge. Uebel carries out his attempt by dividing
Neurath's programme into two parts: one part takes care of the adequacy of
formulating Neurath's ideas in conformity with that of the naturalistic epistemology, while the other part manifests what is lacking in Quine's programme and
is to be found in Neurath's.

3.1 Neurath's Programme of Naturalistic Epistemology

In "Neurath's Programme for Naturalistic Epistemology", Uebel criticizes first
Quine's reading of Neurath's effort in the Vienna Circle debates as merely an
'attitude' rather than a 'full programme' of 'naturalistic epistemology'. According
to Uebel, Quine simply thought that all Neurath did was something slightly
more than provide 'an anti-foundationalist position of a coherentist strategy of
justification' (NPN 638). Its real function to Quine in the endeavor of rejecting
the traditional epistemology was the offer of a 'parable of the boat'. What
Uebel does to Neurath is to "adopt as a distinctive criterion of naturalistic epistemology a point of methodology" (NPN 624). His reason is: "it seems that the
best way of framing its working definition is not in terms of a particular doctrine,
but in how it squares off against the way traditional epistemology is done"
(NPN 624). Clearly, what is at stake here is a methodological concern: how to

---

22   Ibid.
23   Ibid.

hold scientific knowledge claims while rejecting the traditional epistemology. 'Knowledge without foundation' is merely a starting point, but that would not be sufficient to claim scientific knowledge unless further conditions relating to the claims are incorporated into a full programme of new epistemology. This would be a programme of naturalistic epistemology if four conditions proposed by Uebel are incorporated into a full account.

There are four such conditions. They are offered here by Uebel in a somewhat rational sequence reflecting the way traditional epistemology is replaced by its naturalistic version. The sequence goes as follows: 1) Naturalism requires that the *practice of science* be attended to; 2) The 'philosophical' moral of naturalism is that the rationality of science can be shown only by the practices of science, or *from inside* of science; 3) 'Explaining science from within' means that the *epistemological notions employed be explicable in terms of science.* That is to say, epistemological notions should be applicable to and successful in the explanation of processes we antecedently deem natural, namely, processes occurring in the spatio-temporal world; 4) It is not the justification of a claim to truth, but the justification of the *acceptance* of a knowledge claim that is to be provided. The primacy of practice thus becomes *the primacy of theory acceptance.* Naturally the conditions can be further extended, but Uebel thinks that they are sufficient for offering a 'minimalist conception of a consistent naturalism' (NPN 626).

Then, Uebel begins his strategy of proving that these four conditions are all included by Neurath in his 'hidden programme of naturalistic epistemology'. For this purpose, he briefly formulates the previous four conditions as 1) the primacy of practice claim; 2) the replacement (of traditional epistemology) thesis; 3) the explanatory austerity (or the non-justificatory explanation) demand; 4) the primacy of theory acceptance. Obviously, the difficulties lie in the fact that this is not a 'programme' directly set forth by Neurath himself. With this challenge in mind, Uebel nicely selects the banner of 'anti-metaphysics' as the beginning of his arguments. He says as follows.

> Whatever investigation there *may remain* to be pursued as part of the theory of knowledge would have to be such that it finds its place in the totality of sciences, as an *empirical* investigation alongside others (with all the tools provided by formal science). Neurath recognized that the concepts and statements employed by a de-metaphysicalized epistemology must accordingly be capable of explications in scientific terms (NPN 630).

In this paragraph, all four conditions are present. 1) 'The primacy of practice' is represented by the requirement that all investigations are conducted within the extent of science alone. 2. 'The replacement thesis' is characterized by the idea that the inquiry of science becomes an interdisciplinary enterprise in which all empirical investigations alongside others are included. 3. 'The non-justificatory demand' becomes manifest whenever the idea of 'de-metaphysicalization' appears to show the futility of a rigorous and foundational justification. 4. 'The stand of theory acceptance' is consolidated by the combination of all three previous conditions in which a programme of naturalistic epistemology is unveiled by the "austere explanation of the practice of theory acceptance" (NPN 633). However, despite these explanations, Uebel's attribution of a naturalistic epistemology programme to Neurath's position is still not sufficient unless the following question is addressed in the first place: Was Neurath concerned about what would be the pursuit of knowledge after the adoption of an anti-foundationalist position? If Neurath's answer had been negative, then he would not like to see a programme of naturalistic epistemology deriving from his ideas. For in this case, he would not talk about 'truth' of any kind. This is not likely to be the case because Neurath did talk about what he meant by the phrase 'claiming scientific truth', though indirectly.

> 'Induction' that leads to laws is a matter of 'decision', it cannot be deduced. The attempts to give 'induction' a logical foundation are therefore bound to fail. If a statement is made, it is to be confronted with the totality of existing statements. If it agrees with them, it is joined to them; if it does not agree, it is called 'untrue' and rejected; or the existing complex of statements of science is modified so that the new statement can be incorporated; the latter decision is mostly taken with hesitation. *There can be no other concept of 'truth' for science.*[24]

What Neurath says here appears to be pretty similar to that of Popper's 'falsicationism', especially the criticism against the formation of 'inductive assertions'. Indeed, this is precisely what Uebel says in order to fortify Neurath's thesis having a 'normative nature' rather than advancing a purely 'descriptive' exposition of scientific practices. Uebel says: "to encourage a critical attitude was precisely Neurath's intention in promoting the 'scientific world-conception' (NPN 636). Methodologically speaking, this 'attitude' is truly the one which would substantiate not only a full programme of naturalistic epistemology, but also a crucial difference between Neurath's programme from that of Quine's. This difference consists in the addition of two more conditions which are attributed to Neurath by Uebel.

According to Uebel, Neurath's programme does not limit itself within the realm of methodological 'canons'. The four conditions convey further the point that naturalizing epistemology must be understood as being concerned with the human practice of theory acceptance. Doing this would necessarily lead ahead towards a situation in which general determinants of human practices, either historical or sociological, have to be taken into account in order to make the acceptance of any theory accountable. For this reason, Uebel says, Neurath's naturalistic epistemology should include the fifth condition, i.e., 'extra-cognitive factors in theory acceptance' (NPN 634). To Neurath, this approach has to be

---

24   O. Neurath, *Philosophical Papers 1913–1946* (Dordrecht: d. Reidel, 1983), p. 53.

taken as a matter of course. He made all this clear in his concluding paragraph of the Vienna Circle's 'Manifesto':

> We witness the spirit of the scientific world-conception penetrating in growing measure the forms of personal and public life, in education, in upbringing, architecture and the shaping of economic and social life according to rational principles. *The scientific world-conception serves life, and life receives it.*[25]

This is a direct proof demonstrating that science would include anything considered empirically available and adequate into its inquiry. Far more than what Quine says that the naturalistic epistemology is about to be reduced to 'a chapter of psychology' (EN 260), Neurath's programme probably relies more on the extra-cognitive elements than the intra-cognitive ones. With the fifth condition we move to the sixth condition formulated by Uebel, mainly concerned with 'the normativity of scientific claims'.

3.2 The Normativity of Scientific Claims

Not taking the normativity of scientific claims as an indispensable condition for a naturalistic epistemology, the inclusion of extra-cognitive elements would bring about a position of relativized description. This position would be a challenge to Neurath's whole effort since it would make it blindly permissive to everything. For this challenge, Uebel in another paper, deals specifically with the problem concerning how a 'protocol statement' exerts its probative force.[26] For the solution of this problem, Uebel equips protocol statements with two distinct conditions: the formal conditions and the pragmatic condition. The formal conditions refer to the form of protocols (NPS 591), whereas the pragmatic condition refers to a decision of accepting valid protocols as 'binding' (NPS 594). The formal conditions contain four distinguishable parts: 'protocol', 'thought', 'stimulation state', and 'fact'. Uebel puts these four parts together in a 'protocol form' by referring to different stages of forming a protocol from various expressions of empirical content:

> "protocol (thought [stimulation state{'fact'}])" (NPS 590–1).

An example offered by Uebel concerning the structure of protocol statement is this:

> (Abbé Domenico Tata's protocol in 1756 [Prince of Tarsia's Calabrian shepherds' speech-thinking in 1755 {there were stones falling from the sky seen by the prince of Tarsia's Calabrian shepherds in 1755}]) (NPS 605).

---

25   O. Neurath, 'The Scientific Conception of the World: The Vienna Circle' in *Empiricism and Sociology*, M. Neurath & R. Cohen eds. (Dordrecht: D. Reidel, 1973), pp. 317–8.

26   T. Uebel, "Neurath's Protocol Statements: Naturalistic Theory of Data and Pragmatic Theory of Theory Acceptance" in *Philosophy of Science*, 60: 587–607. Underneath abbreviated as 'NPS'.

The hypothetical theory which the protocol statement tests is this one: "All meteorites are fallen meteors" (NPS 605). Nevertheless, due to the fact that in the mid of the 18th century, meteors were widely observed as lightening stones (though unexplained) in the sky, and that the meteorites falling on the ground were much less observed by scientists, the previous statement failed to be considered a protocol merely because the scientific community then would not accept it as one. Note here also that the decision made by the scientific community was not a formal one which concerns only the validity of a protocol statement, but a pragmatic one which concerns whether the valid protocol statement was 'binding'. Uebel further explains what he means by 'binding' here.

> Let us call a valid protocol that we are willing to use in theory testing a 'binding' protocol statement. A valid protocol is considered binding, (a) if a test statement (derived from a theory) is implied by the content sentence of the protocol and the protocol is thus conceived as a *confirming* instance of that theory, or (b) if the test statement is incompatible with the content sentence of the protocol and the protocol is conceived as a *disconfirming* instance of that theory. A valid protocol statement that we are not willing to use in theory testing we call 'nonbinding'. A protocol is nonbinding if it is *not conceived as* a confirming or disconfirming instance of that theory, irrespective of whether the test statement (derived from a theory) is implied by or incompatible with the content sentence of the protocol. In other words, when a protocol is considered binding, we are bound to change the theory to suit the protocol (NPS 594).

The pragmatic condition concerns if a protocol statement is 'binding' in the sense that the statement becomes a 'scientifically respectable assertion', whether confirming or disconfirming. The idea of 'binding' therefore receives its 'normative' status in the sense that it is used "to prevent the unbounded accumulation of anomalies by the emergence of rival theories" (NPS 602). This means that not just any observation statement would be accepted 'scientifically'. There are statements which are 'non-scientific' for failing to be relevant with the empirical basis, which is the major characteristic of science. However, whether a statement is considered to be binding is not a part of the formal conditions; it is decided pragmatically. Apparently a pragmatic decision can accept any statement as a protocol statement depending on the external circumstances. Yet, due to Neurath's distinction added to the formal conditions, he actually adopted a 'normative' stand by rejecting decisions made on the institutionalized basis, and endorsing scientifically sound statements. The scientific soundness refers to the empirical relevance of the facts portrayed in these statements. Uebel explains this stand as follows.

> Neurath's theory rightly neglects this rejection of the probative force of observation statements made as turning on considerations conceptualized under [the pragmatic] condition ... The interest of this historical example (the meteorites example) then lies in showing the following. Rather than sweep all rejections of data or their probative force under one undifferentiated pragmatic rug, Neurath's theory considers as pragmatic in the relevant sense only those decisions about the probative force of data that are made after clearly specifiable and justifiable evidential conditions concerning their validity as data have been deemed met. Neurath's pragmatic approach to theory acceptance is nondogmatic but not unduly permissive (NPS 605).

Only the statements in which 'specifiable and justifiable' evidential conditions are deemed met would be considered 'binding'. Though the consideration itself is pragmatic, the decisions are not permissive in including everything. Evidential conditions referring to the 'facts' of the protocols, need to be specifiable and justifiable in order to prevail. With this additional requirement of 'normative' part, Neurath's programme of naturalistic epistemology is thus a complete one. In what follows, we will further explain this programme by following its line of development from the Vienna Circle up to its full realization in P. Feyerabend's 'pragmatic theory of observation'.

4. Feyerabend, the Pragmatic Naturalist of Observation

The naturalistic programme of Neurath arranged under Uebel's formulation demonstrates its focus on an empirical point: 'the fact'. 'The falling of meteorites on the ground' is the 'observing fact' with which we say what science is. Science is thus a socially institutionalized activity without being blindly permissive, or dogmatic. However, while appreciating Uebel's formulation, we are aware of a fact that he refers to a 'negative way' of setting the normative form such as Neurath's rejection of the denial of the probative force of observation statements made under pragmatic condition (NPS 605). Nevertheless, this way of including statements into the realm of science does not show precisely to what extent some observation statements should be excluded from the territory of 'scientifically respectable assertions', namely protocols. We have to admit that this 'negative way' clearly shows the 'tolerant' part of Neurath's programme, but fails to confront the challenge of relativism. With Uebel's formulation, Neurath remains somewhat an 'epistemological anarchist' (NPS 601) and hence adopts the doctrine of 'anything goes' (NPS 595). Ironically, the two terms, known for being Feyerabend's, might also be added to Neurath's position retrospectively. It could be even more ironic than anything else to assume that Neurath's full programme of naturalistic epistemology might be realized in Feyerabend's philosophy of science. We attempt to argue for this assumption in the rest of this paper by following three lines of thinking: 1) reviewing the development of protocol sentence debates back to the days of Vienna Circle by taking into account Popper's influence on the Circle; 2) taking Feyerabend's ideas as a similar version of naturalistic methodology of science to that of Neurath's; 3) examining Feyerabend's pragmatic theory of observation to demonstrate the 'normative' nature of his methodology.

4.1 Protocol Sentence Debates in the Vienna Circle

Make no mistake, Neurath would not hold the 'factual condition' as a criterion of selecting the 'binding protocols'. We can see this from his explicit stand that: "Thus *statements are always compared with statements*, certainly not with some 'reality', nor with 'things', as the Vienna Circle also thought up till now."[27] Neurath remains firm on his anti-foundationalist position, rejecting any factual basis serving as a criterion. Once again, this position reiterates his difference from the 'mainstream position' of the Vienna Circle. However, though less reputed then, Neurath's group was by no means a small one in the Circle. This was manifested by Kraft who offered an important clue concerning a hidden link among Carnap, Neurath, Popper and even himself. Kraft said that when Carnap held the absolute validity of protocol sentences, Neurath fought this view by holding strongly that "Protocol sentences are no more original than other statements; like others they can be corrected; they, too, are only *hypothetical*".[28] Kraft continued that, Carnap later accepted this view which was rather obvious for Popper as he held that "it was a necessary consequence that the basic sentences are only hypothetical, for they are statements about objective facts which always include theories" (PVC 193). Therefore, a protocol sentence contains no indubitable truth, but only hypothetical validity. All this is further confirmed by Carnap in his paper of "On Protocol Sentences" in which he put both Neurath and Popper into the camp of anti-absolutism, except admitting that Popper's position is even stronger.[29] To this regard, Kraft highly appreciated Popper's role played in the development of the Circle, comparing him with the role played once by Wittgenstein.

> By the insight into the justification of those results the views within the Vienna Circle underwent a considerable change. Popper replaced Wittgenstein in his influence on the Vienna Circle ... It must be attributed to this influence that a rapid and productive development took place within the Vienna Circle by which a new, fruitful movement in epistemology was introduced (PVC 200).

Even before the formation of the Vienna Circle, Kraft and Popper met each other because of their shared view on anti-inductivism.[30] Concerning the shared views of Kraft and Popper, Feyerabend makes it rather clear on his review of Kraft's *Theory of Knowledge* (*Erkenntnislehre*, Springer-Verlag,

---

27   O. Neurath, *Philosophical Papers 1913–1946* (Dordrecht: d. Reidel, 1983), p. 53.
28   Kraft, V. "Popper and the Vienna Circle" in Paul A. Schilpp (ed.), *The Philosophy of Karl Popper* (La Salle, Il.: Open court, 1974), p. 193. Underneath abbreviated as 'PVC'.
29   Popper personally talks about this period of time while he lectured the Vienna Circle once in 1932. He found indeed that there were oppositions concerning his ideas, but he counted Neurath as a member sitting together with Schlick, the two were then considered to be the leading opponents in the Circle by Tsche Hung. We can only understand Popper's words here as a hostile reaction to Neurath who labeled Popper, "the official opponent of the Vienna Circle". See K. Popper, "Replies to My Critics", p. 970.
30   K. Popper, "Replies to My Critics" in Paul A. Schilpp (ed.), *The Philosophy of Karl Popper* (La Salle, Il.: Open court, 1974), p. 975. This point has been made extremely clear by Tsche Hung in a paper written in Chinese, "An Introduction to V. Kraft's Philosophy" in *Essays on Logical Empiricism* (Taipei: Yuan Lieu, 1990), pp. 79–86.

Vienna, 1960).[31] In this review, Feyerabend discussed the problem of induction which includes the probabilistic theories of Carnap and Reichenbach. The conclusion is that "the step beyond experimental results can be made only with the help of *hypotheses* for which little or no justification is given" (RE 321). Though Kraft developed his ideas independently, these ideas have been commonly associated with the name of K. Popper, according to Feyerabend.

We can say, though the persons concerned might not in full awareness of this, what was agreed by all of them was the 'beginning' of a programme for the naturalistic epistemology. If we are allowed to interpret this by the employment of all materials available to us, we are certain that the development of the programme was continued by the efforts of P. Feyerabend. In an 'appendix' of his *magnum opus (Against Method)*[32], Feyerabend notes that though similar to a tremendous extent to T. Kuhn's ideas, the origin of his ideas was still different. He said: "his approach was historical, while mine was abstract. His source was a history of science changed in accordance with his own new ideas, mine was the written debate about protocol statements in the Vienna Circle and, later on, the live debate in the Kraft Circle, its successor in the early fifties (AM 230)". Feyerabend admitted also that the combination of 'the written debate' of the Vienna Circle and 'the live debate' of the Kraft Circle were the original formation of his idea of incommensurability. Though the detail of this idea is not our concern here, the depiction of Feyerabend relating to the development of this idea manifests a crucial relevance to our topic. He says:

> In my thesis (Vienna 1951—written after two years of extensive discussions in the Kraft Circle and supervised by Professor Victor Kraft of the University of Vienna)[33] I examined the meaning of observational statements. I considered the idea that such statements describe 'what is given' and tried to identify this 'given' ... Phenomenologically what is given consists of the same things which can also exist unobserved—it is not a special kind of object ... The given cannot be isolated by observation ... Following this statement I introduced the assumption that the meaning of observation statements depends on the nature of the objects described and, as this nature depends on the most advanced theories about objects, on the content of these theories... In a word: observation statements are not just theory-*laden* but *fully theoretical* and the distinction between observation statements ('protocol statement' in the terminology of the Vienna Circle) and theoretical statements is a pragmatic distinction, not a semantic distinction ... I started from and returned to ideas that had been developed in the Vienna Circle. Quine whose philosophy shows close connections to the philosophy of the Vienna Circle also used a criterion of observability that is rather similar to mine. (AM 228-9)

---

31   P. Feyerabend, "Review of *Erkenntnislehre* by V. Kraft" in *British Journal for the Philosophy of Science*, 13: 319–323. Underneath abbreviated as 'RE'.

32   P. Feyerabend, *Against Method*, the 2nd edition (London: Verso, 1988). Underneath abbreviated as 'AM'.

33   The thesis later on published in an abbreviated version in English, "An Attempt at a Realistic Interpretation of experience" in P. Feyerabend, *Philosophical Papers Vol. 1* (Cambridge: Cambridge University Press, 1981), pp. 17–43.

From this citation, we can say that nothing can be more obvious than Feyerabend's personal admittance that he is the 'orthodox heir' of the Vienna Circle in general and the Kraft Circle in particular. Though, as Kraft said, the 'new epistemology' belongs to only some members of the Vienna Circle, we have enough reasons to believe that the situation changed entirely in the Kraft Circle. In the later Circle around Kraft, the 'new theory of observability' gets the upper hand as stipulated by Feyerabend.

> The new theory of observability which results from the described procedure (and *which was formulated very clearly in the early thirties by Popper, Carnap and Neurath* [my italics]) may be called the *pragmatic theory of observation*. The choice between the pragmatic theory and the semantic theory is of course purely a matter of convention … If we want to be able to derive eternal laws from facts of observation, then the semantic theory will most certainly be a Splendid Thing. However, if it is our intention not to except any part of our knowledge from revision, then we shall have to choose the pragmatic theory.[34]

We see from this that, far from being a so-called post-positivist, Feyerabend holds a view which leans towards the 'naturalistic side' of the Vienna circle. In fact, we would even affirm that Feyerabend is fundamentally different from all his contemporary post-positivists by descending directly from the Vienna Circle.[35] Showing this fact contains not merely a historical significance, but also an implication that the programme of naturalizing epistemology continues its course through the combination of all the efforts. With this combination in mind, we intend to prove in the next section that Feyerabend's pragmatic theory of observation can be argued as a naturalistic methodology of scientific knowledge.

4.2 Feyerabend's Naturalistic Methodology of Scientific Knowledge

Following Uebel's proof of Neurath's programme of naturalistic epistemology, what we should do in the first place is to demonstrate that all six conditions are present in Feyerabend's 'programme' as well. Being equally an 'anti-foundationalist', Feyerabend can be considered to have a 'naturalistic programme' by following those conditions formulated by Uebel. Satisfaction of the first five conditions can be relatively easily fulfilled by many passages of Feyerabend. In what follows, we cite only some passages from his publications ranging from *Against Method* to *Science in a Free Society*.[36]

    1) 'The condition of the primacy of practice' fits Feyerabend's general philosophy of science, especially his insistence that a proper philosophy of

---

34   P. Feyerabend, *Philosophical Papers Vol. 1* (Cambridge: Cambridge University Press, 1981), pp. 125. Underneath abbreviated as 'PP1'.

35   See J. Preston, *Feyerabend: Philosophy, Science and Society* (Cambridge: Polity, 1997), p. 214n.

36   P. Feyerabend, *Science in a Free Society* (London: NLB, 1978); Underneath abbreviated as 'SFS'.

science requires history of science. He says in the beginning of *Against Method* that: "Indeed, one of the most striking features of recent discussions in the history and philosophy of science is the realization that events and developments, such as the invention of atomism in antiquity, the Copernican Revolution, the rise of modern atomism , the general emergence of the wave theory of light, occurred only because some thinkers either *decided* not to be bound by certain 'obvious' methodological rules, or because they *unwittingly* broke them" (AM 16) ; 2) 'The condition of replacement' implies the idea that the rationality of science can be shown only by the practices of science, which are not limited within a pre-established tradition. Feyerabend says in AM that: "*The entities postulated by science are not found, and they do not constitute an 'objective' stage for all cultures and all of history. They are shaped by special groups, cultures, civilizations; and they are shaped from a material which, depending on its treatment, provides us with gods, spirits, a nature that is a partner of humans rather than a laboratory for their experiments, or with quarks, fields, molecules, tectonic plates.*" (AM 260) ; 3) 'The condition of non-justificatory explanation' refers to the idea that "*judging a historical process one may use an as yet unspecified and unspecifiable practice* ... One may base judgements and actions on standards that cannot be specified in advance but are introduced by the very judgements (actions) they are supposed to guide and one may even act without any standards, simply following some natural inclination." (SFS 28) ; 4) 'The condition of theory acceptance' implies the idea that no standard rationality is involved to arbitrate the adoption of a specific tradition; and instead the "tradition adopted by the parties is unspecified in the beginning and develops as the exchange goes along ... The participants get immersed into each others' ways of thinking, feeling, perceiving to such an extent that their ideas, perceptions, world views may be entirely changed." (SFS 29) ; 5) 'The condition of the extra-cognitive factors in theory acceptance' is probably the most obvious one to be satisfied in Feyerabend as he says: "It is time to realize that science, too, is a special tradition and that its predominance must be reversed by an open debate in which all members of the society participate." (SFS 86).

Yet, the real challenge is the satisfaction of the sixth condition, i.e., 'The condition of normativity'. A self-declared 'epistemological anarchist' like Feyerabend would make the condition even more difficult to be satisfied. However, is he really an epistemological anarchist who accepts anything? We are nonetheless inclined to hold a negative answer to this question by taking into account Feyerabend's own words: "'Anything goes' is *not* the one and only 'principle' of a new methodology, recommended by me. It is the only way in which those firmly committed to universal standards and wishing to understand history in their terms can describe my account of traditions and research practices." (SFS 39–40). What then is his account that certainly not everything goes?

We have a good reason to hold that it must be a form of naturalistic methodology which substantiates itself in Feyerabend's 'pragmatic theory of observation'.

Feyerabend's pragmatic theory of observation is set to oppose the 'semantic theory of observation'.[37] The 'semantic theory', according to Feyerabend, is characterized by an assumed logical connection "between the meaning of a term and the fact that it is, or is not, an observational term" (PPI 125). Normally, if we are not aware of the function of the theory, our common sense implies the change of meanings depending on the variations of external circumstances. The semantic theory does not allow the change of meanings of terms employed in the observation statements. It asserts the 'fixed way' of confirming the outside world as 'empiricists' do by either stating what we observe in the world or acquiring meaning from the observed objects. This assertion can be supported by analyses of the 'verbs' (such as to 'see', or to 'observe') or of the 'nouns' (such as 'names' given to observed objects), as long as they form a 'fixed meaning' out of these terms in the related statements. Therefore, the semantic theorists think that the very 'act' of observation is capable of deciding perpetually the meaning of observations. These decisions of meaning in permanent fixation are to Feyerabend not so different from accepting statements in the form of Kant's idea of *a priori* synthetic. However, this form is unacceptable to Feyerabend.

> For consider the principles *P* which guarantee that observational terms can be applied. These principles describe some general features of the world (or of the mind) and are therefore synthetic. On the other hand a theory implying their denial would eliminate its observational basis, and would therefore be unacceptable. We can say in advance that such a theory must not be formulated—which guarantees the perennial correctness of *P* (PP1 125).

So, Feyerabend, following Neurath, Popper and Carnap (PP1 125) adopts 'the pragmatic theory of meaning' instead. According to Preston, the proposition of the pragmatic theory has two purposes: the pluralistic methodology and the materialistic metaphysics.[38] These two purposes will become clear to us as soon as we proceed to the central tenets of the pragmatic theory. Feyerabend begins his analysis of the pragmatic theory with an exposition of the formation of an observational sentence from a specific observer. He says, "The theory admits that observational sentences assume a special position ... not by their meanings, but by the circumstances of their production".[39] In another place, Feyerabend talks about the same thing: "an observation sentence is distinguished from other sentences of a theory... by the cause of its production, or by the fact that its production conforms to certain behavioral patterns" (PP1 50).

---

37   J. Perston, *Feyerabend: Philosophy, Science and Society* (Cambridge: Polity, 1997), p. 45.

38   J. Preston, *op. cit.*, p. 46.

39   P. Feyerabend, "Problem of Empiricism" in R. G. Colodny ed., *Beyond the Edge of Certainty. Essays in Contemporary Science and Philosophy* (Englewood Cliffs, NJ: Prentice-Hall, 1965), p. 212. Underneath abbreviated as 'PE'.

With this, Feyerabend further says that "we must carefully distinguish between the *causes* of the production of a certain observational sentence, or the features of the process of production, on the one side, and the *meaning* of the sentence produced in this manner on the other" (PP1 93). If we do not make this distinction clearly, then it would imply that the physical and psychological processes from which observational sentences are derived would 'speak', "being able to give meaning to sentences that have not yet received any interpretation" (PE 212-3). In fact, they do not. The physical and psychological processes exert observational sentences as appropriate responses to the 'cause' of their production. These responses are 'actual interpretations' adhering to the causal formation of the observational sentences. Now, we have to ask where comes the interpretation which seems to be crucial to the formation of meaning in the observational sentence? The answer to this question is Feyerabend's special meaning of 'theory'.

> In what follows, the term 'theory' will be used in a wide sense, including ordinary beliefs (e.g., the belief in the existence of material objects), myths (e.g., the myth of eternal occurrence), religious beliefs, etc. In short, any sufficiently general point of view concerning matter of fact will be termed a 'theory' (PE 219)

In another place where Feyerabend makes his usage of 'theory' more clearly by referring to the ideas of the others. He says:

> When speaking of theories I shall include myths, political ideas, religious systems, and I shall demand that a point of view so named be applicable to at least some aspects of everything there is. The general theory of relativity is a theory in this sense; "all ravens are black" is not. There are certain similarities between my use of 'theory' and Quine's 'ontology', Carnap's 'linguistic framework', Wittgenstein's 'language games'... Kuhn's 'paradigm' (PP1 105).

With all the ideas of 'ontology', 'linguistic frameworks', 'language games' and 'paradigms', an aura of 'the relativized stand' arises also in Feyerabend's philosophy. Moreover, he attempts without hesitation to put this everywhere. With this aura, Feyerabend thinks he has acquired truly an instrument of emancipation.

> The pragmatic theory of observation restores to science the right to examine human beings according to its own ideas. Moreover, it assumes that the *interpretation* of the observation sentences is determined by the accepted body of theory. This second assumption removes the arbitrary barriers and the a priori elements characteristic of the idea of the observational core. It encourages us to base our interpretations upon the best theory available and not to omit any feature of the theory (PE 213).

To Feyerabend, the most important consequence of the transition to the pragmatic theory is the reversal that takes place in the relation between theory and observation (PE 213). The semantic theory which holds the principle observations as being meaningful *per se* deems theories to be trimmed on the basis of observations. However, the pragmatic theory on the other hand holds that observations, though formed through a physicalistic and psychological process, are pragmatically interpreted and hence naturally determined by a 'theory' in working as an ontological principle. An observation would not be meaningful unless it is caused by a circumstance into which theoretically interpreted possibilities are incorporated. Whenever the observer utters the observation sentence, he acts not like a machine which mechanically reflects to nature, but like an organism which physiologically decides the 'sentence' conforming to certain behavioral patterns. If observation sentences function like the results of a machine, then there would be no possibility of shifting the meaning of one observed object to another. However, as we all know that the same object might be recognized as different 'things' depending on the interpretations added to it (e.g. the meaning attributed to an object before and after the scientific revolution), a pre-established 'logical connection' in the concern would do no good but limit our thinking within the extent of the 'pre-selected establishment'. That is the reason why Feyerabend says: "To express it more radically, each theory will possess its own experience, and there will be no overlap between these experiences" (PE 214).

What can we do if we are limited within the tenacity of a specific theory without being aware of the limit? This is indeed the question which raises the concern of many who think that Feyerabend hence adopts a stand of relativism. To some extent, this is true as Feyerabend says: "Not only is the description of every single fact dependent on *some* theory ..., but there also exist facts that cannot be unearthed except with the help of alternatives to the theory to be tested and that become unavailable as soon as such alternatives are excluded" (PE 175). Therefore, he draws the consequential point from the pragmatic theory by saying: "Clearly, a crucial experiment [to the theory] is now impossible because there is no universally accepted *statement* capable of expressing whatever emerges from observation" (PE 214). What would emerge from observation? 'Human experience', answers Feyerabend. What would be the function of human experiences here? They function as something either beyond or beside the tenacity of the theory and cause the 'observer' to utter certain sentences which do not match the predictions made on the basis of the 'theory'. This means that the observer, though uttering 'meaningful sentences' on the basis of a 'theory', is still able to utter 'other' sentences even without knowing 'another theory'. What would be the function of these 'other sentences'? They reveal the possible discrepancy between the 'physical order' of the theory working as a cosmological point of view and the 'natural order of sensations' (PE 215). The discrepancy can be detected on the basis of sensation despite the fact that theoretical frameworks work here as ontological principles. This reveals Feyerabend's initial ideas concerning the necessity of putting forward a 'pluralistic methodology'.

The processes mimicked by the selected sentences are, of course, the psychological processes going on in an observer who utters the sentences in the circumstances correlated with the initial conditions; the theory—an acceptable theory, that is—has an inbuilt syntactical machinery that *imitates* (but does not describe) certain features of our experience. This is the *only* way in which experience judges a general cosmological point of view. Such a point of view ... is removed if it produces observation *sentences* when observers produce the *negation* of these sentences (PE 215).

Feyerabend here portrays that experience cannot be fully exhausted by the structure of the 'theory'. The way to detect this fact is through the presence of experience which urges the observer to utter a sentence negating what the theory would predict in its tenacity. However, this 'negation' does not hence imply whether the prediction sentences is true or false; all it says is the disagreement between the 'physical order' of a theory and the 'natural order of sensations' (PE 215). So, we should ask at this stage, what would be the function of the 'disagreement' here? Nothing, according to Feyerabend, if it is not accompanied by the guidance of a theory. What kind of guidance? Feyerabend says: "In order to be able to expand our field of action, the theory must guide us into new domains. It must also make us *critical* of our actions so that we may find out which actions are based on strong causal antecedents and which are not. *Only the latter ones will be valuable indicators of external events*" (the italics are mine; PE 215). Here Feyerabend coherently argues his support of a pluralistic methodology.

> The methodological unit to which we must refer when discussing questions of test and empirical content is constituted by a *whole set of partly overlapping, factually adequate, but mutually inconsistent theories* (PE 175).

> Both the relevance and the refuting character of many decisive facts can be established only with the help of other theories that, although factually adequate, are not in agreement with the view to be tested... Empiricism demands that the empirical content of whatever knowledge we possess be increased as much as possible. Hence, *the invention of alternatives in addition to the view that stands in the center of discussion constitutes an essential part of the empirical method* (PE 176).

To this methodology, there remains a problem as pointed out by Shapere. He indicates that in Feyerabend's pragmatic theory of observation, the 'given' is still there, but it is not so different from a 'burp', i.e., a noise without meaning.[40] To Shapere, something without meaning is not useful to be a basis for removing a theory. Therefore, to him, Feyerabend's effort of setting up normativity in his scientific methodology collapses and the growth of scientific knowledge fails to be adequately explained. The attribution of a programme of naturalistic methodology ends in futility. For Shapere, there is a firm reason attributing the stand of 'anything goes' to Feyerabend. He says: "Feyerabend's kind of experience is altogether *too* weak, in its pristine, uninterpreted form, to serve as grounds for 'removal' of any theory; and his view of meaning is too strong to preclude the possibility of any interpretation whatever of what is given in experience".[41]

---

40   D. Shapere, "Meaning and Scientific Change" in I. Hacking ed. *Scientific Revolutions* (Oxford: Oxford University Press, 1981), p. 47.

41   Ibid., pp. 48–49.

We should say this accusation of 'permissive relativism' is correct merely on the superficial level. Underneath the appearance, Feyerabend does propose a normative methodology which relies on criticism in order to remove unsuitable theories.

4.3 The Normative Nature of Pluralistic Methodology

In saying that Feyerabend adopts normative methodology has to be extremely cautious because of his lifelong stand. Feyerabend is well known for his stand of 'against method'. We want however to say that Feyerabend is not merely keen to talk about the empiricism, the 'given' and the theory-independent observation, but inclined to follow the methodological track of Kraft and Popper. When Feyerabend says, "'theory' must make us *critical* of our actions and only the actions which are not based on causal antecedent are valuable indicators of external events", he means that "a philosopher or a scientist ... accepts the principle that every statement of science must be revisable". For this reason, one should notice that this "is grounded in the methodological *decision* to incorporate only refutable statements into science (or into our knowledge in general)".[42] To him, holding everything refutable or revisable is a solution to the general property of epistemological problems which "are not solved by proofs, but by decisions, as well as by the (empirical or logical) evidence that the decisions made are realizable". Therefore, science is only realizable if there are individuals who, other than having a language with a well-developed argumentative function, are capable of rejecting plausible ideas and accepting or inventing implausible ideas. Feyerabend thinks that the role played by the 'decisions' here is essentially necessary for the development of science and he also thinks that this role "has been emphasized with great clarity by Kraft and Popper" (PTE 42).

We see reasonably the presence of Popper's falsificationism in Feyerabend's pluralistic methodology. However, they remain different in the view concerning the thesis that the presence of the 'given' in experience would not be meaningful unless it is incorporated into a 'theory'. The thesis is indeed close to Popper's idea of 'theory impregnation', but the difference is still there as he said: "my empiricism consisted in the view that, though all experience was theory-impregnated, it was experience which in the end could decide the fate of a theory, by knocking it out; and also in the view that only such theories which in principle

---

42   P. Feyerabend, "The Problem of Theoretical Entities" in *Philosophical Papers III*, ed. J. Preston (Cambridge: Cambridge University Press, 1999), p. 42. This paper originally appeared in German as 'Das Problem der Existenz theoretischer Entitäten", trans. by D. Sirtes and E. Oberheim. The paper was a contribution to a *festschrift* for V. Kraft and reflected the twists and turns of Feyerabend's discussion with H. Feigl about reality. See P. Feyerabend, *Killing Time* (Chicago: The University of Chicago Press, 1995), p. 117. Underneath abbreviated as 'PTE'.

were capable of being thus refuted merited to be counted among the theories of 'empirical science'.[43] To Popper, the 'negation' taking place in experience against a theoretically impregnated prediction is enough to remove a theory as a whole. Feyerabend thinks differently by being more cautious about the tenacity of a theory which for him, is an ontological framework and thus practically irrefutable within its own extent of empirical application. So, there is no 'immediate way' of removing a theory which can only be replaced with another theory. Undoubtedly, this is the origin of Feyerabend's pluralistic methodology, but our concern is this: To what extent is this methodology still normative?

The answer to this question is that Feyerabend follows Kraft's anti-inductivism which, according to Feyerabend, was not then dealt with or taken into account by either the German or American books.[44] This 'ignored' theory of knowledge, started with the Vienna Circle, "is a masterpiece of clarity and incisive argument and it should be read by anyone intending to take up a problem of epistemology or of the philosophy of science" (RE 319). In this theory, along with Popper, Kraft argues that "the problem of induction is still without a solution" (RE 320). Yet, Kraft is still different from Popper by holding that perceptions are not theory-independent, but 'test statements' "insofar as they are members of a context regulated by laws, or about *bundles of perceptions*" (RE 321). This is due to the fact that in the experience of the perceiving subject, there are two parts of one observation: the really existing objects and the perceptions. They do not link to each other in principle as we know that they are distinct. However, they are somehow related in the sense that the objects are perceived as 'signs' in experience, which are not identified with either sensations, or with single perception, but with "a *bundle* of perceptions lawfully connected and it is to this bundle that observation sentences refer" (RE 321-2). To Feyerabend, this 'lawfully connected bundle of perceptions' can be held only in hypothetical sense to be further revised. The "methodological, normative considerations are given for the acceptance of the hypothesis of real things of other minds" (RE 322). However, how can we say that merely on the basis of accepting perceptions as hypotheses are we hence engaged with a 'normative methodology'?

The issue boils down to this question. How can we employ the ideas of external things and of others' minds as hypotheses in an epistemic inquiry? Being unfounded conjectures, we will never be able to 'know' exactly what would be the exact nature of external things and others' minds. This impossibility characterizes precisely wherein the problem of induction lies as we can

---

43   K. Popper, "Replies to My Critics" in Paul A. Schilpp (ed.), *The Philosophy of Karl Popper* (La Salle, Il.: Open court, 1974), p. 971.

44   Feyerabend, P. "Review of *Erkenntnislehre* by V. Kraft" in *British Journal for the Philosophy of Science*, 13 (Feb., 1963): 319. Underneath abbreviated as 'RE'.

have either solipsism or mere opinions to be the inevitable results. "Is there a way out of this dilemma?" asks Feyerabend.

> There is, and the solution is purely methodological, or normative. It is also very simple and contains two demands only. First, that our ideas be *testable*. This demand invites us to connect our hypotheses with the domain of experience. Second, that our ideas be capable of giving an explanation of known phenomena. This demand specifies the connection with experience in detail and also puts restrictions upon the ideas to be used: the ideas must not be *ad hoc*; they must be richer in content than what they want to explain, that is they must establish connections in the domain of experience which are either more strict, or more complex, than the connections already known ... The hypothesis of the existence of material objects is therefore not only an essential part of our thinking, [but] a part without which much apparently valuable knowledge would simply collapse ... The support [of this solution] is not by *proof*, nor by 'induction', it is by methodological argumentation that is by reference to some of the norms which constitute our epistemology (RE 322-3).

With the combination of the two demands cited here, we see rather clearly that Feyerabend's pluralistic methodology adopts Kraft's ideas up to a tremendous extent. It contains an essentially normative part which is set to depict the practical effectiveness of scientific growth. Though it is based on conjectures without firm foundation, the practices in science lead to a full programme of naturalistic methodology in which a specific theory and its tenet of explaining the world is accepted on the basis of all elements available. The theory faces challenges as soon as its predictions are negated by the 'given' in experience. In order to proceed to a better explanation of this 'disappointed part' of the previous theory, all we need is not a justificatory criterion to evaluate the theory, but another theory to incorporate all 'anomalous phenomena' into its explanatory tenacity. This is the way through which science naturally develops itself and with this undeniable development we end our exposition of the 'normative' nature of Feyerabend's naturalistic philosophy of science.

5. Conclusion

For the purpose of exposing a valuable part of naturalistic methodology unfortunately eclipsed by historical factors, we have proceeded in this paper to prove the following three points: 1) the stereotypical image of logical positivism is misleading in the sense that an important part of the ideas developed in the Vienna Circle was unfortunately ignored for decades. This ignorance mislead us to hold a view that the naturalistic philosophy of science had its origin in criticizing logical positivism and hence believe its proponents are practically all post-positivists. We have demonstrated that the ignored part of the Vienna Circle is precisely the part preceding the development of a naturalistic methodology in epistemology or in philosophy of science. This part primarily refers to the ideas of O. Neurath. 2) Secondly, we have, mainly following T. Uebel's formulation of Neurath's programme of naturalistic epistemology, demonstrated that these ideas deserve to be a full programme not just for its historical interest, but also for containing a rich interpretation of scientific practices. The 'rich' interpretation leads us to see Neurath's naturalistic epistemology by examining his formal and pragmatic conditions of forming 'protocol sentences'. We then proceed further from here to a detailed examination of the normative part of Neurath's programme. We claim finally that the normative nature of Neurath's methodology has to be founded on the possibility of reflecting the growth of scientific knowledge. 3) From this reason, we move to Feyerabend who, being a direct heir from the Kraft Circle, the immediate follower of the Vienna Circle after the War, sets forth a philosophy of science which can be formulated accordingly as a programme of naturalistic philosophy of science. By examining Feyerabend's philosophy, we show that: A. this programme descends directly from the Vienna Circle via Kraft, Neurath and Popper; B. A similar programme of naturalistic philosophy of science can be attributed to Feyerabend by following the attribution of Uebel to Neurath; C. the normative part of Feyerabend's naturalistic philosophy of science is assured by the adoption of the pluralistic methodology which best corresponds with the growth of scientific knowledge. It is due to this 'correspondence' we claim that the completion of a naturalistic programme of methodology is finally reached in Feyerabend's philosophy.

Bibliography

Carnap, R. *The Logical Structure of the World*, trans. by R. A. George (Berkeley: University of California Press, 1967).

Carnap, R. "On Protocol Sentences", *Noûs* 21 (1987), pp. 457–470 (translated by R. Creath & R. Nollan from "Über Protokollsätze", *Erkenntnis* Bd 3, H. 2–3 (1932), pp. 215–228).

Cartwright, N., Cat, J., Fleck, L. & Uebel, T. *Otto Neurath: Philosophy between Science and Politics* (Cambridge: Cambridge University Press, 1996).

Cirera, R. *Carnap and the Vienna Circle* (Amsterdam/Atlanta, GA.: Rodopi, 1994).

Feyerabend, P. "Review of *Erkenntnislehre* by V. Kraft" in *British Journal for the Philosophy of Science*, 13: 319–323.

Feyerabend, P. "Problem of Empiricism" in R. G. Colodny ed., *Beyond the Edge of Certainty. Essays in Contemporary Science and Philosophy* (Englewood Cliffs, NJ: Prentice-Hall, 1965), pp. 145–260.

Feyerabend, P. *Science in a Free Society* (London: NLB, 1978).

Feyerabend, P. *Realism, Rationalism and Scientific Method. Philosophical Papers Vol. I* (Cambridge: Cambridge University Press, 1981).

Feyerabend, P. *Problems of Empiricism. Philosophical Papers Vol. II* (Cambridge: Cambridge University Press, 1981).

Feyerabend, P. *Against Method* (London: Verso, 1988).

Feyerabend, P. *Killing Time* (Chicago: The University of Chicago Press, 1995).

Feyerabend, P. "*Knowledge* without Foundation" in P. Feyerabend: Knowledge, Science and Relativism, J. Preston ed. (Cambridge: Cambridge university Press, 1999), pp. 50–77.

Feyerabend, P. "The Problem of Theoretical Entities" in *Philosophical Papers III*, ed. J. Preston (Cambridge: Cambridge University Press, 1999), pp. 16–49.

Friedman, M., *Rediscovering Logical Positivism* (Cambridge: Cambridge University Press, 1999).

Giere, R. & Richardson, A. (eds.) *Origins of Logical Empiricism* (Minneapolis MN.: University of Minnesota Press, 1996).

Hacking, I. *Why Does Language Matter to Philosophy?* (Cambridge: Cambridge University Press, 1975).

Haller, R. "The First Vienna circle" in T. E. Uebel (ed.), *Rediscovering the Forgotten Vienna Circle* (Dordrecht: Kluwer, 1991), pp. 95–108.

Hung, Tscha. "Several Problems Concerning Logical Empiricism" in *Journal of New Asian College*, 9: 1–9.

Hung, Tsche in a paper written in Chinese, "An Introduction to V. Kraft's Philosophy" in *Essays on Logical empiricism* (Taipei: Yuan Lieu, 1990), pp. 79–86.

Kitcher, P. "The Naturalists Return" in *The Philosophical Review*, 100: 53–114.

Kraft, V. "Gespräch mit Viktor Kraft" in *Conceptus*, 21:17.

Kraft, V. "Popper and the Vienna Circle" in Paul A. Schilpp (ed.), *The Philosophy of Karl Popper* (La Salle, Il.: Open court, 1974), pp. 185–204.

Kraft, V. *The Vienna Circle* (Westport, Connecticut: Greenwood, 1953).

Lakatos, I. "Lectures on Scientific Method" in *For and Against Method*, M. Motterlini ed. (Chicago: The University of Chicago Press, 1999), p. 19–109.

Neurath, O. *Empiricism and Sociology*, M. Neurath & R. Cohen eds. (Dordrecht: D. Reidel, 1973).

Neurath, O. *Philosophical Papers 1913–1946* (Dordrecht: D. Reidel, 1983).

Oberdan, T. *Protocols, Truth, and Convention* (Amsterdam/Atlanta, GA.: Rodopi, (1993).

Popper, K. "Replies to My Critics" in Paul A. Schilpp (ed.), *The Philosophy of Karl Popper* (La Salle, Il.: Open Court, 1974), pp. 961–1197.

Preston, J. *Feyerabend: Philosophy, Science and Society* (Cambridge: Polity, 1997).

Quine, W. V. O. "Epistemology Naturalized" in *Ontological Relativity & Other Essays* (New York: Columbia University Press, 1969).

Ray, C. in "Logical Positivism" in *A Companion to the Philosophy of Science*, W. H. Newton-Smith ed. (Oxford: Blackwell, 2000), pp. 243–251.

Rescher, N. (ed.) *The Heritage of Logical Positivism* (Lanham, MD: University Press of America, 1985).

Richardson, A. *Carnap's Construction of the World* (Cambridge: Cambridge University Press, 1998).

Rungaldier, E. *Carnap's Early Conventionalism* (Amsterdam/Atlanta, GA.: Rodopi, 1984).

Salmon, W. & Wolters, G. (eds.) *Logic, Language and the Structure of Scientific Theories* (Pittsburgh: University of Pittsburgh Press, 1993).

Sarkar, S. *The Legacy of the Vienna Circle: Modern Appraisals* (New York: Garland, 1996).

Shapere, D. "Meaning and Scientific Change" in I. Hacking ed. *Scientific Revolutions* (Oxford: Oxford University Press, 1981), pp. 28–59.

Solmon, W. "Logical Empiricism" in *A Companion to the Philosophy of Science*, W. H. Newton-Smith ed. (Oxford: Blackwell, 2000), pp. 233–242.

Stadler, F. *Scientific Philosophy: Origins and Developments* (Dordrecht: Kluwer, 1993).

Stadler, F. *The Vienna Circle* (Wien: Springer, 2001).

Uebel, T. "Neurath's Programme for Naturalistic Epistemology" in *Studies in History and Philosophy of Science*, 22, p. 623–646.

Uebel, T. *Rediscovering the Forgotten Vienna Circle* (Dordrecht: Kluwer, 1991).

Uebel, T. *Overcoming Logical Positivism from Within* (Amsterdam/Atlanta, GA.: Rodopi, 1992).

Wartofsky, M. "Positivism and Politics: The Vienna Circle as a Social Movement" in S. Sarkar, *The Legacy of the Vienna Circle: Modern Appraisals* (New York: Garland, 1996), pp. 53–75.